BEHAVIORAL ECONOMICS AND NUCLEAR WEAPONS

 STUDIES IN SECURITY
AND INTERNATIONAL AFFAIRS

SERIES EDITORS

Sara Z. Kutchesfahani
Senior policy analyst, Center for Arms Control and Non-proliferation
Senior program coordinator, Fissile Materials Working Group

Amanda Murdie
Dean Rusk Scholar of International Relations and Professor of International Affairs, University of Georgia

SERIES ADVISORY BOARD

Kristin M. Bakke
Associate professor of political science and international relations, University College London

Fawaz Gerges
Professor of international relations, London School of Economics and Political Science

Rafael M. Grossi
Ambassador of Argentina to Austria and International Organisations in Vienna

Bonnie D. Jenkins
University of Pennsylvania Perry World Center and the Brookings Institute Fellow

Jeffrey W. Knopf
Professor and program chair, nonproliferation and terrorism studies, Middlebury Institute of International Studies at Monterey

Deepa Prakash
Assistant professor of political science, DePauw University

Kenneth Paul Tan
Vice dean of academic affairs and associate professor of public policy, the National University of Singapore's (NUS) Lee Kuan Yew School of Public Policy

Brian Winter
Editor-in-chief, Americas Quarterly

Behavioral Economics and Nuclear Weapons

Edited by
Anne I. Harrington and Jeffrey W. Knopf

The University of Georgia Press
Athens

Paperback edition, 2023
© 2019 by the University of Georgia Press
Athens, Georgia 30602
www.ugapress.org
All rights reserved
Set in Minion Pro by BookComp, Inc.

Most University of Georgia Press titles are
available from popular e-book vendors.

Printed digitally

Library of Congress Cataloging-in-Publication Data
Names: Harrington, Anne (Anne I.), editor. | Knopf, Jeffrey W., editor.
Title: Behavioral economics and nuclear weapons / edited by Anne I. Harrington and
　Jeffrey W. Knopf.
Description: Athens : The University of Georgia Press, [2019] | Series: Studies in security and
　international affairs ; 28 | Includes bibliographical references and index.
Identifiers: LCCN 2018057937| ISBN 9780820355634 (hardcover : alk. paper) |
　ISBN 9780820355641 (ebook)
Subjects: LCSH: Nuclear weapons—Economic aspects. | Economics—Psychological aspects. |
　Nuclear weapons—Government policy. | Deterrence (Strategy) | Nuclear nonproliferation.
　| Military policy—Decision making. | Economic policy—Decision making.
Classification: LCC U264 .B435 2019 | DDC 355.02/17—dc23
LC record available at https://lccn.loc.gov/2018057937

Paperback ISBN 978-0-8203-6483-4

CONTENTS

Acknowledgments   ix

Abbreviations and Acronyms   xi

List of Tables and Figures   xiii

Introduction. Applying Insights from Behavioral Economics to Nuclear Decision Making   1
   Jeffrey W. Knopf and Anne I. Harrington

Chapter One. Testing a Cognitive Theory of Deterrence   25
   Jeffrey D. Berejikian and Florian Justwan

Chapter Two. Disabling Deterrence and Preventing War: Decision Making at the End of the Nuclear Chain   56
   Janice Gross Stein and Morielle I. Lotan

Chapter Three. The Neurobiology of Deterrence: Lessons for U.S. and Chinese Doctrine   78
   Nicholas Wright

Chapter Four. Apocalypse Now: Rational Choice before the Unthinkable   100
   Jean-Pierre Dupuy

Chapter Five. Sanctions, Sequences, and Statecraft: Insights from Behavioral Economics   115
   Etel Solingen

Chapter Six. Justice and the Nonproliferation Regime   135
   Harald Müller

Chapter Seven. Constructing U.S. Ballistic Missile Defense: An Information Processing Account of Technology Innovation   159
   Zachary Zwald

Chapter Eight. *Homo Atomicus*, an Actor Worth Psychologizing?
The Problems of Applying Behavioral Economics
to Nuclear Strategy   187
  Anne I. Harrington and John Downer

Contributors   203

Index   207

ACKNOWLEDGMENTS

When Daniel Kahneman's book *Thinking, Fast and Slow* came out, it created quite a buzz in the U.S. national security community. Participants at U.S. Strategic Command's 2012 Deterrence Symposium came away asking what lessons it had for nuclear deterrence, and the secretary of defense invited Kahneman out to speak in his New Ideas @ OSD seminar series. Kahneman's summary of research on human decision making—research that forms the foundation of the field of behavioral economics—obviously contained implications for the defense community, but the work had not yet been done to draw them out. Given that Kahneman takes on the underlying assumption of rationality within economic models, and that theories of nuclear deterrence share that underlying assumption of rationality, drawing the implications out for questions of nuclear policy and strategy seemed particularly promising.

Miles Pomper, a colleague of ours based at the Center for Nonproliferation Studies in Washington, D.C., participated in early conversations about this project. These conversations led to a decision to seek funding to explore further the implications of behavioral economics for issues related to nuclear strategy and to the nuclear nonproliferation regime. This project would not have happened without him. He helped draft the initial letter of interest and grant proposal and organize the resulting workshop, and we thank Miles for his invaluable contributions to getting this project off the ground.

The work in this volume was supported by a grant from the U.S. Defense Threat Reduction Agency (DTRA) Project on Advanced Systems and Concepts for Countering WMD (PASCC). Initial drafts of the chapters in this volume were presented at a workshop made possible by this grant, and we thank PASCC for its support. We are also grateful to the participants at the initial authors' workshop for their many helpful comments. We should make clear that the views expressed in this volume are those of the authors and are not intended to represent opinions of the U.S. Defense Department.

Last but not least, we would like to thank our significant others for their support and contributions to this project. To Brenda, you are a force of nature. This project exists because of you; you provided the initial inspiration, the motivation, and unwavering moral support. Ultimately, we got it across the finish line despite three cross-country moves in the intervening years to support your military career, and two international moves between academic institutions to support mine. To Christina, your most important contribution to this project was to make sure I occasionally took a break from work to commune with nature. By taking me to see the ocean, magnificent coastal redwoods, and beautiful spring wildflowers, you helped keep me energized.

Anne I. Harrington
Cardiff, Wales

Jeffrey W. Knopf
Santa Cruz, California

July 2018

ABBREVIATIONS AND ACRONYMS

ABM	antiballistic missile
BIP	backward induction paradox
BMD	ballistic missile defense
DEFCON	defense-condition
DoD	Department of Defense
DO-JOC	*Deterrence Operations Joint Operating Concept*
DTRA	Defense Threat Reduction Agency
ED	existential deterrence
EU-3	European Union–3: France, Germany, and the United Kingdom
FAS	Federation of American Scientists
FMA	fear, misperception, and accident
fMRI	functional magnetic resonance imaging
HI	Humanitarian Initiative
IAEA	International Atomic Energy Agency
ICBM	intercontinental ballistic missile
INFCE	international fuel cycle evaluation
IRGC	Islamic Revolutionary Guard Corps
JCPOA	Joint Comprehensive Plan of Action
JOAC	*Joint Operational Access Concept*
LLNL	Lawrence Livermore National Laboratory
LOA	launch on attack
LOW	launch on warning
MAD	mutual assured destruction
MFG	multilateral nuclear fuel guarantees
MID	militarized interstate dispute
MIRV	multiple independently targetable re-entry vehicle
MNA	multilateral nuclear fuel cycle arrangements
NAM	nonaligned movement
NNWS	non-nuclear weapon states
NORAD	North American Aerospace Defense Command
NPR	*Nuclear Posture Review*
NPT	Non-Proliferation Treaty
NSG	Nuclear Suppliers Group

NWS	nuclear weapon states
OTA	Office of Technology Assessment
PALs	permissive action links
PASCC	Project on Advanced Systems and Concepts for Countering WMD
PLA	People's Liberation Army
PLARF	People's Liberation Army Rocket Force
PRC	People's Republic of China
PRPs	personnel reliability programs
QDR	*Quadrennial Defense Review*
RCT	rational choice theory
RDA	rational deliberate action
RevCons	NPT Review Conferences
SAC	Strategic Air Command
SDI	Strategic Defense Initiative
STRATCOM	U.S. Strategic Command
STS	science and technology studies
UCS	Union of Concerned Scientists
UNSC	United Nations Security Council
WMD	weapons of mass destruction

TABLES AND FIGURES

Table 1.1. Mean Number of Peace Years for Loss-Frame Dyads and Gains-Frame Dyads 38

Table 1.2. Regression Results: Models 1–4 39

Table 1.3. Risk of Conflict Initiation at Different Values of Key Independent Variables 41

Table 1.4. Regression Results: Models 5–6 44

Table 1.5. Full Regression Results: Models 1–4 48

Table 1.6. Regression Results: Model 5A 49

Table 1.7. Regression Results: Model 7 (only cases in which the United States is the "target") 50

Table 8.1. Justifications for Assuming Rationality and Their Implications for a Behavioral Approach to Nuclear Strategy 193

Figure 1.1. Predicted Probability of Conflict Initiation (Gains- and Loss-Frame States) 43

Figure 1.2. Probability of Conflict Initiation for Weak-Reputation Challengers 47

Figure 3.1. The Adversary's Decision Calculus in the U.S. *Deterrence Operations Joint Operating Concept* 81

Figure 3.2. Illustrating Prediction Errors 84

Figure 3.3. Fairness Can Limit Deterrence and Cause Escalation 90

Figure 4.1. An Assurance Game Played over Time 105

Figure 4.2. A Mutual Assured Destruction Game 106

Figure 4.3. Occurring Time 107

Figure 4.4. Projected Time 108

BEHAVIORAL ECONOMICS AND NUCLEAR WEAPONS

INTRODUCTION

Applying Insights from Behavioral Economics to Nuclear Decision Making

JEFFREY W. KNOPF AND ANNE I. HARRINGTON

Research in psychology, neuroscience, and other fields has shown that human thinking and decision making often fail to match standard social science assumptions about rationality. Indeed, people often depart in quite systematic ways from the predictions of a rational actor model. These findings form the basis of behavioral economics, an approach that has attracted enormous attention in recent years. Two of the founders of the field—Daniel Kahneman and Richard Thaler—have even been awarded the Nobel Prize in Economics. Given the widespread use of the rational actor model, findings from behavioral economics have potential applications far outside the domain of economics. This book explores the implications of behavioral economics, and the research that informs it, for policies and strategies designed to deal with the challenges posed by nuclear weapons.

Any use of nuclear weapons would have catastrophic consequences, and since the dawn of the nuclear age, a great deal of thought and effort has gone into finding ways to reduce the danger of their use. These concerns can still dominate the headlines: North Korea's nuclear activities, the U.S. decision to pull out of the Iran nuclear deal, and signs of a possible new arms race between Russia and the United States all serve to keep nuclear issues on the agenda. Decisions about whether to acquire or use nuclear arms, and about how to forestall such developments, are made by human beings. For this reason, it is important to have as accurate an understanding as possible about how actual people make such decisions in real-world circumstances. This is also the premise behind behavioral economics: that it is based on a more accurate picture of how people think. Because the field offers a more realistic account of people's likely behavior in real-world situations, it is worthwhile to examine the potential implications of its findings for efforts to manage nuclear risks. In the following chapters, scholars examine how elements of a behavioral approach might affect our understanding of topics ranging from deterrence to economic sanctions, the nuclear nonproliferation regime, and U.S. domestic debates about ballistic missile defense.

In the introduction, we first briefly summarize relevant debates about nuclear strategy in order to put the potential contributions of this volume into context. Next, we give a short overview of behavioral economics. The subsequent section provides an initial introduction to the other chapters in this book. Finally, in lieu of a separate conclusion to the volume, the introduction concludes with a summary of the key findings and their policy implications.

We find that behavioral research has generated a number of specific insights that are relevant to strategic planning and decision making. At present, however, it remains difficult to integrate these insights into a single, comprehensive framework. There are also limits to applying behavioral approaches, which predict average human behavior in the aggregate, to the limited number of actors who are involved in making decisions about nuclear weapons in specific cases. We therefore conclude that behavioral economics does not yet provide a coherent and predictive model that can stand on its own as a framework for analyzing policies intended to minimize nuclear dangers.

At the same time, behavioral research makes it clear that we cannot rely on predictions based on an assumption that others will behave rationally. Even if behavioral economics does not provide a reliable alternative basis for prediction, the research that informs it suggests several valuable insights relevant to nuclear strategy. First, the way choices are framed can have a huge impact on the decisions people make. For this reason, it is vital to learn as much as possible about how others understand their situations and where appropriate to try to shape those framings. Second, emotions can exert a powerful impact on human decisions and behavior. Therefore, we should not assume that decisions about nuclear weapons will be shaped solely by cool calculations of cost and benefit. Third, people are often motivated more strongly by the desire to avoid or minimize loss than by the pursuit of gain. We should not assume that seemingly confrontational moves are necessarily motivated by a desire for expansion, and we should be careful not to act in ways that push others into a loss frame. Fourth, people also tend to care about considerations of justice and fairness but often in self-serving ways. This makes it important to explore the possibilities for developing common standards of fairness that might pave the way for a successful diplomatic negotiation or a stable deterrent relationship. And fifth, time horizons can change how people think. In particular, longer time horizons may allow space for more deliberative reasoning, which in turn can reduce the risks of rash or hasty decision making. Behavioral research also suggests that it can be difficult to get people to give appropriate weight to future outcomes, so the advice to lengthen time horizons will not necessarily be easy to implement.

DEBATES ABOUT RATIONALITY IN THE RESEARCH ON NUCLEAR STRATEGY

The invention of the atom bomb created unprecedented challenges for the world. After World War II, prescient thinkers such as Bernard Brodie recognized that fighting a war with nuclear weapons would be an unimaginable catastrophe for all concerned; for this reason, he argued, the emphasis in military planning had to shift to avoiding such a war.[1] From early in the nuclear age, attention focused on deterrence as a strategy to prevent nuclear war. By the 1960s, key states were also seeking to limit the growth of nuclear arsenals and spread of nuclear arms through tools such as arms control and nonproliferation. More recently, global efforts have also encompassed nuclear security, or measures to keep bomb-making materials out of the hands of nonstate actors such as terrorist groups. While international agreements are central to advancing nonproliferation and nuclear security goals, states sometimes find it advantageous to use other policy tools such as economic sanctions or diplomatic engagement to reinforce their efforts in these areas. And in the United States and a few other countries, efforts to develop ballistic missile defenses also remain an ongoing policy goal.

Given the stakes, it is important to understand when these policy tools do or do not work to reduce nuclear dangers and how to make them as effective as possible. Historically, research has focused primarily on deterrence, and other policy tools have not been the subject of as much systematic investigation. In addition, thinking about deterrence has often been based on a rational actor model. In the first decades of the nuclear age, models based on assuming a generic, rational actor proved remarkably productive in generating crucial insights into the likely workings of nuclear deterrence.[2]

Eventually, however, dissatisfaction began to develop with rational theories of deterrence. In the policy domain, the most influential critique of the rational actor model held that, due to differences in history and form of government, the Soviet Union did not think about nuclear war in the same way as the United States. Because of these differences, threats that would deter the United States might not deter Soviet leaders.[3] This critique targeted the notion of a generic, universal form of rationality.[4] It suggested that different actors can think quite differently, putting a premium on learning as much as possible about what the other side values most. This line of work led to the concept of strategic culture and an assumption that different countries develop different strategic cultures.[5] This way of thinking has provided much of the impetus for an emphasis on "tailored deterrence" in recent U.S. strategic doctrine.[6]

Strategic culture approaches are consistent with an assumption of rationality. They dispute the assumption that all actors share the same values and hence would make the same rational calculations. But once the different value systems and associated utility functions of different actors are understood, it should be possible to predict how each will calculate the relative costs and benefits of acquiring or using nuclear weapons.

A different line of criticism targets the underlying assumption of rationality more directly. By the late 1960s, scholars began to question whether states (and the leaders making decisions for those states) could actually live up to the demanding requirements of the rational actor model.[7] Drawing on findings from psychology and organization theory, these critics argued that deterrence might fail more frequently than we would otherwise expect because of the various limitations on human rationality. Research identified a range of cognitive (or unmotivated) and motivated biases that could lead to misperceptions or miscalculations that might undermine deterrence.[8]

This "psychology and deterrence" research program (discussed more fully below) peaked in the mid-1980s. Although some research along these lines continued after that date, increasingly attention turned elsewhere. The winding down of the Cold War and collapse of the Soviet Union made nuclear deterrence seem like a less urgent problem. Where academic research continued, much of it involved a renewed emphasis on rational actor models. Game theoretic work on situations involving incomplete or asymmetric information attracted particular interest and led to a new wave of deterrence research based on formal models.[9] The critics of rational actor approaches, in turn, found inspiration in the rise of social constructivism in the field of international relations and began exploring how processes of social construction affect deterrence relationships.[10] Finally, for analysts concerned with contemporary policy problems, attention shifted to the challenges posed by rogue states and, after 9/11, to the very difficult problem of whether terrorism by nonstate actors can be deterred. Collectively, these trends have been referred to as a "fourth wave" in deterrence research.[11] Notably, however, they all involved a shift of focus away from psychological and organizational constraints on rationality. Indeed, given frequent assertions that terrorist groups and the leaders of rogue states are crazy or irrational, much of the fourth wave turned to demonstrating that these actors have strategic goals and are capable of being instrumentally rational in pursuit of those goals. Even if their goals are extreme, the fact they still make strategic calculations means they are sufficiently rational that it should be possible to find ways to deter them.[12]

While much of the recent work on deterrence has moved away from a focus on the limits of rationality, policy tools other than deterrence have never received the same level of systematic attention and remain theoretically underdeveloped. Some scholars have examined the use of tools like positive incentives, economic sanctions, diplomatic engagement, or reassurance.[13] However, academic research has focused largely on basic questions such as whether or not such policy tools work. For the most part, this literature has not focused on how limitations on human rationality might affect the operation of such policy tools.[14]

There has been a similar lack of attention to the potential psychological underpinnings of other policy endeavors, such as arms control, nonproliferation, or ballistic missile defenses. Debates about missile defense focus mainly on whether the technology will work. Other critiques rely on the reasoning behind rational deterrence theory to argue that missile defenses could also prove destabilizing.[15] The voluminous literature on arms control and nonproliferation likewise mainly addresses the question of whether such treaties work to reduce arms and seeks to assess the health of the various treaty regimes. Research on the origins of the regimes typically assumes that states are driven by rational assessments of the national interest, although there is also some attention to the roles of norms and domestic politics.[16] Psychological influences on decision making have not been a major concern in these literatures.

Given this background, the research presented in this volume has three goals. First, it aims to update the earlier "psychology and deterrence" literature in light of developments in psychology, neuroscience, and related fields, many of which have informed the field of behavioral economics. More recent findings regarding the effects of framing, the role of emotions, and the importance of fairness considerations all promise new insights into how deterrence operates. Second, this study seeks to extend the reach of behavioral insights beyond a concern with deterrence and into the analysis of other policy tools, particularly as those tools are used to promote nuclear nonproliferation. Third, at the same time that it highlights the potential benefits of applying behavioral economics to strategic questions, this project also seeks to assess the limits and potential pitfalls of this approach. Behavioral economics holds out the promise of being able to predict deviations from rational behavior. This makes it important to consider the possible limits on how much predictability it offers and the potential pitfalls of applying a science that grew out of the study of individual human behavior to a bureaucratic actor like the state.

BEHAVIORAL ECONOMICS: A BRIEF REVIEW

Research in psychology, neuroscience, and other fields has revolutionized our understanding of human decision making in situations involving risk or uncertainty. This research has begun to influence other social science disciplines, most notably through the rise of the behavioral economics perspective in economics. This approach—behavioral economics—applies psychology to economics. Behavioral economics also incorporates some earlier lines of research that have influenced work in international relations, such as applications of social psychology to the study of foreign policy decisions, so we treat behavioral economics as an umbrella term covering a range of psychological influences on decision making. Many of the key findings have been nicely summarized for a general audience in Daniel Kahneman's landmark book, *Thinking, Fast and Slow*, as well as several other books written for a public audience by leading specialists in the field.[17] Several good literature reviews have also summarized key findings for a more academic audience.[18] In 2017, *International Organization*, the premier international relations theory journal, devoted a special issue to "the behavioral revolution and international relations."[19] To date, however, we are not aware of any book that seeks to leverage advances made in the field of behavioral economics—and in particular its critique of the rational actor assumption—to improve our understanding of nuclear deterrence or nonproliferation policies. The essays in this book aim to fill that gap.

The introduction will not provide a full summary of behavioral economics. Subsequent chapters take up specific themes from the literature, and we refer readers who want a complete overview to the sources cited in the preceding paragraph. Here, we highlight a few key aspects of behavioral economics in order to show why it might contain valuable insights for our thinking about policies and strategies to deal with nuclear weapons.

This body of literature starts with the presumption that rational theories of human behavior are wrong to dismiss how individuals make decisions. Rather than assuming that actors are rational, behavioral economists use surveys and experiments to observe how individuals behave in real-world situations when confronted with a choice. In contrast, rational theories of human behavior, such as neoclassical economic theory or traditional deterrence theory, are based on the assumption that actors are "procedurally" rational, by which they mean that actors respond to incentive structures in predictable ways because their preferences are internally consistent (if they prefer A to B and B to C, then they also prefer A to C). Procedural rationality is not meant to be an accurate description of what decision makers do. It describes an ideal type that allows analysts to build simple models that can make predictions about actor behavior in complex environments. Although no individual behaves rationally all the time, the argument goes, in the aggregate enough people behave sufficiently rationally often enough to warrant the assumption of rationality. Therefore, individual acts of irrationality can be dismissed at the level of general theory.

Behavioral economists argue that the ideal type of procedural rationality not only fails to accurately predict outcomes but is also blind to the ways in which these failures themselves are foreseeable. In laboratory experiments, the judgments that subjects make violate the assumption of procedural rationality in predictable, lawlike ways. Humans are capable of rational thought, but rational thought requires calculations and abstract thinking—what Kahneman calls system 2 or slow thinking. These activities absorb time and energy that most people do not have to spare. Instead, humans rely on shortcuts, which Kahneman calls system 1 or fast thinking. Rather than calculating probabilities, they reason in terms of averages, norms, and heuristics. These shortcuts consistently lead individuals to express preferences that are not logically consistent (i.e., they claim to prefer A to B and B to C, but then when asked to make a choice, they choose C over A).

Given that both deterrence theory and nonproliferation policy draw heavily from the field of economics for their conceptual foundations, it is surprising that so little work has been done thus far to draw out the implications of behavioral economics for the nuclear field. The assumption of rationality has long been identified as a weak link in the logic of nuclear deterrence theory. Unlike in economic theory, individual acts of irrationality cannot be dismissed as irrelevant to deterrence theory. The consequences of even a single deterrence failure are too costly.[20]

Starting in the 1960s, deterrence theorists were already looking to psychology for alternatives to rational choice models. Scholars soon created a body of research that employed a decision-making approach based on research in psychology and organization studies. This research identified biases in human decision making that can lead to misperception.[21] It sorted the various biases into two basic categories: cognitive (or unmotivated) and motivated. Cognitive biases reflect the influence of images and beliefs that people already hold. They lead people to filter out information inconsistent with those beliefs so that they see what they already expect to see, even when that image is inaccurate. Motivated biases reflect underlying needs and desires, including needs that political leaders might have that derive from the goal of staying in power. Motivated biases produce wishful thinking, leading people to see what they want to see. Both kinds of bias can lead to deterrence failures as well as missed opportunities for negotiation. The high point of this research was the 1985 publication of *Psychology and Deterrence* by Robert Jervis, Richard Ned Lebow, and Janice Gross Stein.[22] Unfortunately, work on deterrence in this research tradition has flagged since then and has not fully kept up with developments in behavioral economics.

Behavioral economics draws on psychology and recent breakthroughs in the study of the human brain, as well as new experiments conducted by behavioral economists themselves, to develop more accurate models of decision making. The model that has emerged involves three types of deviation from the standard rationality assumption. After describing these three areas of bounding on the rational actor model, we will briefly summarize three bodies of literature that are especially relevant to the study of nuclear decision making. First, we will review prospect theory, which emphasizes the framing of choices and how the motivation to avoid losses can encourage greater risk acceptance. Second, we will discuss research on the impact of emotion on choice and how different emotions can have different effects. Third, we will summarize how certain values can be particularly important, including concerns about fairness.

Three Bounds on Rationality

Behavioral economists trace their approach back to Herbert A. Simon's notion of "bounded rationality."[23] The basic idea is that people often attempt to make rational decisions, but they do so under significant cognitive limitations. The human brain simply cannot process all the information and make all the calculations required for perfectly rational decisions—our efforts to think rationally are inherently bounded.

Behavioral economists have since identified two other types of bounding that lead to deviations from economic rationality: bounded self-interest and bounded willpower.[24] With regard to self-interest, research has shown that people have prosocial concerns that can lead to other-regarding behavior. People are not consistently altruistic, but neither do they always make purely egoistic choices; their self-interest is bounded. In addition, people have a hard time taking the future into account and committing to courses of action that promise the highest payoff over the long run; their willpower to prepare for the future is also bounded. Mainstream economics assumes that future payoffs should be discounted, but research shows that most people engage in excessive discounting. They have a strong bias toward payoffs in the present. The classic example is the failure of most people to save enough for retirement.

The field of behavioral economics, however, grew out of work that built on the notion of bounded rationality. Research by Daniel Kahneman and Amos Tversky lies at the heart of the field, starting with Kahneman and Tversky's work on the various biases and heuristics that influence human judgment and continuing through their development of prospect theory.[25] In a summation of their research program, Kahneman acknowledges that humans can and do engage in "slow thinking," which is characterized by the calculation and analysis required for rational thought. However, humans are much more likely to fall back on shortcuts in order to "think fast," especially when under pressure.[26] Results from laboratory experiments have yielded a list of identifiable ways in which these shortcuts, or "heuristics," cause human decision making to deviate systematically from the ideal-type rational actor model. Some of these heuristics are consistent with and extend the research on cognitive biases that informed an earlier generation of research on psychology and deterrence. Over time, however, work by Kahneman, Tversky, and others has added to the list of heuristics and biases that can lead people into errors in judgment.[27] Repeated experiments have shown, for example, that intuitive judgments based on a piece of vivid or even irrelevant information can affect how people estimate values, probabilities, or causation, often in ways that violate basic rules of statistics and scientific inference.

In short, research has identified a growing list of biases and heuristics that can affect decision making, and our understanding of the psychology of nuclear decisions needs to be updated to take these into account. In addition to the need to update research on cognitive and motivational biases, other developments have produced three significant new lines of work that take us beyond the previous focus on misperception as a potential source of deterrence failure. These developments are the emergence of prospect theory, new research on emotions, and the identification of specific values that can lead people to discount material incentives.

Prospect Theory

Some of the most provocative and best-known findings come from prospect theory, an approach developed by Kahneman and Tversky.[28] In a series of experiments involving alternative choices, these researchers found that people often do not pick the option that promises the highest net utility as an end outcome. Instead of calculating and comparing the expected utility of different end states, people evaluate alternative choices in relation to a reference point. This is often though not always the status quo. Outcomes above the reference point are considered gains, and outcomes below that point are considered losses.

The reason why this matters is because of loss aversion, which is perhaps the most important finding in prospect theory. In short, people are more sensitive to losses than they are to gains. The greater motivation to avoid losses interacts with a second key finding: differences in risk orientation in different domains of choice. People tend to be risk acceptant in the domain of losses, but risk averse in the domain of gains. When given a choice between a certain gain and a chance to gain more but at the risk of getting nothing, most subjects are risk averse; they take the sure thing even when a calculation of expected utility would predict the other choice. But when given a choice between a certain loss and a chance to escape from suffering a loss at the risk of losing more, subjects make the opposite choice and accept the risk of greater loss. In other words, actors will engage in risky gambles in an attempt to avoid losses, but they tend to behave cautiously when they are in the domain of gains.

Because a reference point can frame a decision as being in either the domain of gains or domain of losses, the framing of choice turns out to have powerful effects. Taking two otherwise equivalent pairs of choices and simply altering the wording in ways that move subjects from thinking they are in the domain of gains to seeing themselves in the domain of losses can get them to flip their choice, an observation called preference reversal. In other words, instead of preferences being formed by an individual before a choice is made, the framing of the choice can change one's preferences.[29]

There have been several books and articles written on the application of prospect theory to international relations.[30] Most of these do not address issues directly related to nuclear strategy or proliferation, although Jeffrey Berejikian (a contributor to this project) did explore the potential application of prospect theory to deterrence.[31] And in the area of nonproliferation, Emilie Hafner-Burton, D. Alex Hughes, and David G. Victor wrote an article on elite decision making in which they use insights from behavioral economics to analyze negotiations over the North Korean nuclear program.[32] These examples show the potential exists to apply prospect theory to the study of strategies and policy tools related to nuclear weapons.

Emotion and Emotions

Another relevant strand of research concerns the impact of emotions. This research has shown that rationality and emotions are not necessarily opposed and that different emotions have different effects. First, most specialists now reject the idea that rationality and emotions should be treated as entirely separate and opposed forces. At times, strong emotions do simply override rational calculations. But emotion and reason can also interact in the process of decision making. Considerable research suggests that the ability to make rational decisions depends to some extent on emotions. The feelings people have about alternative outcomes feed into the process of assigning value—or utility—to those outcomes. When people have distinct likes or dislikes, these become part of the yardstick by which they evaluate which choices are better or worse. In contrast, when people have brain damage that reduces their ability to feel emotions, they often cycle endlessly through alternative options and find it difficult to choose one.[33]

In the field of proliferation studies, this provides a possible underpinning for the work of Jacques E. C. Hymans. Hymans argues that some state leaders pursue nuclear weapons because they simply fall in love with the idea of having the bomb.[34] Hymans follows the traditional dichotomy of describing this as an emotional reaction beyond the realm of rational calculation, but behavioral economics suggests a reinterpretation in which emotional reactions to the bomb become one factor in the cost-benefit calculations leaders make about whether to seek nuclear weapons. Beyond its relation to Hymans's theory of proliferation, one can imagine a number of possible implications of the intertwining of rationality and emotions. The way a target state responds to an offer of positive incentives, for example, might be affected by the recipient's feelings about the sender, about the type of good being offered, or even about the acceptability of letting oneself be bribed.

Second, scholars now talk about the impact of "emotions" in the plural, rather than "emotion" in the singular.[35] This reflects the fact that people experience different emotions, such as happiness, sadness, or anger. Research shows that different emotional states have different effects. One of the most important distinctions involves the differences between anger and fear. Fear tends to induce caution, whereas anger makes people more likely to take risks and act without much concern for the consequences. This has potential implications for a strategy like deterrence. A deterrent threat that creates a measure of fear in the target, or that takes advantage of a preexisting fear, has a decent chance of working effectively. In contrast, deterrent threats that anger the target are more likely to backfire and provoke escalation.

Values Can Trump Material Interests

A third intriguing line of research suggests that people take into account other values that can lead them to make choices that depart from material interest calculations. Reflecting the idea of bounded self-interest, this can include concern for the well-being of others, sometimes called social utility. Where social norms exist, people may do things for free out of a sense of obligation to others that they would not do if the same behavior were treated as a matter of monetary incentives.[36] A somewhat different line of work on "sacred values" also suggests that people care about more than just material utility.[37] This concept refers to core values or beliefs that are so deeply internalized they become part of a person's identity. These sacred values are usually beyond the reach of cost-benefit calculations. The classic example involves offering somebody money to change their religion. Such an offer would most likely be seen as offensive and provoke outrage at the person making the offer. Rational actor models will often fail to predict behavior in connection with social norms or sacred values because these are dominated by beliefs about right and wrong, not by calculations of cost and benefit.

Along similar lines, several lines of research suggest that people give significant weight to considerations involving fairness or justice. When people believe they are treated unfairly, this creates particularly strong reactions. This has been shown in experiments involving the well-known ultimatum game. In this game, the experimenter gives two subjects the chance to split some prize, such as ten dollars. Subject one gets to propose the split; if subject two says yes, the players receive the proposed split, but if player two says no both players receive nothing. By the logic of expected utility, the first player could propose to keep nine dollars and give the other player one dollar, and the second player should agree to the split because she or he would still achieve a net gain of one dollar. In practice, however, studies show that people consistently reject highly unequal distributions of benefit even when, in strictly economic terms of expected utility, these choices actually leave them worse off.[38]

This research finding is rich with potential implications for weapons of mass destruction (WMD) nonproliferation. Knopf, for example, has suggested that this might account for the importance some non-nuclear weapon states (NNWS) attach to the disarmament issue in nuclear Non-Proliferation Treaty (NPT) Review Conferences. The NPT recognizes five states as nuclear weapon states, while all others must sign as non-nuclear countries. NPT Article VI requires the nuclear weapon states to make an effort to negotiate nuclear disarmament, but many non-nuclear states have expressed their belief that the nuclear weapon states are not actually committed to eliminating their nuclear arsenals. Because the NPT involves an inherent inequality between nuclear haves and have-nots, perceptions that nuclear weapon states are not complying with nuclear disarmament commitments associated with Article VI, and hence not fulfilling their end of the NPT bargain, are especially likely to rankle non-nuclear nations.[39]

Determining what is fair is not necessarily an objective exercise. Unfortunately, people's views of fairness tend to reflect a self-serving bias.[40] If this bias leads actors to disagree about what counts as fair, then their concerns about not being treated fairly can deepen a conflict. This makes it important to find mechanisms that can produce common or at least overlapping views of what counts as fair. In chapter 6 in this volume, Harald Müller points out that actors can sometimes find agreement on fair procedures in situations where they still have different preferences on substantive issues.

In sum, behavioral economics builds on research in psychology and neuroscience, supplemented by new experiments carried out by the behavioral economists themselves. It has identified a number of ways in which the judgments and choices made by individuals depart in predictable ways from the predictions of a standard rational actor model. The findings that inform behavioral economics have many potential applications when it comes to understanding the decisions actors might make concerning nuclear weapons and the policies associated with them.

OVERVIEW OF THE VOLUME

The chapters in this volume are quite diverse in topic and approach, as we wanted to explore as many ways as possible of applying behavioral economics to issues related to nuclear weapons. We invited a range of scholars with relevant expertise and asked them to extend some appropriate aspect of their previous research. The authors include academics already working in the intersection of psychology and international relations, as well as people with long experience working on topics related to nuclear policy, one individual trained in neuroscience, and a senior scholar from the field of philosophy. We did not seek to impose any specific social science methodology on the authors. We believe it is more important to have a diversity of approaches in the volume and to let individual authors build on their own areas of expertise. Hence, unlike editors who provide contributors with a well-defined list of questions or hypotheses in advance or who assign a specific case study to each author, we chose to leave our contributing authors with a certain amount of discretion. The resulting chapters apply different aspects of behavioral economics to a variety of questions about nuclear decision making. They also employ a range of methods, including statistics, case studies, analysis of texts, and philosophical investigation.

We have grouped the chapters around the following topics: deterrence, nonproliferation, and decision making that involves science and technology such as occurs in debates about missile defenses. The first four chapters provide updates to the earlier literature on psychology and deterrence. Chapter 1, by Jeffrey Berejikian and Florian Justwan, breaks new ground by being the first study to carry out a statistical analysis to test some of the implications of prospect theory for deterrence. As noted above, prospect theory predicts that actors will be risk averse in the domain of gains but risk acceptant when they perceive their choices to lie in the domain of losses. To test this, Berejikian and Justwan analyze a dataset of strategic rivalries from 1816 to 1999. They develop a novel technique to code states as being in either the domain of gains or that of losses. In statistical tests that control for other factors that can influence deterrence outcomes, the authors find that deterrence fails more frequently when one or both states are in a losses frame. Importantly, the authors include a control for when the defender is a nuclear-armed state. The analysis indicates that nuclear weapons possession does not alter the results; a challenger that finds itself in the domain of losses is just as likely to challenge a deterrent commitment when the defender possesses a nuclear arsenal as when it does not. Berejikian and Justwan point out that this result has implications for U.S. deterrence strategy because it can help predict when potential adversaries will be risk acceptant, a condition that makes it harder to apply deterrence effectively.

Chapter 2, by Janice Gross Stein and Morielle I. Lotan, also deals with deterrence. Their chapter addresses a surprising empirical finding. In previous research on nuclear operations, Lotan found that military personnel at lower levels of the nuclear chain of command have often been reluctant to take actions that could lead to a launch of nuclear weapons.[41] Personnel who monitored warning systems did not automatically pass along apparent warnings of nuclear attack out of concern those warnings would turn out to be false alarms. Personnel with nuclear launch responsibilities similarly seem to have been hesitant to respond immediately to warnings of attack or even to launch orders.

Lotan's earlier research focused on U.S. examples. In their chapter for this volume, Stein and Lotan explore in detail an example that took place in the Soviet Union in 1983. In an agonizing decision, Stanislav Petrov, an officer in charge of an early-warning installation, decided to disregard information that seemed to indicate an incoming U.S. missile strike. On the one hand, this decision may have prevented a nuclear war, but on the other, a demonstrated reluctance on the part of nuclear operators to transmit warnings that they expect could lead to a launch of nuclear weapons, or to launch nuclear weapons themselves, destabilizes deterrence. Stein and Lotan show that behavioral economics provides several possible explanations for this reluctance by nuclear operators to pass warnings up the chain of command. One option involves heuristics. It is possible that some early warnings turned out to be due to a computer error or other glitch, leading nuclear operators to develop a heuristic that led them to assume that future warnings during peacetime conditions were similarly likely to be false alarms. The authors place particular weight, however, on the impact of emotions. Research on fear shows that experiencing this emotion tends to make people cautious and risk averse. The possibility of inadvertently starting a nuclear war in response to a false alarm could certainly produce a lot of fear and induce a great deal of hesitation. Stein and Lotan also consider prospect theory as an explanation but find it less persuasive. Whichever explanation or combination of factors is correct, Stein and Lotan point out, we cannot treat nuclear operators as automatons with no discretion; as long as humans are in the loop in nuclear operations, their decision making will matter to the functioning of deterrence.

Nicholas Wright is the author in this volume with training in neurobiology. In chapter 3, he examines doctrinal publications in the United States and China concerned with deterrence, such as the U.S. *Deterrence Operations Joint Operating Concept* (DO-JOC).[42] Wright notes that both China and the United States recognize a psychological component to deterrence, seeing it as a state of mind brought about in one's adversary. But Wright argues that neither country has the psychology quite right, in that their predictions of how the other side will behave in response to deterrent threats or actions are not always based on realistic psychological foundations. Wright highlights in particular the potential impacts of prediction errors and fairness concerns. Prediction errors involve the impact of an incorrect prediction on later behavior. This creates a possible problem because both China and the United States emphasize the value of achieving surprise. But for the other side, a surprise would represent a significant prediction error (i.e., they would not have predicted it), and this could lead them to an extreme action in response. Drawing on his knowledge of neuroscience, Wright closes with some observations about possible limitations of behavioral approaches.

The final chapter dealing with deterrence is written by Jean-Pierre Dupuy, a philosopher who has affiliations with both Stanford University and the Ecole Polytechnique in Paris. In it, he reexamines some classic deterrence paradoxes that previous analysts had sought to address during the Cold War era. He notes that many analysts found it difficult to square deterrence through mutual assured destruction (MAD) with assumptions of rational choice: if one side actually was destroyed in a nuclear attack, it would no longer be rational for that actor to retaliate, and the other side's recognition of this should undermine the credibility of deterrence.

Dupuy discusses a series of possible solutions. It can help if the two actors no longer think in terms of playing the game against each other but instead come to view themselves as playing jointly against a fictitious third entity. This third party would represent the common fate the two actors would share if deterrence failed and they both suffered catastrophic destruction. This potential shared fate creates an interest in the two parties both making sure deterrence succeeds. According to Dupuy, however, this solution still suffers from the problem that it does not appear credible for either side to believe the other. To make it possible for mutual deterrence to work, Dupuy suggests two additional moves.

Part of the solution, Dupuy writes, lies in how we think about time. Dupuy argues we need a notion of "projected time." Normally, we think in terms of "occurring time," in which we can make choices that would take us down different branches to alternative futures. In projected time, in contrast, we treat the future as if it is fixed—in this case fixed on a future in which the two sides avoid nuclear war. This feeds back into the present in a way that leads actors to react to this known future in ways that help produce it. Even this does not fully solve the problem, however. By the logic of backward induction familiar from game theory, if one side knows the other side will be perfectly deterred from using nuclear weapons, it will feel free to behave recklessly.

For this reason, Dupuy argues, we also need an element of indeterminacy in which nuclear Armageddon might or might not happen in the future. But we want to also think in terms of a fixed future in which the outcome is no nuclear war. Getting there, according to Dupuy, requires nearly experiencing the disastrous alternative. It was precisely the experience of going through several near misses during the Cold War that led the two sides to exercise the caution that made it possible for mutual deterrence to work. This leads to the uncomfortable conclusion that perhaps close calls were necessary conditions for nuclear deterrence to succeed.[43]

The next two chapters deal with aspects of nuclear nonproliferation. In chapter 5, Etel Solingen updates her previous work on the impact of economic sanctions. Most research on sanctions has assumed the target state is a unitary state actor. In contrast, Solingen's work has emphasized domestic political coalitions. Solingen has found that ruling coalitions that are outward looking and interested in having their state participate actively in the global economy are more likely to be sensitive to sanctions. In contrast, inward-looking leaderships tend to emphasize nationalism and economic self-reliance and so are less susceptible to being influenced by economic sanctions.

In her chapter, Solingen adds insights from psychology to her previous analysis of domestic coalitions. She suggests that prospect theory shows how the timing of sanctions can be important. Prospect theory has identified an endowment effect, in which actors value something more once they possess it, meaning they will demand a higher payment to give it up than they would be willing to offer to buy the asset before they possessed it. Nuclear programs, as they progress, could create endowment effects. States will become more reluctant to give up capabilities they have achieved than capabilities they have not yet mastered. This makes it harder for sanctions to succeed the further a state has progressed with a nuclear program. Solingen also draws on psychology to reflect back on research and policy debates about economic sanctions, including the possibility that an individual's own beliefs about the efficacy of sanctions could bias how one interprets cases with mixed or ambiguous outcomes.

The other chapter on nonproliferation examines implications of research concerning the importance that people attach to considerations of justice and fairness. Harald Müller, in chapter 6, discusses how justice concerns might affect the nonproliferation regime. Drawing on work by Nancy Fraser, Müller notes that justice concerns can be about distributional, procedural, or recognition (i.e., are people treated as having equal standing) questions. Fairness considerations loom large in nonproliferation because of the inequality baked into the NPT, which recognizes five states as nuclear weapon states while requiring all other states to join as NNWS. Müller identifies several ways in which justice concerns have contributed to frictions in the NPT context. As already mentioned above, one example is complaints by NNWS about a lack of progress toward nuclear disarmament by the nuclear weapon states. Other issues that have justice dimensions include access to peaceful uses of nuclear technology and questions related to the lack of universal membership in the NPT, in particular the perception that India and Israel have received special treatment despite not having signed the NPT. Müller also considers procedural justice issues, including questions about which decisions can be made by bodies in which not all states are members, such as the International Atomic Energy Agency (IAEA) Board of Governors.

Müller's analysis is not wholly pessimistic, however. He notes that justice and fairness concerns can also at times provide a basis for finding common ground. For example, certain norms can become widely accepted and provide a basis for agreement. Müller suggests that concerns about nuclear security became largely accepted once they were taken out of the haves versus have-nots context of many NPT debates. In addition, progress on one dimension of justice can help alleviate concerns on other dimensions. As an example, Müller cites procedural innovations in NPT Review Conferences that helped give NNWS a better sense that their views were represented. Müller concludes that justice concerns have both negative and positive implications for nonproliferation. They can add to the cleavages among states on nonproliferation issues, but they can also create new mechanisms for finding common ground on how to move forward.

Chapter 7 shifts the focus to challenges posed by the importance of science and technology in nuclear decisions. In it, Zachary Zwald examines domestic U.S. debates about ballistic missile defense (BMD). He relates these debates to the larger question of how states choose which new military technologies to develop. Zwald argues that conventional wisdom on this question involves a science versus politics framing. This approach assumes that those who have parochial interests at stake, such as military services or defense contractors that would benefit from missile defense projects, will give biased judgments that exaggerate the technical feasibility and strategic utility of missile defense projects. In contrast, technical experts from the scientific community are expected to give unbiased judgments that identify flaws in proposed missile defense systems.

Zwald challenges this conventional wisdom on two grounds. First, some key participants in missile defense debates do not have obvious parochial interests at stake. For many policymakers and outside analysts, he argues, their views reflect their general beliefs about the scenarios most likely to lead to nuclear war (i.e., deliberate attack or inadvertent escalation) rather than any self-interest related to missile defense programs. Second, research in psychology has shown that all people are prone to certain biases and tend to rely on heuristics. Once people come to hold certain beliefs, their subsequent judgments will be biased by their preexisting beliefs. This does not mean that those with special interests are unbiased, but rather that scientists and political figures on both sides of the missile defense debate are also likely to have biases. Zwald finds support for this in the history of the U.S. debate about candidate missile defense technologies.

Zwald concludes by recommending a more pragmatist approach. This approach takes note of the tremendous uncertainty and complexity involved in predicting whether missile defenses will ultimately help U.S. national security. And it suggests that the democratic political process can be helpful. Rather than trying to insulate military technology decisions from politics and turn them over to supposedly neutral experts, it might be better to encourage open political debate. This would require parties to the debate to better explain their positions and might allow them to look for common ground.

The final chapter is coauthored by Anne I. Harrington and John Downer. Rather than provide a conventional conclusion summarizing the preceding chapters, their final chapter offers a critique of relying on behavioral economics as a foundation for understanding nuclear decision making. Their chapter raises two related criticisms. The first concerns the degree to which the arguments for and against the rationality assumption in economics also apply to the realm of nuclear decision making. Harrington and Downer review several rationales that have been offered in economics for relying on a rational actor model and the degree to which behavioral economics offers a meaningful critique of each. In economics, rational actor predictions are taken to apply on average over a large number of cases or to help explain those business enterprises that prosper, while behavioral factors help explain the exceptions, such as businesses that fail and go out of existence. The world of nuclear strategy, say Harrington and Downer, looks quite different. We are no longer interested in average behavior over a very large number of decisions but rather a much smaller number of key decisions. And the stakes are so high that actors have every incentive to avoid choices that will cause them to "go out of business." Hence, some of the main arguments for invoking psychological factors to explain economic behavior do not map neatly onto the nuclear domain.

Second, Harrington and Downer suggest, applying behavioral economics to nuclear decision making involves a form of category mistake, such as ascribing physical properties to an abstraction, as in attributing emotions to a state. Behavioral economics applies to decisions by individuals. These, however, will not necessarily be the same thing as eventual behaviors by states. As suggested by the level of analysis issue in international relations, there is a difference between an individual and a state. The latter is a collective actor made up of multiple organizational units. The fact that bureaucratic organizations are involved in state decision making means that predictions about individual decisions will not necessarily translate directly into state decisions.[44]

CONCLUSIONS AND RECOMMENDATIONS

Despite the criticisms offered in the final chapter, all of the contributors to this volume concur in finding value in behavioral economics and its critique of the rationality assumption. If the core insight of behavioral economics is correct, it will be important for individuals with policy and planning responsibilities to be aware of the main findings contained in behavioral economics. The chapters in this volume also suggest that the behavioral approach offers a rich vein of potential research opportunities for scholars who study issues related to nuclear weapons.

Behavioral economics, and the bodies of research that inform it, give us good reasons to doubt that human beings can fully live up to the assumptions of a rational actor model. The participants in this project all agree with this skepticism, and they believe it extends to the realm of decision making about nuclear weapons. For this reason, our first conclusion is neither new nor controversial but is still worth remembering: it would not be prudent to rely on theories or models of deterrence or nonproliferation that assume states will make rational choices.

This does not mean rejecting the rationality assumption entirely. Research based on this assumption has generated important insights that justifiably helped shape thinking about issues such as deterrence and nuclear proliferation. While we should not assume perfect rationality in real-world situations, it would be a mistake to jettison expectations of rationality so fully that we end up assuming that other actors are simply irrational. Fortunately, truly irrational actors are fairly rare. The difficulties lie elsewhere. First, rational choice theories often require making assumptions about what actors value (as in the assumption that firms want to maximize profits).[45] But these assumptions can also be inaccurate. This was the essence of the critique of deterrence theory from the perspective of strategic culture, which argued that we have to understand what other actors value most and tailor deterrence to hold those values at risk.

But behavioral economics suggests a second difficulty. Actors strive to be rational, but they are subject to biases and rely on heuristics that lead to systematic deviations from the predictions of rational actor models. The allure of behavioral economics rests in part on this hope for predictability. If we understand the ways in which people systematically deviate from rationality, we can still predict their behavior. Unfortunately, at the end of this project, we conclude that this promise cannot be fully realized, for two reasons. First, behavioral economics contains multiple predictions, some of which are not easily compatible with each other. For instance, work on emotions suggests that fear makes people risk averse, but prospect theory seems to imply that fear of suffering a loss will instead make people risk acceptant. There are disagreements among the proponents of a behavioral approach about which predictions are most valid, and given the multiple options, it can be hard to know which is most likely to apply to a particular decision.

Second, the predictions of behavioral economics are only probabilistic. The models developed by behavioral economists are based mainly on the findings of experiments conducted on groups of people. Within any experiment, some people do not make the same choices as the majority. Similar to mainstream economics, the predictions of behavioral economics suggest what the average behavior will be in a large group of people. In this sense, although behavioral economics has identified predictable deviations from rationality, they are deviations that can be observed only in the aggregate. We still cannot predict if any given actor in a given situation will deviate in that particular way from making a rational choice. Yet, when it comes to deterrence, what we really want to know is whether a particular actor in a particular set of circumstances will be deterred. Behavioral economics might be able to assist us in assessing the probabilities, but because there are likely to be exceptions to almost every prediction, we cannot treat any prediction as completely reliable and ironclad.

In short, although behavioral research has generated a number of specific insights that would be useful to be aware of and keep in mind in strategic planning and decision making, it is difficult to integrate these into a single, comprehensive framework. We conclude, therefore, that behavioral economics does not yet provide a coherent and predictive model that can by itself serve as a basis for designing strategies. While it suggests important insights, behavioral economics does not on its own give us an analytical framework sufficient for identifying policies that will minimize nuclear dangers. At the same time, behavioral research reveals important limitations to relying too heavily on assumptions of rational behavior. Predictions based on the assumption that others will behave rationally will often be frustrated.

Based on the chapters in this volume, we conclude with five specific takeaways that have particular relevance to choosing policies and strategies to reduce nuclear dangers. First, it is vital to learn as much as possible about how others understand their situations and, where appropriate and feasible, to try to shape that understanding. If any theme runs across multiple chapters, it is the effect of how people frame their situations. The framing for choice can have a huge impact on the decisions people make. Frames can affect whether people perceive a question as involving only a simple interest calculation or instead involving a matter of justice or fairness. Frames also affect whether actors perceive themselves to be in a domain of gains or losses. Just as it is important to learn as much as possible about how others frame their circumstances and choice options, it is also important to examine ourselves and try to figure out our own biases. The better we know ourselves and know others, the better we can begin to anticipate how some common psychological tendencies might influence the course of our interactions.

Second, emotions can exert a powerful impact on human decisions and behavior. We should not assume that decisions about nuclear weapons will be shaped solely by cool calculations of cost and benefit. Emotions can also be differentiated, and in most situations, it will be advisable to avoid taking actions that provoke anger in the other side.

Third, people are often motivated more strongly by the desire to avoid or minimize loss than by the pursuit of gain. In situations where we perceive an aggressive actor out to expand its territory or influence, it is worth considering whether in its own thinking that actor views itself as seeking to avoid a future loss or reverse a past loss. As with anger, it is also generally a good idea not to take actions that will put other actors in a loss frame.

Fourth, people also tend to care about considerations of justice and fairness but often in self-serving ways. This makes it important to explore the possibilities for developing common standards of fairness. Such agreements, which might be about fair procedures and not just substantive outcomes, could pave the way for a successful diplomatic negotiation or a stable deterrent relationship.

Fifth, time horizons can change how people think. In particular, longer time horizons may allow space for more deliberative reasoning, which in turn can reduce the risks of rash or hasty decision making. This may be particularly the case with respect to keeping in mind the catastrophic destruction that could result from use of nuclear weapons and imparting a sense of shared danger or shared fate with respect to the urgency of avoiding any use of nuclear weapons in the future. Because individuals tend to heavily discount future payoffs, this advice may be hard to implement. But decisions that involve novel situations or especially high stakes open up the possibility of greater reliance on system 2's slow thinking; so, despite its many troubling implications, behavioral economics also leaves us with grounds for hope as well.

Even if behavioral economics does not provide an obvious solution to minimizing nuclear risks or a ready formula for making strategic choices, it does contain a number of separate insights that are useful and important to know and keep in mind. It is our hope that this book will help to create greater awareness of those insights.

NOTES

This introductory chapter is adapted from a final grant report submitted to the U.S. DTRA PASCC, "Real-World Nuclear Decision Making: Using Behavioral Economics Insights to Adjust Nonproliferation and Deterrence Policies to Predictable Deviations from Rationality" (Monterey, Calif.: James Martin Center for Nonproliferation Studies, January 2016).

1. Bernard Brodie, *The Absolute Weapon* (New York: Harcourt Brace, 1946), 76.

2. The most influential work remains that of Thomas C. Schelling. See his *The Strategy of Conflict* (Cambridge, Mass.: Harvard University Press, 1960) and *Arms and Influence* (New Haven, Conn.: Yale University Press, 1966). For an attempt to formalize earlier work that takes advantage of advances in game theory, see Robert Powell, *Nuclear Deterrence Theory: The Search for Credibility* (Cambridge: Cambridge University Press, 1990).

3. Richard Pipes, "Why the Soviet Union Thinks It Could Fight and Win a Nuclear War," *Commentary* 64, no. 1 (July 1977): 21–34.

4. Keith Payne, "The Fallacies of Cold War Deterrence and a New Direction," *Comparative Strategy* 22, no. 5 (December 2003): 411–28.

5. Jack L. Snyder, *The Soviet Strategic Culture: Implications for Limited Nuclear Operations*, RAND report R-2154-AF (Santa Monica, Calif.: RAND, 1977).

6. See M. Elaine Bunn, "Can Deterrence Be Tailored?" *Strategic Forum*, no. 225 (January 2007): 1–8, for a good short summary of this approach. On the relationship between strategic culture and tailored deterrence, see Jeffrey S. Lantis, "Strategic Culture and Tailored Deterrence," *Contemporary Security Policy* 30, no. 3 (December 2009): 467–85.

7. Stephen Maxwell, "Rationality in Deterrence," *Adelphi Papers*, no. 50 (1968): 1–19; Alexander L. George and Richard Smoke, *Deterrence in American Foreign Policy: Theory and Practice* (New York: Columbia University Press, 1974).

8. Richard Ned Lebow, *Between Peace and War: The Nature of International Crisis* (Baltimore: Johns Hopkins University Press, 1981).

9. For a good review, see Vesna Danilovic and Joe Clare, "Deterrence and Crisis Bargaining," in *International Studies Compendium*, ed. Robert E. Denemark (New York: Wiley-Blackwell, 2010), http://internationalstudies.oxfordre.com/view/10.1093/acrefore/9780190846626.001.0001/acrefore-9780190846626-e-78/version/0.

10. Amir Lupovici, "The Emerging Fourth Wave of Deterrence Theory: Toward a New Research Agenda," *International Studies Quarterly* 54, no. 3 (September 2010): 705-32.

11. Jeffrey W. Knopf, "The Fourth Wave in Deterrence Research," *Contemporary Security Policy* 31, no. 1 (April 2010): 1-33.

12. Colin S. Gray, "Maintaining Effective Deterrence," Strategic Studies Institute, U.S. Army War College, Carlisle, Penn., August 2003; Robert F. Trager and Dessislava P. Zagorcheva, "Deterring Terrorism: It Can Be Done," *International Security* 30, no. 3 (Winter 2005/6): 87-123; James H. Lebovic, *Deterring International Terrorism and Rogue States: US National Security Policy after 9/11* (London: Routledge, 2007).

13. Thomas Bernauer and Dieter Ruloff, eds., *The Politics of Positive Incentives in Arms Control* (Columbia: University of South Carolina Press, 1999); Etel Solingen, ed., *Sanctions, Statecraft, and Nuclear Proliferation* (Cambridge: Cambridge University Press, 2012); Jeffrey W. Knopf, ed. *Security Assurances and Nuclear Nonproliferation* (Stanford, Calif.: Stanford University Press, 2012); Nicholas L. Miller, "The Secret Success of Nonproliferation Sanctions," *International Organization* 68, no. 4 (Fall 2014): 913-44.

14. An important exception is the work of Janice Gross Stein on reassurance. See her "Deterrence and Reassurance," in *Behavior, Society and Nuclear War*, vol. 2, ed. Philip Tetlock, Jo L. Husbands, Robert Jervis, Paul C. Stern, and Charles Tilly (New York: Oxford University Press, 1991), 8-72.

15. Charles L. Glaser, "Why Even Good Defenses May Be Bad," *International Security* 9, no. 2 (Fall 1984): 92-123.

16. For an example on norms, see Maria Rost Rublee, *Nonproliferation Norms: Why States Choose Nuclear Restraint* (Athens: University of Georgia Press, 2009). For domestic politics, see Steven E. Miller, "Politics over Promise: Domestic Impediments to Arms Control," *International Security* 8, no. 4 (Spring 1984): 67-90

17. Daniel Kahneman, *Thinking, Fast and Slow* (New York: Farrar, Straus and Giroux, 2011); Richard Thaler and Cass Sunstein, *Nudge* (New Haven, Conn.: Yale University Press, 2008); Daniel Gilbert, *Stumbling on Happiness* (New York: Vintage Books, 2007); Dan Ariely, *Predictably Irrational* (New York: Harper Collins, 2008); Nassim Taleb, *The Black Swan* (New York: Penguin, 2008).

18. Colin F. Camerer and George Loewenstein, "Behavioral Economics: Past, Present, Future," in *Advances in Behavioral Economics*, ed. Colin F. Camerer, George Loewenstein, and Matthew Rabin (Princeton. N.J.: Princeton University Press, 2004), 3-51; Rick K. Wilson, "The Contribution of Behavioral Economics to Political Science," *Annual Review of Political Science* vol. 14 (2011): 201-23.

19. "The Behavioral Revolution and International Relations," *International Organization* 71, no. S1 (Supplement 2017), see especially the introduction by Emilie M. Hafner-Burton, Stephan Haggard, David A. Lake, and David G. Victor.

20. In an earlier collection on psychology and deterrence, Robert Jervis made a similar point, arguing that we have to care about individual cases that might be exceptions to a generalized prediction of rational behavior. See "Introduction: Approach and Assumptions," in Robert Jervis, Richard Ned Lebow, and Janice Gross Stein, *Psychology and Deterrence* (Baltimore: Johns Hopkins University Press, 1985), 10-11.

21. The classic study remains Robert Jervis, *Perception and Misperception in International Politics* (Princeton, N.J.: Princeton University Press, 1976).

22. Jervis, Lebow, and Stein, *Psychology and Deterrence*.

23. Herbert A. Simon, *Models of Man, Social and Rational: Mathematical Essays on Rational Human Behavior in a Social Setting* (New York: John Wiley and Sons, 1957).

24. Christine Jolls, Cass R. Sunstein, and Richard Thaler, "A Behavioral Approach to Law and Economics," *Stanford Law Review* vol. 50 (May 1998): 1471–1550.

25. The story of Tversky and Kahneman's collaboration is related in Michael Lewis, *The Undoing Project: A Friendship That Changed Our Minds* (New York: W. W. Norton, 2016).

26. Kahneman, "Part 1: Two Systems," *Thinking, Fast and Slow*, 19–105.

27. These are summarized in Kahneman, *Thinking, Fast and Slow*, part 2.

28. The authors summarized the theory initially in Daniel Kahneman and Amos Tversky, "Prospect Theory: An Analysis of Decision under Risk," *Econometrica* 47 (1979): 263–91. For a revised and updated version that added further wrinkles to the approach and that remains the standard model today, see Tversky and Kahneman, "Advances in Prospect Theory: Cumulative Representation of Uncertainty," *Journal of Risk and Uncertainty* 5, no. 4 (1992): 297–323.

29. Amos Tversky and Daniel Kahneman, "The Framing of Decisions and the Psychology of Choice," *Science* 211, no. 4481 (January 30, 1981): 453–58.

30. Jan Faber, "On Bounded Rationality and the Framing of Decision in International Relations: Towards a Dynamic Network Model of World Politics," *Journal of Peace Research* 27, no. 3 (1990): 307–19; Janice Gross Stein and Louis W. Pauly, eds., *Choosing to Co-operate: How States Avoid Loss* (Baltimore: Johns Hopkins University Press, 1993); Barbara Farnham, ed., *Avoiding Losses/Taking Risks: Prospect Theory in International Politics* (Ann Arbor: University of Michigan Press, 1994); Jack Levy, "Prospect Theory, Rational Choice, and International Relations," *International Studies Quarterly* 41, no. 1 (1997): 87–112; Robert Jervis, "The Implications of Prospect Theory for Human Nature," *Political Psychology* 25, no. 2 (2002): 163–76; Jeffrey Berejikian, "The Gains Debate: Framing State Choice," *American Political Science Review* 91, no. 4 (1997): 789–805; Rose McDermott, *Risk Taking in International Politics: Prospect Theory in American Foreign Policy* (Ann Arbor: University of Michigan Press, 1998); Rose McDermott, "Prospect Theory in Political Science: Gains and Losses from the First Decade," *Political Psychology* 25, no. 2 (2004): 289–312.

31. Jeffrey Berejikian, "A Cognitive Theory of Deterrence," *Journal of Peace Research* 39, no. 2 (2002): 165–83.

32. Emilie M. Hafner-Burton, D. Alex Hughes, and David G. Victor, "The Cognitive Revolution and the Political Psychology of Elite Decision Making," *Perspectives on Politics* 11, no. 2 (June 2013): 368–86.

33. The pathbreaking work was by Antonio Damasio. Its implications for international relations are discussed in Jonathan Mercer, "Rationality and Psychology in International Politics," *International Organization* 59, no. 1 (Winter 2005): 77–106. See also Todd H. Hall and Andrew A. G. Ross, "Affective Politics after 9/11," *International Organization* 69, no. 4 (Fall 2015), 847–79.

34. Jacques E. C. Hymans, *The Psychology of Nuclear Proliferation* (Cambridge: Cambridge University Press, 2006).

35. Janice Gross Stein, "The Psychology of Assurance: An Emotional Tale," in *Security Assurances and Nuclear Nonproliferation*, ed. Jeffrey W. Knopf (Stanford, Calif.: Stanford University Press, 2012), 39–56.

36. For example, in one experiment, parents mostly arrived on time to pick up children from a day care center because they did not want to inconvenience the day care staff by making them stay late. But when the day care center added a fine for late pickups, more parents came late because they were willing to pay a financial penalty and no longer felt the social obligation to be on time. Camerer and Loewenstein, "Behavioral Economics," 27 (see also the relevant experiment described on 34); Ariely, *Predictably Irrational*, ch. 4.

37. For a nice summary, see Frank Rose, "Don't Mess with My 'Sacred Values,'" *New York Times*, Sunday Review, November 16, 2013. Relevant studies include J. Baron and M. Spranca, "Protected Values," *Organizational Behavior and Human Decision Processes* 70, no. 1 (April 1997): 1–16; Philipp Tetlock, "Thinking the Unthinkable: Sacred Values and Taboo Cognitions," *Trends in Cognitive Sciences* 7, no. 7 (July 2003): 320–24; Scott Atran and Robert Axelrod, "Reframing Sacred Values," *Negotiation Journal* 24, no. 3 (July 2008): 221–46.

38. David A. Welch, *Justice and the Genesis of War* (Cambridge: Cambridge University Press, 1993); Jonathan Mercer, "Emotional Beliefs," *International Organization* 64, no. 1 (Winter 2010): 10–11; Stein, "Psychology of Assurance."

39. Jeffrey W. Knopf, "Disarmament and Nonproliferation: Examining the Linkage Hypothesis," *International Security* 37, no. 3 (Winter 2012/13): 92–132.

40. Linda Babcock and George Loewenstein, "Explaining Bargaining Impasse: The Role of Self-Serving Biases," *Journal of Economic Perspectives* 11, no. 1 (1997): 109–26.

41. Morielle I. Lotan, "Strategic Dilemmas of WMD Operators," *Comparative Strategy* 34, no. 4 (2015): 345–66.

42. U.S. Department of Defense, *Deterrence Operations Joint Operating Concept*, version 2.0 (Offutt Air Force Base, Neb.: U.S. Strategic Command, December 2006).

43. A similar conclusion has been argued from a different psychological foundation in Michael D. Cohen, *When Proliferation Causes Peace: The Psychology of Nuclear Crises* (Washington, D.C.: Georgetown University Press, 2017).

44. This critique dovetails with a major theme in the *International Organization* special issue devoted to behavioral approaches, which identifies aggregation from individuals to states as an ongoing problem in attempts to use psychology to explain international outcomes. See especially Robert Powell, "Research Bets and Behavioral IR," *International Organization* 71, no. S1 (Supplement 2017): S265–77.

45. Herbert Simon refers to these as *auxiliary assumptions* and argues that they often do much of the work in rational choice theories (see Herbert A. Simon, "Human Nature in Politics: The Dialogue of Psychology with Political Science," *American Political Science Review* 79, no. 2 [June 1985]: 293–304).

CHAPTER ONE

Testing a Cognitive Theory of Deterrence

JEFFREY D. BEREJIKIAN AND FLORIAN JUSTWAN

In this chapter, we evaluate the potential of prospect theory to explain risky decisions that lead to deterrence failures. Our analysis is based on experimental findings in behavioral economics about the factors shaping human risk disposition and is motivated by both academic and policy concerns. Specifically, we are interested in examining important but untested assumptions about risk and deterrence stability that underpin the American approach to deterrence. As echoes of the Cold War faded, scholars and policymakers increasingly argued that deterrence strategies needed to incorporate as much information as possible about the perceptions, values, and decision making of potential deterrence targets.[1] In 2006, the United States signaled a significant shift toward tailored deterrence policies that emphasize the psychological dimensions of deterrence stability.[2] This change accompanied a reconsideration of decades-old assumptions about decision making that had served as the cornerstone of deterrence thinking during the Cold War. Rather than assuming that deterrence threats are perceived objectively by rational actors, the U.S. view is now that successful deterrence requires "getting into the heads" of rival decision makers to understand how the world looks from their perspective.[3]

For deterrence planners, understanding rival risk perceptions—both the level of risk acceptance and the timing of shifts in risk preferences—emerged as a central concern. For example, the U.S. *Deterrence Operations Joint Operating Concept* (DO-JOC) states that "deterrence policies must account for both risk-averse and risk-acceptant" governments because "[a]n adversary's risk-taking propensity affects the relationship between values and probabilities of benefits and costs when in the process of reaching a decision. Risk-averse adversaries will see very low probability, but severe costs as a powerful deterrent, while risk-acceptant adversaries will discount costs in their pursuit of significant gains."[4]

The implication here is that the level of deterrence credibility sufficient to deter risk-averse governments may be insufficient to deter those that are risk acceptant. Interestingly, according to the DO-JOC, the intellectual underpinning for this assertion "incorporates elements of prospect theory in its approach."[5]

However, the academic research literature provides little empirical evidence for the relationship between risk disposition and deterrence stability that has been incorporated in American security documents. While there is some conceptual scholarship linking prospect theory to deterrence outcomes, this work is theoretical and remains untested.[6] We do not know, for example, if there is a set of conditions under which an adversary's decision making shifts from conservative to risk acceptant. Nor do we know if, or when, such risk acceptance leads to a breakdown of stable deterrence relationships.

Our analysis constitutes the first statistical test of deterrence outcomes explicitly grounded in prospect theory. Because the United States is the dominant military power on the planet, assessing the veracity of cognitive assumptions embedded in American security doctrine is important for policy reasons. An analysis of prospect theory and deterrence is hence relevant to both deterrence scholars and policymakers.

For academics, our results show that governments are more likely to risk provoking deterrence rivals when the status quo ante for security—what we call the *security frame*—is unacceptable. These results hold even when controlling for a standard set of covariates identified in the academic literature as precipitating a deterrence failure. Furthermore, in additional statistical tests we find that our results are *not* moderated by the nuclear status of the defender. In other words, our empirical analysis suggests that the effect of security frames is not limited to non-nuclear dyads. This is noteworthy because it demonstrates that our cognitive theory of deterrence has explanatory value for deterrence failures in both nuclear and non-nuclear settings.

For policymakers, our results reveal that measurable shifts in the security environment can affect risk disposition and, therefore, undermine deterrence stability.[7] This insight can be folded into a tailored deterrence framework.

We divide the remainder of this chapter into five sections. First, we provide a selective overview of traditional deterrence theory with an emphasis on risk. Second, we develop a cognitive theory of deterrence anchored to prospect theory and derive testable hypotheses. Third, we summarize alternative explanations for the breakdown of deterrence so that we can control for their effects. Fourth, we test our claims against the deterrence behavior of strategic rivals during the period 1816–1999. The discussion concludes by identifying some of the practical implications of our analysis for deterrence policymaking and by suggesting topics for future research.

CLASSICAL DETERRENCE THEORY

Traditional deterrence scholarship can be divided into two broad camps, structural and decision theoretic.[8] While both camps assume that policymakers respond rationally to deterrence incentives, neither develops an explicit theory of risk disposition that can explain when and why risk preferences shift. Structural deterrence arguments focus on the material distribution of military capabilities and the balance of threats between deterrence partners.[9] Deterrence success, then, reduces to relative capability, and assumptions about shifting risk preferences recede into the background. The objective distribution of power across antagonists defines the incentives for conflict. According to this structural approach, power parity supports stability because it increases the potential costs of conflict as neither side has a distinct advantage. When the distribution of power becomes unbalanced, in contrast, weaker states can no longer credibly deter stronger rivals and the situation becomes unstable. As the cost of conflict increases for other reasons (e.g., through the destructive capacity of weapons systems), the stabilizing influence of parity is enhanced. As Mearsheimer puts it, the more "horrible" the costs of war, "the less likely it is to occur."[10] While structural arguments have tended to focus on great power conflict and the presumed stability of a bipolar distribution of power, the same logic can be generalized to most types of rivalry including competition between nuclear powers.[11]

For decision theorists, defender reputation, resolve, and motivation affect deterrence stability. Thomas Schelling argues that a state's past conflict behavior can deter future conflict by credibly signaling a willingness to defend core values.[12] While foreign policy scholarship has largely rejected an unqualified version of this reputational argument, research supports the more modest claim that defender reputations accrue in dyads.[13] Research also suggests that states with many rivals have an incentive to engage in conflictual behavior (often short of war) as part of a proactive reputation-building strategy.[14] In addition, challengers have greater reason to believe deterrence threats when rivals pursue policies in a way that engages domestic actors. Leaders in democratic regimes, for example, face domestic political costs when they do not follow through on their commitments.[15] These "audience costs" increase the credibility of public deterrent threats and explain why governments sometimes deliberately tie their hands through the forward deployment of resources. While scholars still debate some of the assumptions surrounding the concept of audience costs, Weeks provides evidence for their existence even in autocratic regimes.[16] Public commitments can also bolster deterrence credibility in defense pacts. Transparent defensive alliances are significantly less likely to become the targets of military aggression.[17] Fuhrmann and Sechser extend this logic to alliances that include nuclear powers, and find that credibility is enhanced when an ally "stands to incur damage to its reputation if it does not fulfill its obligation."[18]

While contemporary deterrence scholarship has forged a consensus on the structural and reputational factors associated with deterrence outcomes, there is little agreement about the determinants and impact of shifting risk dispositions.

Many studies simply do not explicitly theorize about risk.[19] Still, ignoring the fact that risk preferences do shift is often less worrisome than deliberately assuming away variation in risk disposition altogether. For example, Fearon asserts that states are either "risk-averse or risk-neutral over the issues" because "[a] risk-acceptant leader is analogous to a compulsive gambler—willing to accept a sequence of gambles that has the expected outcome of eliminating the state and regime. Even if we admitted such a leader as rational, it seems doubtful that many have held such preferences."[20] Any theory anchored to such an assumption cannot explain deterrence failures that are in fact the result of risk-acceptant decision making. Excluding even the possibility of risky decisions, therefore, directs our attention away from what is perhaps the central challenge in deterrence planning.

This lack of attention to the issue of shifting risk preferences is not a problem inherent to the underlying logic of deterrence politics. Instead, simply ignoring risky decisions or bracketing risk acceptance as "compulsive" is a *theoretic* choice. We believe it to be a mistake. Instead, our objective here is to explain the circumstances under which risk-acceptant behavior is most likely to emerge and determine the degree to which it undermines deterrence stability. Prospect theory views changing risk dispositions as a natural and predictable component of human choice, rather than as a pathological compulsion, an error that can be dismissed as irrational, or an idiosyncratic characteristic of individual decision makers. In this way, prospect theory provides a solid foundation on which to begin an investigation into the conditions that produce risk-acceptant deterrence decision making.

PROSPECT THEORY, STATUS QUO EVALUATIONS, AND DETERRENCE

Prospect theory stands as the leading alternative to rational choice in explaining why decision makers take risks. The approach builds upon underlying empirical observations about human decision making.[21] Loss aversion describes the observation that the subjective sting from losses hurts more than the enjoyment derived from equivalent gains. As a result, people usually expend more effort and demonstrate greater resolve when trying to avoid losses compared to when they attempt to secure new gains. Reference dependence captures the finding that decision makers are quite sensitive to deviations from a reference point, which often though not always reflects their status quo endowment. People evaluate alternative strategies in terms of the potential to produce gains or losses against a reference point, rather than against their final net asset positions.

Prospect theory thus describes decision making in a two-step process. The first step involves the framing of options. Here, individuals consider the potential consequences of their decisions and place these outcomes in a domain of gains or losses. The second stage involves an evaluation of options and a decision. The central finding under prospect theory is that the initial frame affects one's willingness to tolerate risk. That is, an individual's risk disposition is influenced by whether the outcomes are perceived as gains or losses relative to their reference point.[22] In gains frames, individuals consistently exhibit risk aversion: they will choose a no-risk option with a guaranteed payoff over a gamble that could lead to a higher payoff but with a chance of ending up with nothing, even when the gamble has an equal or greater expected value. By contrast, in loss frames, decision makers display risk acceptance: they prefer a gamble that could eliminate losses but also lead to greater losses over a no-risk prospect of equal or greater value.

A simple example demonstrates the consequences of framing:

> *Gains frame*: Imagine a choice between two options that imply personal gains.
> - Option 1: a sure gain of eighty dollars
> - Option 2: a risky venture with an 85 percent chance of winning one hundred dollars and a 15 percent chance of winning nothing
>
> *Losses frame*: Now imagine a second set of options that imply personal losses.
> - Option 1: a sure loss of eighty dollars
> - Option 2: an 85 percent chance of losing one hundred dollars and a 15 percent chance of losing nothing

In the gains-frame condition, most decision makers prefer the certain outcome (option 1) over the risky venture even though the expected monetary outcome is five dollars less. By contrast, in the loss-frame condition, most individuals prefer the gamble (option 2) over the sure thing even though the expected financial loss is five dollars greater. The impact of decision frames on risk preferences is notable because it produces choices that confound rational decision making. For deterrence, loss frames are important because they produce decisions wherein individuals consistently forgo the option that should be expected to produce the largest level of benefit.[23] As we will describe, this kind of risk taking can undermine stable deterrence even when both governments have crafted credible deterrence policies and when the expected benefits of the deterrence status quo are greater than the potential gains from conflict initiation.

Operationalizing decision frames is then the central conceptual task when using prospect theory as a foundation for foreign policy analysis. In laboratory experiments it is relatively easy to manipulate gains and loss frames, but this kind of direct experimentation is not possible outside a lab. Unfortunately, prospect theory does not itself offer a "theory of framing." Kahneman and Tversky note, for example, that "the reference point is the state to which one has become adapted." This implies that the reference point and the status quo are one in the same. However, they also suggest that there are many cases in which "the reference point is determined by events that are only imagined."[24] Moreover, there is evidence that actors treat the recent past as a reference point, against which they only partially adjust an evaluation of current value.[25] Decision-maker aspirations can also define reference points. For example, unmet aspirations can produce loss frames and risk-acceptant, nonmaximizing choices.[26]

The difficulty in establishing reference points and decision frames is not, however, an insurmountable task. Prospect theory has enjoyed considerable success in explaining risky choices in the real world. Much of this research is in the field of behavioral economics, where several decades of investigation demonstrate that framing is pervasive and that it influences a wide range of economic decisions.[27] There is also good reason to believe that the cognitive mechanisms underlying prospect theory emerged in response to evolutionary pressures in the early human environment and are thus part of a shared biological legacy.[28] Indeed, cognitive neuroscience appears to confirm that shifts in risk disposition are anchored to the structure of the human brain and that framing is attached to basic and fundamental emotional processing.[29]

In the foreign policy literature, a relationship between decision frame, risk tolerance, and foreign policy is now well established and points to the promise of deploying prospect theory to understand deterrence politics.[30] Early applications of prospect theory in foreign policy analysis were conceptual and intended to demonstrate its potential to explain behavior that defied conventional explanations.[31] The first wave of empirical research confirmed that loss frames propel governments into risky decisions as they pursue their foreign policy goals.[32] More recently, scholars have used prospect theory to explain the content of the goals themselves. Kahneman and Renshon argue that risk acceptance under loss frames produces a bias for hawkish foreign policies.[33] Berejikian demonstrates that the onset of loss frames elicits a shift from liberal to realist policy preferences.[34] Garrison, and Fuhrmann and Early, show that shifting decision frames can undermine government support for arms control negotiations.[35] Domestic decision frames also shape foreign policy behavior. For example, when leaders are trapped in an eroding political position, they are likely to adopt risk-acceptant foreign policies.[36] Elites can also manipulate public attitudes about conflict by creating loss frames.[37] Finally, the onset of a loss frame can propel states into risky wars. Levy and Whyte show how an eroding security position produced a high risk tolerance among Japan's elite in the lead up to World War II.[38] Under loss frames, great powers are more likely to enter into risky conflicts with lesser rivals and remain bogged down in such disputes long after the costs of continuing outstrip any further gains in security.[39]

All of this suggests that there is now robust empirical evidence to support the contention that policymakers operating in the domain of losses are more likely to adopt risk-acceptant foreign policy strategies. Below, we extend this logic to deterrence and argue that government assessments about the status quo for security shape the decision frame for deterrence relationships. According to prospect theory, these security frames affect risk disposition and, therefore, calculations about the utility of escalation in the face of deterrent threats.[40]

Defining the Frame

While the concept of a frame takes many meanings in the foreign policy literature, the integration of prospect theory into deterrence logic requires that we commit to a single definition and a set of associated propositions.[41] Here, we adopt the concept of evaluative framing from Mintz and Redd because it is most consistent with the cognitive processes associated with prospect theory. Evaluative framing "occurs when the frame manipulates the reference point to which the external environment is compared" so that "the frame operates as an evaluative anchor in the assessment of the environment."[42] Evaluative frames provide the reference against which decision makers assess alternative strategies and their associated outcomes. We assume that governments continually evaluate the effectiveness of their security policies and that the sum of these examinations constitutes a state's evaluative frame for security. When the status quo ante for security is unacceptable, prospect theory predicts that decision makers become more willing to accept gambles to "catch up" and minimize their potential losses. As we will discuss, these shifts in frame-induced risk influence the policies that governments adopt as they manage their relationships with strategic rivals.[43]

Because prospect theory cannot predict the content of an evaluative frame, that is, whether a state views the status quo as acceptable or unacceptable, we also assume a relationship between a government's objective condition and its self-understanding of the security environment. The notion that states construct evaluative frames to assess their overall security potential against their actual position has deep roots in the study of foreign policy. For example, balance of power theory, power transition theory, and hegemonic conflict theory all incorporate elements of this idea.[44] The shared insight in these approaches is that governments assess their overall security position relative to their rivals and then calibrate their strategies accordingly. Power transition theory, in particular, emphasizes the importance of status quo evaluations and their impact on foreign policy choices.[45] While scholars have tended to focus on great powers, the evidence is clear that lesser states make similar assessments on a regional basis.[46]

This means that we treat decision-maker assessments of the status quo as an empirical matter. In our approach, decision frames are defined by the objective, material consequences of a government's foreign policy choices.[47] It is axiomatic that all states cannot achieve the same level of security because security endowments and external constraints differ across countries and over time. Instead, we assume that governments evaluate their security performance against realistic possibilities. This evaluative frame for security is defined by the comparison of a state's actual security position to its potential, given the security endowments and regional constraints at each point in time. States that are closer to maximizing their potential are more likely to judge that they are doing well, while states near the opposite end of the continuum are more likely to be dissatisfied with the status quo ante for security.

Frames and Deterrence Stability

The integration of evaluative framing with prospect theory produces a set of hypotheses that are amenable to statistical testing. When the status quo ante for security is acceptable, governments can opt for the benefits of the status quo through inaction, or they can pursue an escalation gamble intended to improve their position through a policy of confrontation. Such governments confront a gains-frame choice, and according to prospect theory, they are more likely to adopt risk-averse policies. Under gains frames, we should then observe that challengers will more often prefer the status quo over the gamble, even in circumstances where a defender's reputation is questionable and/or confrontation contains an expected value of further gain. Conversely, when the status quo ante for security is unacceptable, governments face a choice between accepting the losses inherent to the status quo and a gamble intended to improve their position. Here, policymakers face a loss-frame choice, and according to prospect theory, they would be more risk acceptant. We should observe that such governments more often opt for the gamble in an attempt to upend the status quo, even if a defender's deterrence threats are credible and/or confrontation carries an expected value of further loss beyond the status quo ante.

This logic formalizes the relationship between decision frame, risk, and deterrence stability that is (often implicitly) assumed in U.S. deterrence planning. Specifically, deterrence is more likely to be effective when both states are in a gains frame, and less likely to be effective when either or both are in a losses frame. Under gains frames, even less than credible deterrence threats will provide a sufficient deterrent. By contrast, under a loss frame, even largely credible deterrence threats may not suffice. This framework also allows us to formulate two specific testable hypotheses about prospect theory and the stability of deterrence relationships.[48]

> Hypothesis 1: Dyads with two states in gains frames are more stable than dyads with one or both states in a loss frame.
>
> Hypothesis 2: Within dyads, states in a loss frame are more likely to destabilize an existing deterrence relationship than are states in a gains frame.

TESTING THE ARGUMENT

To test these hypotheses, we need a dataset identifying the universe of general deterrence relationships. Previous scholarship suggests that dyadic rivalries are the appropriate sample.[49] Our analysis begins with the dataset constructed by Clare and Danilovic, who focus on cases of strategic rivalries from 1816 to 1999 as developed by Thompson.[50] Here, the dyad qualifies as a rivalry if three criteria are met: "The actors in question must regard each other as (a) competitors, (b) the source of actual or latent threats that pose some possibility of becoming militarized, and (c) enemies."[51] Clare and Danilovic supplement Thompson's original dataset with militarized interstate dispute (MID) data.[52] This step allows for the analysis of disputes within all 174 rivalries. Our unit of analysis in the dataset is the directed-rivalry-dyad-year.[53] The dependent variable is a binary indicator that captures the destabilization of an existing deterrence relationship. It is coded as "1" when the challenger threatens, displays, or uses force against its opponent. Since the dependent variable is dichotomous in nature, we estimate the model with binary probit.

Operationalizing the Security Frame

Bueno de Mesquita provides a useful metric for assessing a state's overall security position.[54] A key innovation in this framework is the use of alliance patterns as a proxy for the degree to which states broadly share common foreign policy goals and the extent to which they differ. Because alliance patterns are (at least in part) malleable, we adopt Bueno de Mesquita's assumption that alliances signal a country's security interests and that over time governments alter these policies in order to express affiliation or disagreement with the security objectives of other states. Utilizing the method described by Bueno de Mesquita in *The War Trap* for operationalizing the utility of conflict, we construct a continuum from best to worst possible regional security environments for all states j versus each target i.[55] This continuum is bracketed at the high end by the hypothetical interstate alliance pattern and relative power configuration that would leave i most vulnerable to defeat, and at the low end by the pattern that leaves i most secure. That is, we can define the endpoints on the continuum as the sum of expected utilities for j versus i, $\Sigma E(U_{ji})_{max}$ and $\Sigma E(U_{ji})_{min}$ respectively. State i's actual security $\Sigma_{j \neq i} E(U_{ji})$ moves between the extremes of this continuum as alliance patterns and relative power shift over time. By this conceptualization, i is least secure when the summed expected utilities for conflict are at their maximum (because its potential opponents j are at their relatively most powerful), and i is most secure when they at their minimum.

For example, for Spain in 1990 the security continuum ranges from 95.15 (worst security environment) to −31.02 (best security environment). That is, the worst possible outcome for Spain in 1990 would be if the observed expected utilities for conflict for j states in Europe summed to 95.15.[56] Spain's observed security score for 1990 was −29.54, indicating that the country was about as secure as possible, given the constraints it faced. By contrast, the observed score for Chile in 1960 was 87.53, with a range from 87.75 (worst security) to −101.55 (best security), indicating that Chile operated in a very threatening international environment in which the summed expected utility for conflict for Chile's neighbors was near its maximum.

To construct our loss-frame variable, we use the method above to first identify the midpoint on a state's security continuum for each year. If a country's actual security score for a given year is below this point, we code the state as being in a gains frame (coded as loss frame = 0). Conversely, if the yearly score is above the midpoint, the state falls short of its security potential. Consistent with our argument that the evaluative frame for security is defined by the comparison between a state's actual security position and its overall potential, these governments are more likely to be unsatisfied with the status quo. We therefore code these states as being in a loss frame (coded as loss frame = 1).

We acknowledge that decision makers do not always perceive their country's strategic position in the same way that outside observers would define it and that there is a distinguished tradition in international relations scholarship on leader perception.[57] However, because our operationalization of the decision frame is tied to objective conditions, any perceptual variation or bias (systematic or random) would serve to weaken correlations between the security frame as we measure it and deterrence outcomes and therefore work against the statistical test we describe later. We will also offer an additional analysis to determine the degree to which perception might affect our results.

A quick look at diplomatic history suggests that governments are quite aware of their country's overall position on the security spectrum and that they pay close attention to the central components that are in our operationalization of the strategic frame. For example, at the beginning of the twentieth century, our variable codes Germany as being in a loss frame. Indeed, policymakers in Berlin were quite dissatisfied with the international status quo—specifically the deepening cooperation between France, Great Britain, and Russia. On numerous occasions German chancellor von Bülow expressed his unease about "encirclement" by the Triple Entente, and he suggested that this policy was potentially "very dangerous for peace."[58] Diplomatic correspondence reveals that Emperor Wilhelm shared this pessimistic interpretation of Germany's strategic frame during the early 1900s.[59] The monarch was particularly concerned about the possibility of a binding Anglo-French agreement regarding the distribution of naval forces, and he feared that the entente members were prepared to "fight and arm together against [Germany]."[60]

Decision makers in London were equally dissatisfied with their country's status quo at the beginning of the twentieth century. Britain experienced a period of relative decline between 1895 and 1905.[61] For many years, the kingdom had been operating under the "two-power standard," which stipulated that its naval strength was to be equal with the maritime capabilities of the two next greatest powers. This formula was seen as the primary method to protect the overall security of the British Empire. In the early 1900s, however, this long-standing policy had become inadequate as countries like Japan, Russia, France, and Germany had made significant efforts to upgrade their militaries and—in the case of Russia and France—increased their diplomatic cooperation. Politicians in London felt uneasy about the new distribution of power and underlying alliance patterns on the continent.[62] The First Lord of the Admiralty, the Earl of Selborne, summarized salient British concerns in a memorandum composed in September 1901: "The recognized standard for the naval strength of Great Britain has hitherto been equality with the ships of the two next greatest naval Powers. [T]his standard would be beyond the strength of this country if the United States were to use all their resources to develop this naval strength, and . . . it is inadequate if applied to a possible war against France in alliance with Russia."[63] Walter Kerr, the first sea lord of the British Empire, expressed similar feelings about Britain's strategic frame. In a letter to Selborne, he lamented "the strain which is being put upon" Britain because of the "feverish developments of other nations" that threatened to overwhelm their country.[64]

These (albeit brief) descriptions of the German and the British cases demonstrate that the indicators used by decision makers to construct their evaluative frames are captured by the measure we describe above. By our measure, both Britain and Germany fell significantly short of their security potential at the beginning of the twentieth century, and the language used by foreign policy elites suggests that this objective condition influenced how they perceived their security performance.

Alternative Explanations

As noted, previous research has suggested several additional variables that can influence the stability of deterrence relationships. To place our statistical analysis on the broadest possible foundation and to test the robustness of our independent variable against potentially confounding factors, we surveyed the literature on conflict and military deterrence for potential alternative explanations. We group these explanations into four categories.[65]

Geopolitical interests. The first set of alternative explanations for deterrence breakdown is related to the geopolitical interests of both states. While strategic rivals can be assumed to have conflictual interests toward each other, additional dissimilarity of broader geopolitical interests may make conflict even more likely. We include a measure of both states' alliance portfolio (weighted global s-score) as a proxy for the similarity of security interests.[66] Furthermore, a state's close relationship with a superpower can have a tangible impact on its willingness to fight. For targets, close ties with the system leader may serve as a deterrent. For challengers, close alliance ties with the most powerful state can either restrain or incentivize conflict, depending on the specific policy preferences and behavior of the superpower. To account for these possibilities, we include each state's alliance portfolio similarity with the system leader into our model (portfolio similarity leader).

Reputations. The next set of variables in our model is related to the reputation of both states. These covariates are included in the original Clare and Danilovic dataset. They argue that challengers with weak reputations and many competitors have an incentive to "appear strong" and engage in proactive reputation building. While reputation building is a long-run rational strategy, the short-run mechanism by which it is pursued involves a policy of heightened confrontation. This is, then, an alternative explanation for the disruption of established deterrent relationships within the context of strategic rivalries. Clare and Danilovic developed a two-part scheme for operationalizing the incentive to build reputations. The first is a count of the total number of rivalries with which a country is involved in a given year (number of rivals). The second is the challenger's reputation. This variable is based on the state's behavior in its most recent dispute. It is considered to be irresolute if it acquiesced to its opponent or if the opponent won the dispute without the application of force. Since reputation can be assumed to decline over time, the final reputation variable is calculated by raising 0.9 to the x-th power, where x is the number of years since a state acted irresolutely. We add these two variables and an interaction term (reputation x number of rivals) to the model since the effect of a challenger's reputation has been shown to be conditional on the total number of potential opponents. Furthermore, previous scholarship has identified the reputation of defenders as an important explanatory variable. To account for this, we also include an indicator for defender reputation. The coding procedure follows the approach outlined above.

Capabilities. As mentioned, structural theories of deterrence emphasize the impact of capabilities on threat credibility. To capture the balance of power between two states in a dyad, we control for the ratio of the challenger's capabilities to the combined capabilities of both states in a dyad (relative capabilities). In addition, there is reason to believe that absolute capabilities have an independent effect on the stability of deterrence: even if the balance of forces favors one side over the other one, this advantage might be insignificant if a country is weak in absolute terms. We therefore also include a separate measure of the power of both states in the dyad in our model (capabilities challenger and capabilities target). Furthermore, a state's power may be directly affected by its current dispute involvement. In an analysis of general deterrence between enduring rivals, Huth and Russett show that deterrence breakdown is significantly less likely if the challenger is already engaged in a dispute with another state.[67] Conversely, a defender that is involved in a conflict with a third party may appear as an "easy target," which may motivate its rivals to initiate a dispute. To account for these processes, we add two dummy variables to our dataset (ongoing dispute initiator and ongoing dispute defender) that are coded as 1 if the challenger or target respectively has an ongoing extradyadic dispute at the start of a given year. A final set of capability-related variables is taken from the literature on military alliances. Recent scholarship in this area has demonstrated that formalized agreements between states directly affect deterrence outcomes. Specifically, Johnson and Leeds show that the initiation of interstate disputes is significantly less likely if the defender has a defensive alliance that is relevant for a given dyad.[68] They attribute this to a deterrent effect of these agreements. They also demonstrate that challengers with relevant offensive alliances and neutrality pacts are more likely to initiate conflict. Building on these insights, we use alliance data from Johnson and Leeds and introduce three variables to our dataset. Defense pact target captures whether the target has a defensive alliance with another state that is relevant against the challenger. Offensive alliance challenger and neutrality pact challenger are coded as 1 if the initiator has signed a relevant offensive alliance or neutrality pact with a third state.

Domestic politics. According to audience cost theory, the threats issued by democracies are more credible than statements by nondemocratic leaders since decision makers who are accountable to the public will face domestic punishment if they do not follow through on their public announcements. Here, we control for the regime type of both challenger and target. We include two dummy variables (democracy initiator and democracy target), which are coded as 1 if the initiator or target scores above +5 in the polity IV dataset and 0 otherwise. Since numerous studies in the field of international relations have found that democracies tend to be more peaceful toward each other, we also add a control variable to the dataset that indicates whether both states in a dyad are democracies according to the operationalization above.[69]

Finally, we add a set of standard control variables from the literature on conflict and military deterrence to our model. We control for the minor/major power status of the dyad, the logged distance between both states' capitals, and geographic contiguity.[70] We also include cubic splines of the number of peace years in a particular dyad in order to address the problem of temporal dependency.[71]

RESULTS AND DISCUSSION

Hypothesis 1 suggests that gains-frame dyads are more stable than dyads in which one or both states are in a loss frame. To investigate this claim, we conducted a simple t-test and compared the mean number of peace years for pairs of states that were constantly in a gains frame and dyads in which at least one state was constantly in a loss frame. From the forty dyads that fit this description, twenty-one were gains-frame dyads and nineteen loss-frame dyads. The results can be found in table 1.1 and provide initial support for our theory. The mean number of peace years for gains-frame dyads is 20.1 and 12.8 for loss-frame dyads. The difference between these two values is statistically significant at the 0.05 level in a one-tailed test.

These statistics are suggestive and provide initial empirical support for our cognitive theory of deterrence. However, in order to convincingly show that loss frames undermine deterrence, we need to move beyond these bivariate relationships. We next estimated a series of four statistical models to test hypothesis 2 (table 1.2). We chose an incremental procedure to investigate the robustness of our findings and to get a deeper understanding of the relationships between the variables in our dataset: in model 1, we included only our main independent variable, the variables related to states' geopolitical interests and the standard controls. In models 2–4 we then successively added the variables related to reputation, capabilities, and domestic politics. Model 4 is the fully specified analysis with all the covariates we have described.

This approach reveals the most important finding of our analysis: our main independent variable, "loss frame," is significant at the 0.01 level and the effect is robust to various model specifications. Furthermore, the size of the coefficient remains stable across all four models, suggesting that loss frames represent an important factor that existing research has neglected. Several of the alternative explanations also receive support in our statistical analysis. Models 1, 2, and 3 provide evidence for the claims that strategic rivals with similar geopolitical interests are slightly less likely to initiate disputes than rivals with very dissimilar

Table 1.1
Mean Number of Peace Years for Loss-Frame Dyads and Gains-Frame Dyads

	Number of dyads	Mean number of peace years
Both states in gains frame	21	20.9
At least one state in loss frame	19	12.8
Difference (std. error)		8.1** (4.56)
Degrees of freedom		38

** = $p \leq 0.05$ (one-tailed test)

Table 1.2
Regression Results: Models 1–4

Coefficient (std. error)	Probit Regression on Conflict Initiation (0/1)			
	Model 1	Model 2	Model 3	Model 4
Frames				
Loss frame (initiator)	0.21 (0.05)**	0.21 (0.05)**	0.21 (0.05)**	0.17 (0.05)**
Interests				
Portfolio similarity	−0.25 (0.09)**	−0.24 (0.09)**	−0.25 (0.09)**	−0.17 (0.11)
Portfolio similarity with system leader (initiator)	−0.29 (0.14)**	−0.29 (0.13)**	−0.22 (0.13)*	−0.24 (0.17)
Portfolio similarity with system leader (defender)	−0.09 (0.14)	−0.10 (0.13)	−0.09 (0.13)	−0.11 (0.17)
Reputation				
Weak reputation (initiator)		−0.14 (0.17)	−0.21 (0.18)	−0.32 (0.20)
Number of rivals (initiator)		−0.01 (0.02)	−0.02 (0.02)	−0.01 (0.02)
Reputation × number of rivals		0.05 (0.04)	0.07 (0.04)*	0.09 (0.04)**
Weak reputation (defender)		0.24 (0.09)**	0.19 (0.09)**	0.31 (0.09)**
Capabilities				
Relative capabilities (initiator)			0.07 (0.13)	0.11 (0.13)
Capabilities (initiator)			−0.35 (0.65)	−0.93 (0.73)
Capabilities (defender)			1.09 (0.78)	0.71 (0.89)
Ongoing dispute (initiator)			0.06 (0.05)	0.02 (0.05)
Ongoing dispute (defender)			0.07 (0.05)	0.05 (0.05)
Defense pact (defender)			0.06 (0.06)	0.03 (0.06)
Offensive alliance (initiator)			−0.19 (0.08)**	−0.20 (0.10)**
Neutrality pact (initiator)			0.13 (0.07)*	0.10 (0.09)
Domestic politics				
Democracy (initiator)				0.21 (0.06)**
Democracy (defender)				0.24 (0.07)**
Joint democracy				−0.23 (0.13)*
Constant	−1.45**	−1.40**	−1.52**	−1.40**
Observations	12,456	12,456	12,113	10,437
Log likelihood	−3114.03	−3107.46	−3014.76	−2603.15

Additional controls in models 1–4 (omitted due to space constraints): minor/major power status of the dyad, logged distance between capitals, contiguity, years since last conflict initiation (including cubic splines). A full table with all coefficient estimates can be found in the appendix to this chapter.

* = $p \leq 0.10$
** = $p \leq 0.05$

alliance portfolios. Furthermore, the global system leader appears to have a constraining effect on strategic rivals since challengers with interests similar to the system leader are less likely to initiate conflict. We must note, however, that these findings are not very robust. In the fully specified model, the effects related to geopolitical interests are indistinguishable from zero. Instead, seven substantive variables (including loss frame) are statistically significant.

First, the model provides evidence for the importance of a defender's reputation. Challengers appear to be more likely to initiate conflict when the behavior of the defender in the most recent dispute was irresolute. Second, the significant interaction term of challenger reputation and its number of rivals confirms previous research by Clare and Danilovic, who suggest that governments with weak reputations and many rivals have an incentive to bolster their reputations proactively and are more likely to initiate disputes with their competitors.[72]

The third finding obtained from model 4 is that only one variable related to states' capabilities is statistically significant. The data analysis shows that challengers are less likely to destabilize a deterrence relationship if they have a relevant offensive alliance against the defender. This finding is puzzling and goes against earlier research conducted by Johnson and Leeds.[73] These divergent results can be partly traced back to differences in case selection criteria. Johnson and Leeds use data from all directed dyads between 1816 and 2000, and their number of observations is therefore significantly higher than ours. We suggest that future research should focus on the effect of offensive alliances in general deterrence relationships among strategic rivals, and we suspect that an in-depth analysis of the alliance treaties would reveal the underlying mechanisms behind the relationship uncovered in our statistical analysis.

A final set of findings suggested by model 4 is related to domestic politics. All three variables in this category are statistically significant. There is some evidence for a democratic peace argument since joint democracies are slightly less likely to destabilize deterrence relationships than mixed dyads or joint autocracies ($p < 0.10$). Furthermore, the probability of conflict initiation increases both for democratic targets and for democratic challengers. While this result is at odds with audience cost theory, it is not entirely surprising. Only a small proportion of the countries in our dataset are democracies, and most of our observations are therefore mixed dyads. In previous studies, such pairs of states have been found to be especially prone to conflict, and our results lend support to this argument.[74]

We now move to an investigation of the substantive effect of our loss-frame variable. Using the software package Clarify,[75] we can compare the effects of the six alternative explanations from model 4 and our primary variable of interest. Since conflict initiation is a very rare event, even relatively robust explanatory variables add only a few percentage points to the overall likelihood of deterrence

Table 1.3
Risk of Conflict Initiation at Different Values of Key Independent Variables

	Minimum	Maximum	Change in probability of conflict initiation = 1[a]	Change in relative risk
Loss frame (initiator)	0	1	+2.0%	+41.0%
Weak reputation (defender)	0	0.9	+3.5%	+74.0%
Offensive alliance (initiator)	0	1	−1.6%	−34.5%
Democracy (initiator)	0	1	+2.5%	+53.6%
Democracy (defender)	0	1	+2.5%	+60.4%
Joint democracy	0	1	−1.6%	−36.0%
Weak reputation (initiator)[b]; four rivals	0.9[c]	3.6	+1.7%	+36.0%
Weak reputation (initiator)[b]; seven rivals	0.9[c]	6.3	+4.4%	+136.0%

[a] Predicted probabilities are significant at the 0.05-level (except for joint democracy [p = 0.08]). Continuous variables are at their means, all other variables are at their medians.
[b] Weak reputation operationalized as: initiator behaved irresolutely within the last year.
[c] Baseline specification for comparison: weak reputation (0.9) with only one strategic rivalry.

breakdown. Changes in the relative risk of conflict initiation (calculated by dividing the risk at a given variable configuration from the baseline risk) are therefore a more informative measure than absolute changes in predicted probabilities. Setting all other variables to their median values, the relative risk of a state deciding to actively destabilize an existing deterrence relationship increases by about 41 percent when a state moves from a gains frame to a losses frame. This change is both statistically significant and substantively powerful. Furthermore, it is important to note that this value is on par with the impact of some of the other statistically significant variables in model 4. Table 1.3 gives an overview of changes in relative risks and associated predicted probabilities for different values of relevant variables.

Holding all continuous covariates at their means and all other variables at the median values, states with a relevant offensive alliance have a 34 percent lower relative risk to initiate a conflict in a strategic rivalry than other countries. The variables related to domestic politics have a similar substantive effect. Democratic challengers are about 53 percent more likely to initiate disputes in deterrence relationships than nondemocratic states. Conversely, democratic targets are at a 60 percent higher risk to attract conflict than autocratic defenders. The effect of joint democracy in a dyad is a bit smaller: if both states score above +5 on polity IV, the relative risk of deterrence breakdown decreases by about 36 percent compared to joint autocracies and mixed dyads. Thus, joint democracy and the challenger's decision frame are roughly equal contributors to the stability/breakdown of deterrence. Our analysis thus supports both of our hypotheses and demonstrates why neglecting decision frames is a serious shortcoming in the existing literature on deterrence.

A few other variables exhibit noteworthy effects. As table 1.3 shows, a challenger's risk of deterrence destabilization is also crucially influenced by the reputation of the target. Specifically, it is about 74 percent higher if the defender has acted irresolutely within the past twelve months than when the target has a strong reputation. Furthermore, the support for Clare and Danilovic's reputation building argument is substantial. The positive and significant interaction composed of the challenger's weak reputation and its number of rivals suggests that the effect of a weak reputation is contingent on the overall number of rivalries. To investigate the substantive impact of these two variables, we calculated the predicted probabilities of conflict initiation for challengers with weak reputations and one, four, and seven rivals.[76] The differences are striking. A challenger who acted irresolutely within the past year has a 3.2 percent probability of dispute initiation if it only has one rival. At four rivals, the probability increases to 4.9 percent, and at seven rivals (the maximum value in the dataset), it reaches 7.6 percent. Expressed in relative risks, this means that weak reputation states with one rival are about 136 percent less likely to initiate conflict than weak reputation states with seven rivals.

It is worth noting that model 4 also reveals that quite a few variables that have been proposed by previous scholarship as important predictors of deterrence stability and breakdown do not seem to influence general deterrence among strategic rivals. Neither defense pacts nor relative capabilities, nor the current dispute involvement of challenger or target, have a statistically significant effect on conflict initiation. This, by itself, is an interesting finding and suggests that deterrence among strategic rivals is qualitatively different from some other deterrence relationships studied in previous research.

Additional Analysis: The Role of (Mis)Perception

As operationalized here, our measure of decision frames is anchored to the objective condition of a state's security environment. However, as we have noted, it is widely acknowledged that material capabilities are also filtered through decision-maker perceptions. Our argument offers no claims about the factors that might influence perceptions, so we assume that variation in perception is randomly distributed. It seems reasonable to assume that perception matters less as states move away from the middle of security spectrum and toward the extremes because the objective security condition of the state becomes more transparent. That is, decision-maker perceptions should be more likely to add "noise" to the data and decrease the substantive impact of being in a gains/loss frame for states close to the midpoint. While perceptual noise stacks the deck against the statistical analysis described above, we conducted an additional test to investigate the degree to which perception might affect our results.

We estimated a model (model 5) in which we interacted our loss-frame variable with a state's relative position on its security spectrum. We calculated this second variable by dividing the distance of a country's actual security score in a given year from the midpoint by the total length of its security spectrum. This procedure allows us to compare distances from the midpoint across countries and years. We expect that the effect of a country's strategic frame increases at the tail ends of the security spectrum, where the consequences of its security position would be clearest. For states coded in a loss frame, those in the middle range should be less likely to initiate because of random perceptual errors compared to loss-frame states at the tail end. Conversely, gains-frame states that are close the midpoint should be more likely to destabilize a deterrence relationship than countries that are relatively close to their best hypothetical security situation. Since model 4 has demonstrated that not all explanations suggested by the deterrence literature necessarily apply to strategic rivals, we controlled only for those substantive variables that had a significant effect in model 4.[77] The results of our analysis are shown in table 1.4.

The signs and significance levels of most control variables and alternative explanations remain unchanged.[78] The most important insight from model 5 is that the effect of our loss-frame variable is, in fact, conditional on a state's position on the security spectrum. A graphical representation of the results is informative. Figure 1.1 plots the predicted probability of conflict initiation for gains- and loss-frame states across different distances from the midpoint

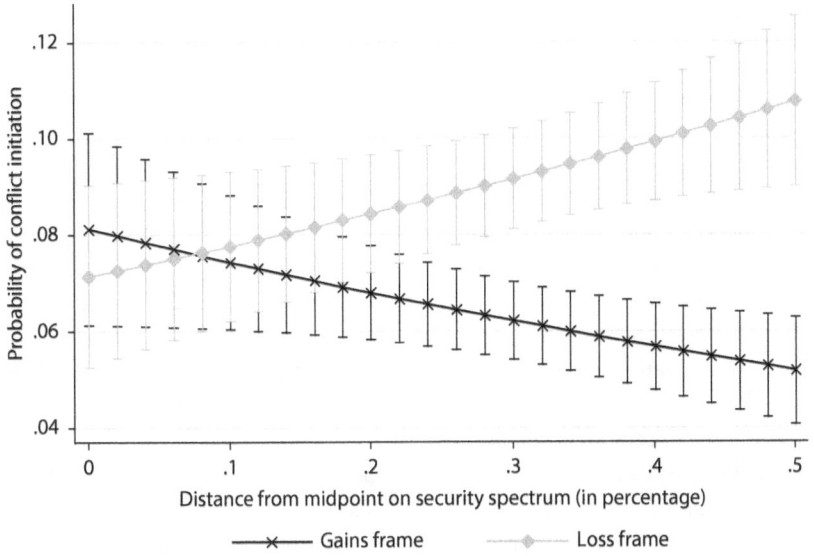

Figure 1.1. Predicted Probability of Conflict Initiation (Gains- and Loss-Frame States)

Table 1.4
Regression Results: Models 5–6

Coefficient (std. error)	Probit Regression on Conflict Initiation (0/1)	
	Model 5	Model 6
Frames		
Loss frame (initiator)	−0.08 (0.10)	0.22 (0.05)**
Distance from midpoint	−0.51 (0.22)**	
Loss frame x distance	0.97 (0.32)**	
Nuclear-armed defender		−0.10 (0.36)
Loss frame x nuclear-armed defender		0.12 (0.35)
Reputation		
Weak reputation (initiator)	−0.44 (0.19)**	−0.38 (0.19)**
Number of rivals (initiator)	−0.01 (0.02)	−0.01 (0.02)
Reputation x number of rivals	0.11 (0.05)**	0.10 (0.04)**
Weak reputation (defender)	0.31 (0.10)**	0.31 (0.10)**
Capabilities		
Offensive alliance (initiator)	−0.16 (0.10)*	−0.16 (0.10)
Neutrality pact (initiator)	0.11 (0.09)	0.08 (0.09)
Domestic politics		
Democracy (initiator)	0.21 (0.06)**	0.22 (0.06)**
Democracy (defender)	0.26 (0.08)**	0.26 (0.08)**
Joint democracy	−0.31 (0.14)**	−0.31 (0.14)**
Additional controls		
Contiguity	0.24 (0.08)**	0.25 (0.08)**
Distance between capitals	−0.04 (0.04)	−0.02 (0.04)
Major versus major power	−0.04 (0.11)	−0.03 (0.12)
Minor versus minor power	0.02 (0.10)	0.02 (0.11)
Major versus minor power	0.29 (0.11)**	0.30 (0.12)**
Constant	−1.09**	−1.35
Observations	10,437	10,437
Log likelihood	−2601.28	−2620.69

Splines omitted due to space constraints.

* = $p \leq 0.10$

** = $p \leq 0.05$

of the security spectrum. The patterns are consistent with the predictions of our theory: gains and loss frames do not have an effect on deterrence destabilization for countries that are very close to the center of their security spectrum (between 0 and 20 percent of its total length). However, as states move closer to the tail ends, we see that conflict initiation becomes significantly more likely for loss-frame states and less likely for gains-frame states. The differences in predicted probabilities at the tail ends of the security spectrum are striking. States in "clear" loss frames are about 6 percent more likely to initiate a conflict compared to states in "clear" gains frames. This amounts to a more than 100 percent increase in the relative risk of deterrence destabilization. These results suggest that the implications of the strategic frame are clearest as states populate the outer boundaries of the security continuum, as we expected.

Additional Analysis: Nuclear versus Non-nuclear Deterrence

Some studies suggest that nuclear and non-nuclear deterrence relationships are qualitatively different from each other.[79] According to this argument, the potential consequences of nuclear retaliation severely diminish the base probability of conflict initiation against a nuclear-armed defender. It is thus theoretically possible that nuclear capabilities mute the effect of our main variable of interest. In other words, it may be the case that strategic frames lose some or all of their predictive power in nuclear deterrence relationships. In order to investigate this idea empirically, we estimated an additional model (model 6) in which we interacted our loss-frame variable with a binary indicator that is coded as 1 if a defender was a nuclear-armed state during a given year and 0 otherwise. The results are presented in table 1.4. If nuclear weapons indeed moderate the effect of our main independent variable, we would expect to find a statistically significant interaction between loss frame and the nuclear defender dummy. This is not the case. The interaction term in model 6 is statistically insignificant and does not improve the overall fit of the model. This shows that our empirical results do *not* differ between nuclear and non-nuclear deterrence relationships. This finding is substantively important since it suggests that shifting risk dispositions affect conflict onset against both nuclear and non-nuclear defender states.

CONCLUSION

The goal of this chapter was to analyze the breakdown of general deterrence from a prospect theory perspective. We argue that previous scholarship in the field of international relations has neglected the impact of strategic frames on the risk disposition of policymakers as they contemplate escalation policies within the context of settled deterrence relationships. Policymakers' assessments of the acceptability of the status quo affect their willingness to embrace risk. Our analysis shows that dyads with two states in gains frames are more stable than dyads with one or both states in a loss frame. Furthermore, in our main statistical model we were able to demonstrate that governments in loss frames are significantly more likely to destabilize existing deterrence relationships than are states in gains frames.

As a policy matter, perhaps the central empirical implication of cognitive deterrence is that a state's assessment of the status quo should be given greater attention. Typically, the credibility of threats is viewed to be the key independent variable explaining the success or failure of deterrence. Under cognitive deterrence, status quo evaluations are at least as important a variable as threat credibility. Our findings suggest that governments should pay close attention to the security conditions of deterrence rivals because this can help predict a rival government's risk disposition. Governments rightfully focus on the credibility of their deterrence threats including, as we examined in this study, reputation. However, as the target security frame changes, defenders may confront more aggressive rivals even when the credibility of deterrence commitments remain unchanged. Under a gains frame, even less than perfectly credible deterrence threats support successful deterrence. By contrast, in a loss frame, rivals accept greater risks. Here, even largely credible deterrence threats do not guarantee stability. Successful deterrence management requires both attention to one's own credibility and reputation (as decision-theoretical theories have long noted) and, to the extent possible, managing the strategic frame within the relationship.

Indeed, our research indicates that American policymakers currently promoting tailored deterrence should take notice of our findings. Shifting risk dispositions of strategic rivals do appear to influence the stability of deterrence. For example, while it is not the primary focus of our study, examining only cases in which the United States is coded as "target" reveals that challengers in loss frames are about 50 percent more likely to threaten, display, or use force than challengers who are satisfied with their strategic status quo.[80]

Perhaps the most intriguing implication here is that frame manipulation may turn out to be a central component of effective deterrence tailoring. A core concept in the DO-JOC is to "encourage adversary restraint."[81] Our study demonstrates clearly that governments (including rivals of the United States) operating in the domain of gains are risk averse and much easier to restrain. Deliberately seeking to alter loss frames by targeting rivals with positive security incentives should, by the results of this study, elicit a desirable shift in risk disposition. The broad goal of such "deterrence framing" would be to deliver a package of policies that include both "carrots" and "sticks," thereby inoculating rivals against the kind of risky decision making that settled loss frames appear to produce. Such a policy, were it to be pursued, would doubtless confront policymakers with domestic political challenges. Charges of being "soft" on rivals or giving into "blackmail" are inevitable. Indeed, there is the distinct possibility of creating a moral hazard for rivals to communicate resolve. Examining the trade-offs between the benefits of frame manipulation and the risk of incentivizing bad behavior remains open and fertile terrain for deterrence scholars and policymakers alike.

This study also contains important implications for the study of international relations. First, traditional theories of deterrence are incomplete if they ignore the fact that risk disposition can shift dramatically within and across governments. Second, we demonstrate that objective loss-frame variables, like the one presented in this chapter, can be applied to other analyses of prospect theory in the study of foreign policy. So far, the rich literature on prospect theory and foreign policy behavior almost exclusively relies on case studies. This research can now be supplemented by statistical analyses, giving scholars another way to analyze the generalizability of previous findings. Importantly, the concern that decision-maker perception mediates objective security conditions is not an insurmountable hurdle to the statistical testing of foreign policy frameworks grounded in cognitive principles.

Appendix

In this appendix, we present additional information and robustness checks.

1) Figure 1.2 is a graphical representation of the results obtained in the interaction term in model 4 (reputation × number of rivals).
2) Table 1.5 contains all coefficient estimates for models 1–4. Due to space constraints, the tables in the main text did not contain information on all control variables.
3) Table 1.6 presents the results of model 5A, which is an alternative specification of model 5. In this regression, we include all of the covariates included in model 4.
4) Table 1.7 (model 7) shows the results for the cases in our dataset in which the United States is coded as "target." Note that *neutrality pact, democracy (initiator)*, and *democracy (defender)* had to be dropped due to perfect collinearity.

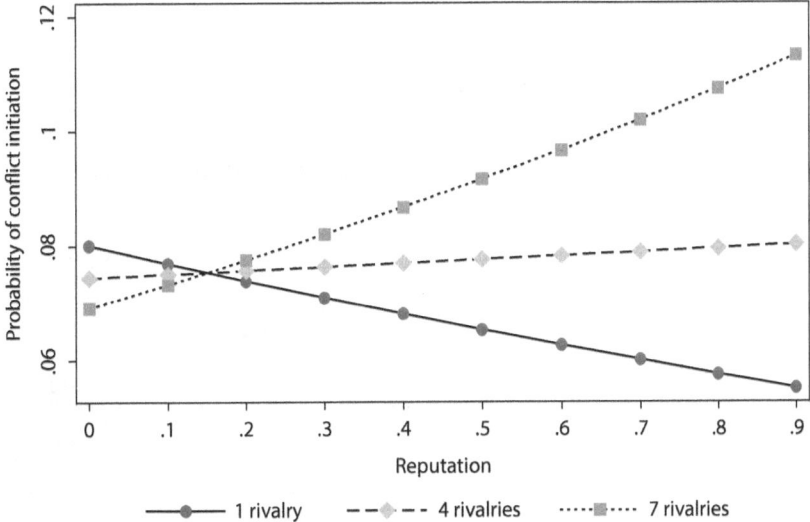

Figure 1.2. Probability of Conflict Initiation for Weak-Reputation Challengers

Table 1.5
Full Regression Results: Models 1–4

Coefficient (std. error)	Model 1	Model 2	Model 3	Model 4
Frames				
Loss frame (initiator)	0.21 (0.05)**	0.21 (0.05)**	0.21 (0.05)**	0.17 (0.05)**
Interests				
Portfolio similarity	−0.25 (0.09)**	−0.24 (0.09)**	−0.25 (0.09)**	−0.17 (0.11)
Portfolio similarity leader (initiator)	−0.29 (0.14)**	−0.29 (0.13)**	−0.22 (0.13)*	−0.24 (0.17)
Portfolio similarity leader (defender)	−0.09 (0.14)	−0.10 (0.13)	−0.09 (0.13)	−0.11 (0.17)
Reputation				
Weak reputation (initiator)		−0.14 (0.17)	−0.21 (0.18)	−0.32 (0.20)
Number of rivals (initiator)		−0.01 (0.02)	−0.02 (0.02)	−0.01 (0.02)
Reputation x number of rivals		0.05 (0.04)	0.07 (0.04)*	0.09 (0.04)**
Weak reputation (defender)		0.24 (0.09)**	0.19 (0.09)**	0.31 (0.09)**
Capabilities				
Relative capabilities (initiator)			0.07 (0.13)	0.11 (0.13)
Capabilities (initiator)			−0.35 (0.65)	−0.93 (0.73)
Capabilities (defender)			1.09 (0.78)	0.71 (0.89)
Ongoing dispute (initiator)			0.06 (0.05)	0.02 (0.05)
Ongoing dispute (defender)			0.07 (0.05)	0.05 (0.05)
Defense pact (defender)			0.06 (0.06)	0.03 (0.06)
Offensive alliance (initiator)			−0.19 (0.08)**	−0.20 (0.10)**
Neutrality pact (initiator)			0.13 (0.07)*	0.10 (0.09)
Domestic politics				
Democracy (initiator)				0.21 (0.06)**
Democracy (defender)				0.24 (0.07)**
Joint democracy				−0.23 (0.13)*
Additional controls				
Major/major power dyad	0.05 (0.10)	0.07 (0.10)	0.06 (0.11)	0.05 (0.11)
Minor/minor power dyad	0.16 (0.11)	0.15 (0.11)	0.24 (0.12)	0.10 (0.12)
Major/minor power dyad	0.35 (0.12)**	0.34 (0.11)**	0.43 (0.15)**	0.40 (0.16)**
Contiguity	0.31 (0.08)**	0.31 (0.07)**	0.31 (0.07)**	0.28 (0.08)**
Logged distance between capitals	0.04 (0.03)	0.03 (0.03)	0.02 (0.03)	0.01 (0.03)
Peace years	−0.05 (0.01)**	−0.05 (0.01)**	−0.05 (0.01)**	−0.04 (0.01)**
Peace years^2	0.01 (0.01)**	0.01 (0.01)**	0.01 (0.01)**	0.01 (0.01)**
Peace years^3	−0.01 (0.01)**	−0.01 (0.01)**	−0.01 (0.01)**	−0.01 (0.01)**
Constant	−1.45**	−1.40**	−1.52**	−1.40**
Observations	12,456	12,456	12,113	10,437
Log likelihood	−3114.03	−3107.46	−3014.76	−2603.15

* = $p \leq 0.10$

** = $p \leq 0.05$

Table 1.6
Regression Results: Model 5A

Coefficient (std. error)	Model 5A
Frames	
Loss frame (initiator)	−0.08 (0.10)
Distance from midpoint	−0.30 (0.23)
Loss frame x distance from midpoint	0.81 (0.23)**
Interests	
Portfolio similarity	−0.19 (0.11)*
Portfolio similarity leader (initiator)	−0.21 (0.18)
Portfolio similarity leader (defender)	−0.13 (0.17)
Reputation	
Weak reputation (initiator)	−0.37 (0.20)*
Number of rivals (initiator)	−0.01 (0.02)
Reputation x number of rivals	0.11 (0.05)**
Weak reputation (defender)	0.31 (0.09)**
Capabilities	
Relative capabilities (initiator)	0.06 (0.13)
Capabilities (initiator)	−1.00 (0.72)
Capabilities (defender)	0.60 (0.87)
Ongoing dispute (initiator)	0.02 (0.05)
Ongoing dispute (defender)	0.05 (0.05)
Defense pact (defender)	0.02 (0.06)
Offensive alliance (initiator)	−0.21 (0.10)**
Neutrality pact (initiator)	0.11 (0.09)
Domestic politics	
Democracy (initiator)	0.20 (0.07)**
Democracy (defender)	0.23 (0.07)**
Joint democracy	−0.22 (0.13)*
Additional controls	
Major/major power dyad	0.05 (0.11)
Minor/minor power dyad	0.10 (0.12)
Major/minor power dyad	0.41 (0.15)**
Contiguity	0.27 (0.08)**
Logged distance between capitals	−0.01 (0.03)
Peace years	−0.04 (0.01)**
Peace years^2	0.01 (0.01)**
Peace years^3	−0.01 (0.01)**
Constant	−1.21**
Observations	10,437
Log likelihood	−2598.39

* = p ≤ 0.10
** = p ≤ 0.05

Table 1.7

Regression Results: Model 7 (only cases in which the United States is the "target")

Coefficient (std. error)	Probit Regression on Conflict Initiation (0/1)
	Model 7
Frames	
Loss frame (initiator)	0.28 (0.11)**
Interests	
Portfolio similarity	0.13 (0.71)
Portfolio similarity leader (initiator)	−1.69 (1.27)
Portfolio similarity leader (defender)	−1.17 (0.94)
Reputation	
Weak reputation (initiator)	0.22 (1.19)
Number of rivals (initiator)	0.09 (0.18)
Reputation x number of rivals	−0.28 (0.22)
Weak reputation (defender)	−0.46 (0.34)
Capabilities	
Relative capabilities	1.14 (2.68)
Capabilities (initiator)	4.39 (5.19)
Capabilities (defender)	1.33 (5.58)
Ongoing dispute (initiator)	0.25 (0.20)
Ongoing dispute (defender)	0.05 (0.05)
Defense pact (defender)	0.01 (0.26)
Offensive alliance (initiator)	0.07 (0.28)
Domestic politics	
Joint democracy	0.24 (0.36)
Additional controls	
Major/major power dyad	−2.37 (0.98)**
Minor/minor power dyad	−1.71 (0.98)*
Major/minor power dyad	−2.58 (1.08)**
Contiguity	0.99 (0.38)**
Logged distance between capitals	0.38 (0.57)
Peace years	−0.04 (0.05)
Peace years^2	0.01 (0.01)
Peace years^3	−0.01 (0.01)
Constant	−2.33 (4.34)
Observations	357
Log likelihood	−96.98

* = p ≤ 0.10

** = p ≤ 0.05

NOTES

1. For example, Payne has forcefully argued that the version of deterrence theory developed during the Cold War is now conceptually deficient to the extent that "various factors that may be unique to the context and the challenger ... can be decisive in determining" deterrence outcomes. Keith Payne, *The Fallacies of Cold War Deterrence and a New Direction* (Lexington: University Press of Kentucky, 2001), 98.

2. U.S. Department of Defense, *Quadrennial Defense Review (QDR) Report* (Washington, D.C.: Department of Defense, 2006). Moreover, the most recent *Nuclear Posture Review (NPR)* explicitly notes that "there is no 'one size fits all' for deterrence" and therefore "the United States will apply a tailored and flexible approach to effectively deter across a spectrum of adversaries, threats, and contexts." U.S. Department of Defense, *Nuclear Posture Review* (Washington, D.C.: Department of Defense, 2018), executive summary.

3. Elaine Bunn, "Can Deterrence Be Tailored?" *Strategic Forum* 225 (2007): 2. Bunn provides an excellent conceptual overview of "tailored deterrence." For additional information, see Jeffrey Lantis, "Strategic Culture and Tailored Deterrence: Bridging the Gap between Theory and Practice," *Contemporary Security Policy* 30 (2009): 467–85, and Karl-Heinz Kamp and David S. Yost, eds., *NATO and 21st Century Deterrence* (Rome: NATO Defense College, 2009). Sean Larkin, "The Limits of Tailored Deterrence," *Joint Force Quarterly* 63 (2011): 47–57, offers a critical analysis. In 2013, the United States and South Korea established a bilateral framework for tailored deterrence on the Korean peninsula. See "U.S. South Korea Announce Tailored Deterrence Policy," http://www.defense.gov/news/newsarticle.aspx?id=120896, October 2, 2013.

4. U.S. Strategic Command, *Deterrence Operations Joint Operating Concept* (DO-JOC) (Washington, D.C.: U.S. Department of Defense, 2006), 21.

5. Ibid., 21.

6. Jeffrey D. Berejikian, "A Cognitive Theory of Deterrence," *Journal of Peace Research* 39, no. 2 (2002): 165–83; Gary Schaub, "Deterrence, Compellence, and Prospect Theory," *Political Psychology* 25, no. 3 (2004): 389–411.

7. Our focus on deterrence stability means that we are interested here in general rather than immediate deterrence. Immediate deterrence refers to a crisis situation in which a challenger is perceived as making preparations to strike, whereas general deterrence is characterized by an "adversarial relationship with no particular overt challenge" yet initiated, Paul Huth and Bruce M. Russett, "Deterrence Failure and Crisis Escalation," *International Studies Quarterly* 32, no. 1 (1988): 29.

8. Frank C. Zagare, "Reconciling Rationality with Deterrence: A Re-Examination of the Logical Foundations of Deterrence Theory," *Journal of Theoretical Politics* 16, no. 2 (2004): 107–41.

9. John Mearsheimer, *Conventional Deterrence* (Ithaca, N.Y.: Cornell University Press, 1983); Huth and Russett, "Deterrence Failure and Crisis Escalation."

10. John Mearsheimer, "Back to the Future: Instability in Europe after the Cold War," *International Security* 15, no. 1 (1990): 19.

11. Paul Huth and Bruce Russett, "General Deterrence between Enduring Rivals: Testing Three Competing Models," *American Political Science Review* 87, no. 1 (1993): 61–73.

12. Thomas C. Schelling, *Arms and Influence* (New Haven, Conn.: Yale University Press, 1966).

13. Vesna Danilovic, *When the Stakes Are High: Deterrence and Conflict among Major Powers* (Ann Arbor: University of Michigan Press, 2002).

14. Joe Clare and Vesna Danilovic, "Multiple Audiences and Reputation Building in International Conflicts," *Journal of Conflict Resolution* 54, no. 6 (2010): 860–82.

15. James Fearon, "Domestic Political Audiences and the Escalation of International Disputes," *American Political Science Review* 88, no. 3 (1994): 577–92.

16. Michael Tomz, "Domestic Audience Costs and International Relations: An Experimental Approach," *International Organization* 61, no. 4 (2007): 821–40; Jack Snyder and Erica D. Borghard, "The Cost of Empty Threats: A Penny, Not a Pound," *American Political Science Review* 105, no. 3 (2011): 437–56; Jessica L. Weeks, "Autocratic Audience Costs: Regime Type and Signaling Resolve," *International Organization* 62, no. 1 (2008): 35–64.

17. Jesse C. Johnson and Brett Ashley Leeds, "Defense Pacts, a Prescription for Peace?" *Foreign Policy Analysis* 7, no. 1 (2011): 45–65.

18. Matthew Fuhrmann and Todd Sechser, "Signaling Alliance Commitments: Hand-Tying and Sunk Costs in Extended Nuclear Deterrence," *American Journal of Political Science* 58, no. 4 (October 2014): 922.

19. For example, Walter Petersen, "Deterrence and Compellence: A Critical Assessment of Conventional Wisdom," *International Studies Quarterly* 30, no. 3 (1986): 269–94; Curtis S. Signorino and Ahmer Tarar, "A Unified Theory and Test of Extended Immediate Deterrence," *American Journal of Political Science* 50, no. 3 (2006): 586–605; Clare and Danilovic, "Multiple Audiences and Reputation Building."

20. James Fearon, "Rationalist Explanations for War," *International Organization* 49, no. 3 (1995): 388.

21. Daniel Kahneman and Amos Tversky, "Prospect Theory: An Analysis of Decision under Risk," *Econometrica* 47 (1979): 263–91.

22. George Quattrone and Amos Tversky, "Contrasting Rational and Psychological Analyses of Political Choice," *American Political Science Review* 82, no. 3 (1988): 719–36.

23. Daniel Kahneman and Amos Tversky, "The Psychology of Preferences," *Scientific American* 246 (January 1982): 160.

24. Ibid., 171–72.

25. Amos Tversky and Daniel Kahneman, "Judgment under Uncertainty: Heuristics and Biases," *Science* 185, no. 4157 (September 27, 1974): 1124–31; William F. Wright and Urton Anderson, "Effects of Situation Familiarity and Financial Incentives on Use of the Anchoring and Adjustment Heuristic for Probability Assessment," *Organizational Behavior and Human Decision Processes* 44, no. 1 (1989): 68–82.

26. Chip Heath, Richard P. Larrick, and George Wu, "Goals as Reference Points," *Cognitive Psychology* 38, no. 1 (1999): 79–109. We will return to this question of framing and argue that a government's basic desire for security sets the "security frame" for deterrence and that this determines the decision frame that governments use to evaluate their options.

27. Nicholas C. Barberis, "Thirty Years of Prospect Theory in Economics: A Review and Assessment," *Journal of Economic Perspectives* 27, no. 1 (2013): 173–95; Colin F. Camerer, "Prospect Theory in the Wild: Evidence from the Field," *Advances in Behavioral Economics* (2004): 148–61.

28. Rose McDermott, James H. Fowler, and Oleg Smirnov, "On the Evolutionary Origin of Prospect Theory Preferences," *Journal of Politics* 70, no. 2 (2008): 335–50.

29. Camelia M. Kuhnen and Brian Knutson, "The Neural Basis of Financial Risk Taking," *Neuron* 47, no. 5 (2005): 763–70; Christopher Trepel, Craig R. Fox, and Russell A. Poldrack, "Prospect Theory on the Brain? Toward a Cognitive Neuroscience of Decision under Risk," *Cognitive Brain Research* 23, no. 1 (2005): 34–50; Sabrina M. Tom, Craig R. Fox, Christopher Trepel, and Russell A. Poldrack, "The Neural Basis of Loss Aversion in Decision-Making

under Risk," *Science* 315 (2007): 515–18. Qingguo Ma, Yandong Feng, Qing Xu, Jun Bian, and Huixian Tang, "Brain Potentials Associated with the Outcome Processing in Framing Effects," *Neuroscience Letters* 528 (2012): 110–13.

30. For a comprehensive summary of prospect theory research in international relations, see Jeffrey D. Berejikian, "Prospect Theory in International Relations," in *Oxford Bibliographies in International Relations*, ed. Patrick James, last modified February 25, 2016, http://www.oxfordbibliographies.com/view/document/obo-9780199743292/obo-9780199743292-0163.xml.

31. Jack S. Levy, "Loss Aversion, Framing, and Bargaining: The Implications of Prospect Theory for International Conflict," *International Political Science Review* 17, no. 2 (1996): 179–95; Robert Jervis, "The Implications of Prospect Theory for Human Nature and Values," *Political Psychology* 25, no. 2 (2004): 163–76.

32. Barbara Farnham, *Avoiding Losses/Taking Risks: Prospect Theory and International Conflict* (Ann Arbor: University of Michigan Press, 1994); Rose McDermott, *Risk-Taking in International Politics: Prospect Theory in American Foreign Policy* (Ann Arbor: University of Michigan Press, 1998).

33. Daniel Kahneman and Jonathan Renshon, "Why Hawks Win," *Foreign Policy* (2007): 34–38.

34. Jeffrey D. Berejikian, *International Relations under Risk: Framing State Choice* (Albany: State University of New York Press, 2004).

35. Jean A. Garrison, "Framing Foreign Policy Alternatives in the Inner Circle: President Carter, His Advisors, and the Struggle for the Arms Control Agenda," *Political Psychology* 22, no. 4 (2001): 775–807; Matthew Fuhrmann and Bryan R. Early, "Following START: Risk Acceptance and the 1991–1992 Presidential Nuclear Initiatives," *Foreign Policy Analysis* 4, no. 1 (2008): 21–43.

36. Steven B. Rothman, "Domestic Politics and Prospect Theory in International Conflict: Explaining Japan's War Decision in the 1904 Russo-Japanese War," *Asia Pacific World* 2, no. 2 (2011), 66–84.

37. Daniel Masters and Robert M. Alexander, "Prospecting for War: 9/11 and Selling the Iraq War," *Contemporary Security Policy* 29, no. 3 (2008): 434–52.

38. Ariel S. Levi and Glen Whyte, "A Cross-Cultural Exploration of the Reference Dependence of Crucial Group Decisions under Risk: Japan's 1941 Decision for War," *Journal of Conflict Resolution* 41, no. 6 (1997): 792–813.

39. Rose McDermott and Jacek Kugler, "Comparing Rational Choice and Prospect Theory Analyses: The US Decision to Launch Operation 'Desert Storm,' January 1991," *Journal of Strategic Studies* 24, no. 3 (2001): 49–85; Jeffrey W. Taliaferro, "Quagmires in the Periphery: Foreign Wars and Escalating Commitment in International Conflict," *Security Studies* 7, no. 3 (1998): 94–144.

40. The core logic for this argument can be found in Berejikian, "Cognitive Theory of Deterrence."

41. For a discussion, see Alex Mintz and Steven B. Redd, "Framing Effects in International Relations," *Synthese* 135, no. 2 (2003): 193–213; and Denis Chong and James N. Druckman, "Framing Theory," *Annual Review of Political Science* 10 (2007): 103–26.

42. Mintz and Redd, "Framing Effects," 195.

43. An important implication of our argument is that we would observe greater risk acceptance across a range of foreign policy issues when states slip into loss frames.

44. For balance of power theory, see Kenneth Waltz, *Theory of International Politics* (Reading, Mass.: Addison-Wesley 1979). For power transition theory, see Abramo F. K. Organski,

World Politics (New York: Knopf, 1968). For hegemonic conflict theory, see Robert Gilpin, *War and Change in World Politics* (Cambridge: Cambridge University Press, 1981).

45. Douglass Lemke and William Reed, "Regime Types and Status Quo Evaluations: Power Transition Theory and the Democratic Peace," *International Interactions* 22, no. 2 (1996): 143–64.

46. Douglass Lemke, *Regions of War and Peace* (Cambridge: Cambridge University Press, 2002).

47. The assumption that governments assess their physical security accurately is embedded in most theories of classical deterrence. However, it does potentially run counter to some "fourth wave" deterrence theories that emphasize the role played by human subjectivity and argue that deterrence relationships are largely socially constructed. See Amir Lupovici, "The Emerging Fourth Wave of Deterrence Theory: Toward a New Research Agenda," *International Studies Quarterly* 54, no. 3 (2010): 705–32.

48. Our argument is about the stability of general deterrence relationships. As we describe, we are interested in identifying the conditions under which one side moves to destabilize a settled status quo. Once this has happened, governments enter an immediate deterrence game, which we hope to examine in a separate study.

49. Huth and Russett, "General Deterrence between Enduring Rivals."

50. Clare and Danilovic, "Multiple Audiences and Reputation Building"; William Thompson, "Identifying Rivals and Rivalries in World Politics," *International Studies Quarterly* 45, no. 4 (2001): 557–86.

51. Thompson, "Identifying Rivals and Rivalries," 560.

52. Daniel M. Jones, Stuart A. Bremer, and David Singer, "Militarized Interstate Disputes, 1816–1992: Rationale, Coding Rules, and Empirical Patterns," *Conflict Management and Peace Science* 15, no. 2 (1996): 163–213.

53. The base data set for our analysis of strategic rivalry comes from Clare and Danilovic, "Multiple Audiences and Reputation Building."

54. Bruce Bueno de Mesquita, *The War Trap* (New Haven, Conn.: Yale University Press, 1981).

55. The set of states for j are those in i's region. Expected Utility scores are generated by the software package Eugene. D. Scott Bennett and Allan C. Stam, "Eugene: A Conceptual Manual," *International Interactions* 26, no. 2 (2000): 179–204.

56. At first glance, the polarity of this score seems backward. However, the score $\sum_{j \neq i} E(U_{ji})$ captures the sum of bilateral conflict utilities for each state in the region, so high positive scores represent net positive utility for j states. As we describe, to aid our interpretation we reverse the polarity when constructing the loss frame variable.

57. For example, Robert Jervis, *Perception and Misperception in International Politics* (Princeton, N.J.: Princeton University Press, 1976).

58. Bernhard von Bülow, *Fürst Bülows Reden nebst urkundlichen Beiträgen zu seiner Politik* (Berlin: Georg Reimer, 1907), 310.

59. Germany, Auswärtiges Amt, Johannes Lepsius, et al., *Die Grosse Politik der Europäischen Kabinette, 1871–1914*. Sammlung der diplomatischen Akten des Auswärtigen Amtes, im Auftrage des Auswärtigen Amtes (Berlin: Deutsche Verlagsgesellschaft für Politik und Geschichte, 1922), 64.

60. Germany, Auswärtiges Amt, Edgar T. S. Dugdale, *German Diplomatic Documents, 1871–1914* (New York: Barnes and Noble, 1969), 105.

61. Aaron L. Friedberg, *The Weary Titan: Britain and the Experience of Relative Decline, 1895–1905* (Princeton, N.J.: Princeton University Press, 1988).

62. Ibid., 156.

63. Quoted in Iestyn Adams, *Brothers across the Ocean: British Foreign Policy and the Origins of Anglo-American "Special Relationship,"* 1900–1905 (London: Tauris Academic Studies, 2005), 83.

64. Quoted in Friedberg, *The Weary Titan*, 175.

65. Unless otherwise indicated, all variables are obtained through the software package Eugene.

66. Jessica Weeks, "Strongmen and Straw Men: Authoritarian Regimes and the Initiation of International Conflict," *American Political Science Review* 106, no. 2 (2012): 326–47.

67. Huth and Russett, "General Deterrence between Enduring Rivals."

68. Johnson and Leeds, "Defense Pacts."

69. Zeev Maoz and Bruce M. Russett, "Normative and Structural Causes of Democratic Peace, 1946–1986," *American Political Science Review* 87, no. 3 (1993): 624–38.

70. Instead of controlling for contiguity and major power status of a dyad separately, Clare and Danilovic add a variable for "politically relevant dyads," which is coded as 1 if the states are contiguous and/or at least one state is a major power and 0 otherwise. The results of our statistical analysis do not change if we only control for politically relevant dyads.

71. David B. Carter and Curtis S. Signorino, "Back to the Future: Modeling Time Dependence in Binary Data," *Political Analysis* 18, no. 3 (2010): 271–92.

72. Clare and Danilovic, "Multiple Audiences and Reputation Building."

73. Johnson and Leeds, "Defense Pacts."

74. John R. Oneal and Bruce M. Russett, "The Classical Liberals Were Right: Democracy, Interdependence, and Conflict, 1950–1985," *International Studies Quarterly* 41, no. 2 (1997): 267–94; Karen Rasler and William Thompson, "Contested Territory, Strategic Rivalries, and Conflict Escalation," *International Studies Quarterly* 50, no. 1 (2006): 145–67.

75. Gary King, Michael Tomz, and Jason Wittenberg, "Making the Most of Statistical Analyses: Improving Interpretation and Presentation," *American Journal of Political Science* 44, no. 2 (2000): 341–55.

76. In the appendix to this chapter, we also offer a graphical representation of the results for this interaction.

77. The signs and significance levels of our results in model 5 do not change if we add all of the omitted variables from model 4. We present this alternative statistical analysis in the appendix to this chapter.

78. The main effect for the initiator's weak reputation becomes significant in this specification, but the general interactive relationship between this variable and the initiator's number of rivals does not change.

79. Matthew Fuhrmann and Todd Sechser, "Signaling Alliance Commitments: Hand-Tying and Sunk Costs in Extended Nuclear Deterrence," *American Journal of Political Science* 58, no. 4 (October 2014): 922. In this article, the authors focus specifically on extended nuclear deterrence. Conceptually however, the logic can also be applied to direct deterrence relationships.

80. The predicted probability of conflict initiation against the United States increases from 8.1 percent to 12.1 percent. The statistical model used to estimate these results can be found in the appendix to this chapter.

81. U.S. Strategic Command, *Deterrence Operations*, 20.

CHAPTER TWO

Disabling Deterrence and Preventing War

Decision Making at the End of the Nuclear Chain

JANICE GROSS STEIN AND MORIELLE I. LOTAN

This chapter examines the behavior of nuclear operators, those military officers responsible for warning of a possible nuclear attack or executing orders to launch a nuclear response. We argue that their behavior is generally not consistent with rational theories of deterrence. Modern theories of deterrence were developed to prevent nuclear war in a world of uncertainty. Unlike risk, which relies on known probability distributions, uncertainty is indeterminate, and largely for this reason, theorists quickly moved to model uncertainty as risk in decisions about war. That conflation of uncertainty with risk masked the challenges those charged with making decisions about the use of nuclear weapons face. The limited evidence available suggests that when confronted with a decision about whether to transmit evidence of an imminent attack up the chain of command or even to order the use of nuclear weapons in response to evidence of an imminent use of nuclear force by an adversary, nuclear operators at the end of the chain generally discounted warnings of an imminent attack and chose not to transmit warnings up the chain. In so doing, they effectively disabled deterrence even as, at the same time, they prevented nuclear war.

We begin by looking at the way nuclear operators responded to incoming evidence that the other side had attacked or was about to attack. We then examine risk and uncertainty as constraints on decision making and look at how successive waves of deterrence theorists conflated uncertainty with risk. Psychology helps in the first instance to explain this seemingly anomalous behavior. Decision makers create highly simplified subjective expected probability estimates that enable false certainty and overconfidence. An ill-structured and deeply unsettling decision is transformed into a tractable problem that makes a decision possible. Operators also tended to gravitate to the extreme end of the probability curve, using heuristics such as anchoring, availability, and representativeness.

The chapter then identifies other candidate explanations that may amplify or minimize this paradoxical behavior by operators in the future. Prospect theory treats uncertainty as risk and predicts that when decision makers are in the domain of loss, they will choose the risk-acceptant option when they think that losses are highly probable.[1] Those who study emotions generate a diametrically opposite prediction; they expect that decision makers who are frightened will become risk averse. Sociologists predict that in the face of uncertainty, decision makers will resort to social conventions to make their choice. We conclude with a discussion of the implications of the choices of nuclear operators for theory, strategy, and policy.

NUCLEAR OPERATORS AND THEORIES OF NUCLEAR DETERRENCE

Deterrence theory developed in successive waves in response to the buildup of larger and more complex stockpiles of nuclear weapons by the United States and the Soviet Union. Although the nuclear world became multipolar after the United Kingdom joined the club in 1952, the dominant relationship between the two superpowers structured thinking about nuclear weapons. Not surprisingly, the theoretical debate was most vigorous and fertile in the United States, where theorists moved from theories of mutual assured destruction (MAD) to those of escalation dominance in a bipolar world.

At the core of all these models were a decision and a paradox. The decision was to import assumptions from microeconomic rationality to develop models of nuclear decision making. Theorists modeled decision making under conditions of risk and extended these models to interactive games and sequences of play to demonstrate the challenges confronting nuclear decision makers. There was also a paradox: the likely consequences of the use of nuclear weapons were so awful, the negative values were so high, that it was difficult to demonstrate the rationality of a choice to use nuclear weapons. Deterrence thus became a theory of psychological manipulation that wrestled in creative ways with, as Thomas Schelling put it, the "rationality of irrationality."[2] This paradox became obvious when nuclear umbrellas were opened and deterrence was extended to smaller allies. President de Gaulle of France was only the first to worry that no president of the United States would sacrifice Paris for Washington. Leaders in Tokyo, Riyadh, Tel Aviv, Warsaw, and Riga likely share that same worry today. Deterrence theorists accordingly became overwhelmingly preoccupied with the psychological concepts of credibility and reputation for resolve as the most important assets in nuclear deterrence.

The direct relationship between the two superpowers was the first, most urgent, and least complicated to model. From the mid-1960s, when the Soviet

Union developed a robust second-strike capability, until 1991, when the Soviet Union broke apart, deterrence rested on MAD. For MAD to be credible, it had to be believable that operators, who receive information of a launch by an adversary, would rapidly transmit the warning up the chain of command and, following an executive decision, would have the delegated authority and the resolve to launch quickly, before the first strike arrived and decimated command and control. Out of these constraints came doctrines of launch on attack (LOA) and launch on warning (LOW).

Time lines for decision are very short. LOA requires U.S. operators to detect a launch of Russia's intercontinental ballistic missiles (ICBMs) and launch an attack within a window of thirty minutes, before the Russian ICBMs hit American missiles. The window for a presidential decision is estimated to be only eight minutes: the North American Aerospace Defense Command (NORAD) needs approximately four minutes after a launch to confirm that an attack is underway and notify the person designated by the president; at the other end, transmitting an emergency action message, authenticating that message by launch crews, running through the launch sequence, and firing the ICBMs so that they clear their silos before Russian missiles arrive is estimated to consume another eighteen minutes. That leaves only eight minutes for the presidential advisor to decide whether or not to warn the president and the president to decide whether or not to issue the order to attack.[3]

This chapter focuses on operators lower in the chain of command. It is nevertheless instructive to look at how designated advisors at the center behave on the rare occasions when they do receive such a warning from nuclear operators. In November 1979, Zbigniew Brzezinski, then the national security advisor to President Jimmy Carter, received a call from his military advisor at 3:00 a.m. that the Soviet Union had launched two hundred missiles at the United States. He knew that he had three minutes before he had to call the president and that the president would only have four minutes to make a difficult decision among several options given the nature of the "selective strike" that the Soviet Union appeared to have launched. Within two minutes, since the necessary confirmations did not arrive, it was clear to Brzezinski that it was a false alarm. He subsequently learned that the alert was the result of an exercise and "some sort of glitch." He informed the president the next morning who, Brzezinski alleges, was displeased that he had not been awakened, but Brzezinski insisted that he was following the required procedure.[4]

This story highlights an important feature of the environment in which nuclear operators work. Based on the best available evidence, false alarms were not unusual. The Center for Defense Information, drawing on data obtained under the Freedom of Information Act, reported that in the seven years between 1977 and 1984, there were 1,152 moderately serious false alarms of an impending

Soviet attack or an average of almost three alarms per week.[5] Operators received alarms of impending attack in an almost routine way.

The routine occurrence of false alarms sets the context for nuclear operators even as it creates a challenge. On the one hand, if nuclear operators do not behave in expected ways, if they do not transmit warnings up the chain of command or do not launch when ordered, then credibility and resolve, essential building blocks in the larger conceptual and psychological architecture of MAD, break down. Nuclear operators are an essential link in the logic chain of deterrence. On the other hand, that essential link led theorists to worry that nuclear war could break out accidentally through misunderstanding, machine malfunction, malfunction at the human-machine interface, or the unauthorized action of a rogue subordinate.[6] System designers struggled to calibrate between these two errors, with little evidence to guide the decisions that they made.

Given these constraints, it is not surprising that theorists of nuclear deterrence paid little or no attention to the calculus of nuclear operators down the chain of command. Operators at the lowest level in the chain of command were treated conceptually as if they had zero degrees of freedom and no autonomous choice, as executors, not as decision makers.[7] Indeed, theorists paid no attention to individual variance even among central decision makers at the top. Rather they modeled states as unitary rational actors and affirmed the rationality of a nuclear response if nuclear deterrence were to be credible in a relationship where both powers had a second-strike capacity.

Theorizing away autonomous choice is questionable, however, as long as human beings have some role in decision making. Lotan argues that operators are not simply passive executors but decision makers situated in critical positions at the beginning of the nuclear chain when they receive alarming intelligence information or at the end when they are required to launch nuclear missiles.[8] Once we treat operators as decision makers with some degrees of freedom, however, it becomes important to understand how command and control systems are configured. Both the United States and the Soviet Union, despite declaratory policies of "launch on warning," built human choice into the final decision to avoid the possibility that a machine would automatically commit the state to nuclear war.[9] Once decision makers were inserted into the choice loop, some degree of freedom was introduced into the system.

The Soviet and American systems were configured somewhat differently. In theory, nuclear decision making in the Soviet Union was controlled by a very small circle of high-level decision makers in the Politburo and the General Staff. Nuclear operators were required automatically to pass computer-generated warnings up the chain of command.[10] In the United States, permissive action links (PALs) and personnel reliability programs (PRPs) were introduced into the U.S. system to safeguard against an unreliable nuclear operator who would violate instructions. American operators were not, however, required automatically to transmit computer-generated warnings; the requirement to transmit information up the chain was partially a function of the level of defense-condition (DEFCON). Operators had the authority to conclude that a warning was false.[11] At least formally, operators within the U.S. system had greater autonomy than their Soviet counterparts to take context into account. Analysts recognized that these systems, while valuable, could not eliminate human error.[12] What received less theoretical attention was that these systems could not eliminate decision autonomy at the lowest level of the chain.

What does the evidence tell us about the behavior of operators at the bottom of the nuclear chain of command and control? Evidence is partial and fragmentary on both systems. During the period of greatest tension and highest level of DEFCON, during the Cuban missile crisis, U.S. operators did pass up the chain of command what turned out to be false warnings; these warnings were discounted by senior decision makers.[13] There is also evidence that a pilot accidentally sounded an alert of nuclear sabotage; that warning was also discounted.[14] And as we have seen, operators at NORAD headquarters report that they have repeatedly discounted warnings of a Russian missile launch against the United States. These warnings occurred during periods of low tension, and it is therefore not surprising that operators exercised their autonomy to decide that these were machine errors and did not transmit the information up the chain of command.

Information about the Soviet system is even more limited than the American. In 1962, during the Cuban missile crisis, the American destroyer USS *Beale* dropped depth charges on the nuclear-armed Soviet submarine *B-59*. It appears that, at that time, Soviet submarine commanders had considerable delegated authority to fire their nuclear torpedo. They were able to monitor U.S. submarines' extensive use of depth charges but were unable to communicate with Moscow. Although the charges were nonlethal explosives, the commander was convinced that an all-out war was about to begin, and he ordered his men to arm the submarine's single nuclear-tipped torpedo and prepare to attack.

Soviet regulations at the time required that all three of the submarine's senior officers sign off on a launch of a nuclear torpedo. The captain was clearly in favor of a launch, but Vasili Arkhipov, the second in command, refused to consent. He calmed the captain down and convinced his fellow officers to bring the *B-59* to the surface and request new orders from Moscow.[15] That decision not to launch very likely prevented nuclear war. It also destabilized Soviet deterrence and mutual assured destruction.

A second major incident occurred in September 1983. A decision by a single Soviet military officer may have been all that prevented the Soviet Union from launching nuclear weapons in response to a false warning of a U.S. attack. A gap in Soviet capabilities was an important part of the context at the time. In the preceding years, the United States had moved away from a countervalue strategy to a counterforce strategy that focused on a decapitating strike that would compromise Soviet command and control. In response, the Soviet leadership charged early warning officers with the explicit responsibility of passing information of an incoming attack up the chain of command. The Soviets had deployed the first generation of early-warning radar, but deployment of a more sophisticated phased-array radar would not be completed until 1985. The satellite component of the early-warning radar doubled the ten minutes of decision time provided by ground-based radars but was not reliable.[16] Moreover, the nuclear command and control system did not provide enough time for the leadership to receive the warning and communicate the launch order. Soviet designers were working hard on the guaranteed transmission of retaliation orders under a nuclear attack but were aware that their speed and reliability were not adequate.[17] Under these conditions, early warning was especially important.

The gap in deploying more sophisticated radar was not the only factor contributing to a very tense environment in Moscow. In the run-up to the September incident, a number of developments had exacerbated Cold War tensions. In the spring of 1983, President Reagan had announced plans for a missile defense system, which the Kremlin saw as a major threat to its nuclear arsenal. President Reagan had also called the Soviet Union an "evil empire." In early September, the Soviets had shot down a Korean Air Lines commercial flight when it crossed into Soviet airspace, killing all 269 people on board. The United States also conducted an elaborate annual exercise—Global Shield—in the summer of 1983 that the Soviets feared might be a cover for a U.S. attack. Intelligence agencies in the United States reported that General Secretary Andropov was obsessed with the possibility of a surprise nuclear attack by the West and had sent instructions to Soviet spies around the world to look for evidence of preparations.[18]

The incident that occurred in September 1983 is worth exploring in some detail because the key Soviet officer, Stanislav Petrov, then a lieutenant-colonel in the Soviet Air Defense Forces, subsequently gave extensive interviews about his thinking.[19] These interviews, while done after the fact, nevertheless shed light on how Petrov remembers his decision at the time. All the elements of an acutely high-stress decision are here; the loss was potentially very large but the probability was uncertain and time was very short, just minutes. In the face of that deep uncertainty, and pressed to make a decision, it was the fear of starting a nuclear war that shaped his decision.

On September 26, 1983, Petrov was on duty at Serpukhov-15, the secret command center just south of Moscow where the Soviet military monitored Oko, its system of early-warning satellites over the United States. Petrov had helped to design the system, which was newly installed. He was at a pivotal point in the chain of command, overseeing a staff that monitored incoming signals from the satellites. He reported to superiors at warning system headquarters; they in turn reported to the general staff of the Soviet military, who would consult with General Secretary Andropov on the possibility of launching a retaliatory attack.

On the night of September 26, an alarm went off. On the panel in front of Petrov was a red pulsating button, flashing "Start." The warning system's computer, weighing the signal against static, concluded that a missile had been launched from a base in the United States. "The siren howled," Petrov recalled, "but I just sat there for a few seconds, staring at the big, back-lit, red screen with the word 'launch' on it." At first, the satellite reported that one missile had been launched—then another, then another. Soon, the system was "roaring," he recalled. The system warned that five Minuteman ICBMs had been launched. The computer systems in front of him changed their alert from "launch" to "missile strike" and insisted that the reliability of the information was at the "highest" level.

When the alarms went off, Petrov remembered, "For 15 seconds, we were in a state of shock. We needed to understand, what's next?" Usually, Petrov said, one report of a lone rocket launch did not immediately go up the chain to the general staff and the electronic command system there, known as Krokus. But in this case, the reports of a missile salvo were coming so quickly that an alert had already gone to general staff headquarters automatically, even before he could judge if the warning was genuine. A determination by the general staff was critical because, at the time, the nuclear suitcase that would give a Soviet leader remote control in such decisions was still under development.

The pressure was intense. "There was no rule about how long we were allowed to think," Petrov remembered, "before we reported a strike. But we knew that every second of procrastination took away valuable time; that the military and political leadership needed to be informed without delay. All I had to do was reach for the phone, to raise the direct line to our top commanders, but *I couldn't move. I felt like I was sitting on a hot frying pan*" (emphasis added). "We built the system to rule out the possibility of false alarms," Petrov told his interviewer in 2015. "And that day the satellites told us with the highest degree of certainty that these rockets were on the way."

After five minutes, with electronic maps and screens flashing as he held a phone in one hand and an intercom in the other, trying to absorb streams of information, Petrov decided that the launch reports were probably a false alarm. He recalled making the decision under enormous stress; another officer at the early-warning facility was shouting into the phone to him to remain calm and do his job. As he subsequently explained, it was a "gut" decision, at best a "50–50" guess, based both on his distrust of the newly installed early-warning system and the information that only five missiles were launched. "I had a funny feeling in my gut," he told the *Washington Post*.

The enormous risks of the choice that he had to make were apparent to Petrov. In interviews with the *Washington Post* in 1999 and BBC Russia in 2013, he recalled: "I didn't want to make a mistake. I knew perfectly well that nobody would be able to correct my mistake if I had made one. I thought the chances were 50–50 that the warnings were real"—"*But I didn't want to be the one responsible for starting a third world war*" (emphasis added). His probability estimate, offered after the fact even when he knew the outcome of the decision, is evidence of extraordinary uncertainty: 50–50 is an estimate of random chance, a feeling that the warning was equally likely to be true or false.

Petrov attributed the decision he made to both his training and his intuition. He had been told that a nuclear first strike by the Americans would come in the form of an overwhelming attack. "When people start a war, they don't start it with only five missiles," he said. Another factor, he said, was that Soviet ground-based radar installations—which searched for missiles rising above the horizon—showed no evidence of an attack. The ground radar units were controlled from a different command center, however, and because they could not see beyond the horizon, they would not spot incoming missiles until some minutes after the satellites had. "But these people were only a support service. The protocol said, very clearly, that the decision had to be based on computer readouts. And the decision rested with me, the duty officer."

In a very sophisticated and counterintuitive pattern of thinking, he later explained that what made him suspicious was just how strong and clear the alert was. "There were 28 or 29 security levels. After the target was identified, it had to pass all of those 'checkpoints.' I was not quite sure it was possible, under those circumstances." Petrov said the system had been rushed into service in response to the introduction by the U.S. of a similar system. He knew that it was not 100 percent reliable and had flaws. It was, he said, "raw. . . . We are wiser than computers. We created them."

Petrov also explained his decision in part as a consequence of his civilian education. He was the only officer on his team who had received a civilian education. "My colleagues were all professional soldiers, they were taught to give and obey orders." He believed that if somebody else had been on shift, the alarm would have been raised. "They were lucky it was me on shift that night."

Petrov called the duty officer in the Soviet army's headquarters and reported a system malfunction. If he was wrong, the first nuclear explosions would have happened minutes later. "Twenty-three minutes later, I realized that nothing had happened. If there had been a real strike, then I would already know about it. It was such a relief." After a six-month investigation, Petrov and his colleagues discovered that Soviet satellites had mistaken the sun's reflection in some clouds for the start of an American missile salvo. "Can you imagine?" he asked. Petrov was subsequently reprimanded because his logbook entries at the time were not complete.

An additional noteworthy yet very different kind of incident occurred on January 25, 1995, when Norway launched a four-stage rocket as part of a scientific experiment. The paperwork announcing the planned launch was apparently misplaced and when Russian operators spotted the rocket on their radar, they did report up the chain of command. Their alarm led to the first-ever opening of the nuclear briefcase by President Boris Yeltsin. Within several minutes, it became evident that the rocket was headed toward the North Pole, and twenty-two minutes after launch, it splashed into the ocean. Fortunately, despite the short time available for decision, Yeltsin took no action.[20] As in Russia and the United States, more fragmented and limited evidence from crises between India and Pakistan suggests similar kinds of decision-making behavior.[21]

In sum, in the face of warnings, human decision makers generally, although not always, chose not to transmit warnings that they expected could lead to a launch of nuclear weapons or, when they received warnings, decided not to launch nuclear weapons. In these cases, operators' decisions on both sides had contradictory consequences: they prevented war but destabilized the deterrent posture of their own government and the deterrence regime that governed the relationship between the two superpowers.

How can we explain this puzzling behavior? Before grappling with the potentially relevant explanations, it is important first to distinguish analytically between risk and uncertainty.

RISK AND UNCERTAINTY

Risk and uncertainty pose very different kinds of analytical challenges to decision makers. When people make decisions under conditions of risk, they can estimate the likely consequences of different options. These consequences are governed by a known probability distribution, and estimates of probability therefore are more or less closely related to "objective" probabilities. These kinds of probability distributions depend on a large number of random trials over time. After a machine gun has been fired thousands of times, we can be reasonably confident, given knowledge of range and velocity, in an estimate of the likelihood that a shell will reach its target. Decisions with options with known consequences that are governed by probability distributions are (relatively) easy to structure.

Any decision that has as one of its potential consequences nuclear war, however, cannot be governed in any meaningful sense by a probability distribution.

Even the assessment of value, though far less challenging than probability, is still not straightforward. Nuclear weapons have been used only twice, more than seventy years ago, and those devices were primitive in comparison to the weapons that are currently deployed and being developed. Scientists can estimate the likely scope and scale of damage from the use of nuclear weapons, but their estimates are theoretical, developed, fortunately, in the absence of any empirical evidence. Because the order of magnitude of damage is so large, error matters little in framing the decision problem and in shaping the calculus of leaders—once leaders understand how destructive the consequences of a nuclear war would be, a margin of error in the estimate of the damage would not change how leaders assess the consequences of a nuclear exchange. On the contrary, analysts have speculated that precisely because of these large orders of magnitude, it is threshold effects that matter. The "nuclear taboo," theorists suggest, functions as a decision heuristic, a shortcut that guides decision makers under conditions of uncertainty. There is some evidence that a nuclear taboo did serve as a threshold marker for the highest level of decision makers in Washington and Moscow during the Cold War.[22] Is that taboo also relevant for operators at the ends of the chain of command? Evidence from Petrov's decision—he clearly did not want to be responsible for the first use of nuclear weapons since 1945—suggests that it is.

More difficult still is estimating the consequences of a decision to launch a nuclear weapon in response to a machine-based warning that a foreign missile has been or is about to be launched. Uncertainties abound at every critical juncture. First, is the intelligence accurate? Was a missile indeed launched or did the warning systems malfunction? Was there "machine error"? How should the human interface with the machine? This is of fundamental concern today to defense analysts struggling with the legal and ethical dimensions as well as the effectiveness of autonomously targeted robotic weapons. For nuclear operators, there are currently no resources that can, within the very short time available, narrow the uncertainty.

Second, if a missile were launched, was it done on central orders or was it the act of a rogue operator? Here too, there are no relevant probability distributions to structure estimates, yet the meaning attached to the evidence in context will be critical to the way the decision maker structures the problem. Once we conceive of nuclear operators as decision makers situated at the beginning or at the end of the chain of command, we have to go outside deterrence theory to understand the ways in which they structure the problem and frame their choices.

How have decision makers in other spheres dealt with uncertainty? They have managed uncertainty in multiple ways with varying degrees of effectiveness under different conditions. The usual and least conceptually satisfactory way is to blur the distinction between the two and conflate uncertainty with risk. Because uncertainty is so difficult to structure analytically and so uncomfortable to tolerate psychologically, decision makers make probability estimates even when there are no underlying probability distributions available. These "subjectively expected" consequences become the artifacts that decision makers can use to structure the problem and make choices. The benefits of these artificial subjective probability estimates are clear. Decision makers can take an ill-structured problem and make it tractable. For nuclear operators, who have very little time to make a decision, making a problem tractable has a clear advantage.

But this structured traction masks a harsh reality and can lead to pathologies in decision making.[23] First, it enables overconfidence, always a risk among expert decision makers. Overconfidence is enabled in part by masking the limitations on the ability to estimate the likelihood of consequences with even reasonable confidence. The false certainty that comes from estimating the likelihood, for example, of a rogue operator obscures the underlying challenge that an operator has no reasonable way of generating an estimate. That deeply unsettling knowledge is simply too disturbing to entertain so it is easier to take the false comfort that comes from subjective probabilities. Stanislav Petrov stood out in his capacity to resist the comfort of false certainty and recognize the intense uncertainty of the situation and the difficulty of his decision.

There is a second pathology. People are not intuitive probability thinkers. "Human performance suffers," argues Tetlock, "because we are, deep down, deterministic thinkers with an aversion to probabilistic strategies that accept the inevitability of error."[24] When people generate these kinds of evidence-free estimates, they routinely produce simplified estimates. They decide that a consequence is either very likely or very unlikely. People tend to gravitate to the extreme end of the probability curve, basing their estimates on what is available and easily accessed in memory or on the last such estimate that they made, which then artificially anchors their judgments.[25] Unlike flawed estimates of risk that analysts can document against available probability distributions, when the estimates are subjective in a world of uncertainty, there are no grounds for determining whether an estimate is reasonable or not. Since there is no basis for any estimate in a world of uncertainty because they are unrelated to underlying probability distributions, these estimates simply are. And because they are, and nothing else is available, they have an outsized influence on operators' choices.

Cognitive psychology has demonstrated important differences between the expectations of rational decision models and the processes of attribution and estimation that people frequently use. It explains these differences by the need for simple rules of information processing and judgment that are necessary to make sense of environments that are both uncertain and complex. People have a preference for simplicity, they are averse to ambiguity and dissonance, and they misunderstand fundamentally the essence of probability.[26] We are not intuitively good at estimating probabilities.

Cognitive psychology has identified a number of heuristics and biases that people use in environments of risk and uncertainty that can impair processes of judgment.[27] Heuristics are convenient shortcuts or rules of thumb for processing information. Three of the best-documented heuristics are *availability*, *representativeness*, and *anchoring*. The availability heuristic refers to people's tendency to interpret ambiguous information in terms of what is most easily available in their cognitive repertoire.[28] The heuristic of representativeness refers to people's proclivity to exaggerate similarities between one event and a prior class of events, typically leading to significant errors in probability judgments or estimates of frequency.[29] The heuristic of anchoring refers to an estimation of magnitude or degree by comparing it with an "available" initial value (often an inaccurate one) as a reference point and making a comparison.[30] In a world of uncertainty, leaders search for the relevant reference classes to anchor their judgments.[31] Initial judgments or prior beliefs serve as a conceptual anchor on the processing of new information and the revision of estimates.

If we were to draw on the knowledge that availability, anchoring, and representativeness, three prominent cognitive shortcuts, are likely to influence subjective probability estimates, what can we expect nuclear operators to choose in the face of machine-generated information that a nuclear missile has been launched? These heuristics work to magnify the impact of past decisions on present-day operators, to the extent that they are knowledgeable about prior events. *We should consequently expect operators who receive warnings of imminent launch or a missile on the way to infer machine error and to discount the likelihood of a nuclear attack by an adversary, as their predecessors generally have done in the past.* Standing instructions and a vigorous attempt to close off choice are not likely to have an impact on these choices; they did not in the past, and there is consequently little reason to expect that they will in the future. On the contrary, knowledge that operators were correct to trump the machine in the past can only reinforce their confidence in the future. We can make the same point using different language: cognitive psychologists would expect nuclear operators to treat the past as prologue. This pattern of inference should reassure those who worry most about accidental or miscalculated nuclear war and trouble those who worry that an absence of credibility and a reputation for resolve are most likely to lead to war.

This expectation is drawn from a limited but nevertheless generally consistent pattern of behavior that is interpreted through the lens of some of the most robust findings of cognitive psychology. There are, of course, other perspectives within psychology that are candidate explanations and yield quite different, even contradictory expectations. Two of the most prominent are prospect theory and emotions, particularly fear, as drivers of decisions.

PROSPECT THEORY

Foreign policy decision makers, like people generally, are not neutral about the likelihood of gain and loss. Prospect theorists posit that people are more sensitive to relative changes in assets than to net asset levels, that they frame choice around a reference point, and that they give more weight to expected losses from that reference point than to expected comparable gains in constructing their subjective estimates of risk when they think losses are likely to be high.[32]

Prospect theory has considerable implications for rational theories of deterrence. Theories of deterrence are premised on the expectation that a deterrer will threaten harmful consequences that will exceed the benefits of what a would-be challenger wants to do. Challengers calculate their subjective expected utility, understand that the likely costs would exceed the benefits, and refrain from action. Prospect theory expects quite different behavior: it expects leaders to be risk averse in the domain of gain and risk acceptant in the domain of loss, when they perceive a heightened threat or the strong likelihood of loss of something that matters to them.

What kind of behavior would prospect theory expect when a nuclear operator receives alarming intelligence that an adversary has launched or is about to launch a nuclear weapon? If we treat the status quo as the reference point, then that nuclear operator is plunged immediately into the domain of loss. Prospect theory would suggest then that the operator choose the risk-acceptant rather than the risk-averse option. Much depends on how nuclear operators frame the problem, on whether individual or collective risk drives the framing of the problem, and on how they estimate short-term versus long-term risk.[33] Other things being equal, nuclear operators in the domain of highly probable loss should choose the risk-acceptant option. If they had, then they should have communicated the warnings or launched the nuclear torpedo, but as we showed, operators did not behave that way. Indeed, contrary to the expectations of prospect theory, nuclear operators who were in the domain of highly probable loss were risk averse in the face of frightening intelligence.

EMOTION

Cognitive psychologists and prospect theorists, despite their evidence-based critique of models of (microeconomic) rationality, have moved only one degree away from the fundamental assumption of utility-maximizing rationality. They continue to set rationality as the default and then explore the consequences of systematic "errors" and "deviations," of "constrained" or "bounded" rationality. These deviations from rationality only make sense against a background of a narrowly conceived microeconomic concept of rationality as an account of probability and value. Recent scholarship on emotion provides a more compelling explanation of risk aversion in a deeply uncertain environment.

Neuroscientists and neuropsychologists start with the powerful impact of emotion on behavior. Evidence from two decades of research emphasizes first that information processing seems to be the result not only of a deliberative thought process but largely of preconscious neurological processes. The brain can absorb about eleven million pieces of information a second but can only process forty consciously. The unconscious brain manages the rest. Second, emotion is primary and plays a dominant role in driving behavior.[34] Research on emotion is having a significant impact on theories of deterrence, reputation and signaling, and nuclear proliferation.[35]

There is growing consensus that emotion is "first" because it is automatic and fast. Operating below the threshold of conscious awareness, it plays a dominant role in shaping perception and behavior.[36] We generally feel before we think, and what is even more surprising, often we act before we think.[37]

The brain implements "automatic processes," which are faster than conscious deliberations, with little or no awareness or feeling of effort.[38] Not surprisingly, the conscious brain then interprets behavior that emerges from automatic, affective processes as the outcome of perception and deliberation. Kahneman calls the first, emotion-based system of processing "intuitive" and "associative" and the second system "reasoned" and "rule-governed." The first system is preconscious, automatic, fast, effortless, associative, unreflective, usually with strong emotional bonds, and slow to change. The second system is conscious, slow, effortful, reflective, rule-governed, and flexible. The vast majority of processing occurs through the first system, which draws heavily on emotions, and in a competition between the two, always trumps the rule-governed, reasoned system. It is extraordinarily difficult, Kahneman concludes, for the second system to educate the first.[39]

Among the emotions generally considered to be basic, the impact of fear is the most widely studied. Fear has been central to the study of foreign policy and international politics. Since Thucydides, the great student of the Peloponnesian Wars, realists have premised their analyses of war on the ubiquity of fear. In these realist and rationalist accounts, however, fear remains an assumption, unexplored, rather than a dynamic process that is experienced.

Neuropsychologists treat fear very differently. Fear is conditioned in part by our evolutionary makeup and is frequently evoked by crude or subliminal cues. It is, of course, highly adaptive; fear heightens attention and vigilance and prepares people to respond to what they perceive as imminent danger.

Nevertheless, fear prompts hesitation and risk-averse behavior.[40] Indeed, fear can be so powerful in its impact that it can overwhelm the usual risk acceptance associated with loss aversion.[41]

For nuclear operators who receive warning of an impending attack, emotion is likely to be a powerful driver. Very high stakes are at play, and operators understand that the consequences of error are potentially enormous and that they have only minutes to decide. Neuroscience research related to risk suggests the likely impact of emotion in such a scenario. Neuroscience treats risk not only as subjective cognitive assessment—as thinking—but also treats *risk as feeling*. The risk-as-feeling argument contends that responses to risky situations result in part from direct, unmediated emotion. The intense feeling of risk that nuclear operators are likely to experience is likely to evoke, quickly and in unmediated ways, feelings of fear. Under these conditions, decision research suggests, emotion is likely to swamp cognition and shape risk preferences.[42] Fear of the consequences of nuclear war would generate the consistent pattern of risk aversion that we have observed among nuclear operators who face these terrible choices. Petrov made reference to precisely that fear when he looked back at his decision years later.

Those who study the impact of emotion, particularly fear, on behavior do a better job than does prospect theory in capturing the risk-averse behavior of nuclear operators.[43] We would need far more granular data than we currently have to disentangle the impact of cognitive heuristics from the powerful impact of fear in shaping their risk-averse behavior, but behavioral decision theory and research from neuroscience are helpful. Both treat *risk as feeling*. The risk-as-feeling argument contends that responses to risky situations result in part from direct, unmediated emotion and in part indirectly from emotion mediated through cognition. Feelings—fear, anger, sadness—respond directly to a sense of risk. Petrov remembers feeling shocked, frozen in place, unable initially to process the signals he was seeing, a reaction consistent with the "freeze" in the fight, flight, and freeze response evoked by fear.

People also evaluate risky alternatives through cognitive processes, based largely on the probability and desirability of associated consequences. These cognitive evaluations generate affective consequences, which exert a reciprocal influence on cognitive evaluations. Although the two reactions are reciprocal and interdependent, they come from different sources and can, at times, diverge. What we do know is that when emotion and cognition diverge, emotion often swamps cognition and then risk preference is determined by emotions.[44]

CONVENTIONS

Is this behavior invariant across strategic cultures and social conventions? As our understanding of subjective risk assessments deepens, for example, we have become more aware of how these assessments—well explained by basic psychological processes—are also embedded in culture and convention.

Cultures and conventions matter in the way people frame problems, but they are especially important in an environment that is radically uncertain. Nelson and Katzenstein argue that in the presence of uncertainty, decision makers rely on social conventions to make decisions. Conventions are shared templates, sometimes tacit, sometimes conscious, that serve to simplify uncertain situations and organize and coordinate actions in predictable ways. Conventions, they argue, stabilize but do not eliminate uncertainty by giving decision makers a sense of control over a necessarily uncertain future.[45]

How can the concept of conventions help us understand the generally risk-averse choices of nuclear operators? We can argue as a first approximation that conventions are embedded in strategic cultures, in the informal rules that govern the command, control, and communications systems that are put in place around nuclear operators. That argument would be convincing if Soviet and American systems had been configured in similar ways; but they were not. There were important differences in standard operating procedures as well as significant differences in levels of trust. Yet these differences cannot explain the variation that occurred among Soviet officers in 1962 and Russian officers in 1995.

More convincing is the existence of a "nuclear taboo," a deeply internalized horror about the consequences of the use of nuclear weapons.[46] There is an accompanying sense that once the injunction against the use of nuclear weapons is violated, even in the mildest way, the constraints against their use will collapse and there will be no retreat. That knowledge is not fully articulated, not fully reasoned, and clearly never tested against the evidence. It is tacit, yet all the more powerful as a guiding framework when operators have mere moments to decide in a deeply uncertain environment. That taboo has strengthened over time.

This argument challenges the primacy of cognitive explanations. In none of these cases did one side intentionally and deliberately initiate the use of a nuclear weapon as part of an attack against the other. Rather, the simplified and intuitive decision making of nuclear operators was congruent with their environments. Emotional arguments fare better: the fear of and aversion to the use of nuclear weapons is consistent with arguments about social convention, a taboo that seems, at least for the moment, to be deeply engrained across cultures. The fear and the taboo are mutually reinforcing; the one strengthens the other and they worked together to prevent escalation through miscalculation.

DETERRENCE AND THE PREVENTION OF NUCLEAR WAR

We make an argument in this chapter that is paradoxical and troubling.[47] We find that psychological habits and emotions as well as social conventions converge to explain why, during the Cold War, nuclear operators generally chose not to launch nuclear weapons or transmit alarming information that an adversary had attacked. They made these choices in a context where both parties had second-strike capability and where a willingness to respond if attacked was an essential component of nuclear deterrence embedded in a strategic culture of mutual assured destruction. In at least one case if not more, a decision by a nuclear operator likely prevented war and, in others, operators' choices likely prevented miscalculated escalation.

Preventing a nuclear attack is the objective of all doctrines of nuclear deterrence. Yet, once the pattern of these choices by nuclear operators becomes widely known, deterrence is potentially destabilized. If operators will not transmit frightening evidence up the chain of command, or launch nuclear weapons in response to an alleged attack as ordered, then deterrence as a strategy loses its credibility. There is a second layer of contradiction. If deterrence theory is valid, dissemination of knowledge of this patterned response could lead to the kind of risk taking that deterrence theories and strategies seek above all to avoid.

Our conclusions are tentative given the small number of cases, the thinness of the evidence, and the growing pool of proliferators and would-be proliferators who do not have obvious second-strike capability. Within these constraints, however, it appears that the evidence drawn from the practices of nuclear operators that we have examined challenges both the theory and the strategy of deterrence.

It can be argued that this pattern is an artifact of the Cold War and cannot be generalized to the future. At least two arguments could be advanced. First, unlike the routinized, well-structured rules that characterized the latter half of the Cold War, proliferators and would-be proliferators today do not necessarily accept these rules. Some are deeply revisionist, unaccepting of the present system, and at times apocalyptic in their outlook. It is important to note that exactly these arguments were made about the Soviet Union by American strategists throughout much of the Cold War.

Second, and this is a far more compelling argument, with the development of more tailored weapons that produce more limited and targeted damage, the threshold between nuclear and conventional weapons diminishes. It consequently becomes more likely that nuclear weapons will be used on the battlefield. The nuclear taboo will fade, the argument goes, as the damage from nuclear weapons becomes more limited.

There is, of course, no evidence that can confirm or deny this argument. What we can say is that the evidence we have from the past is troubling to theories of deterrence. Proponents of deterrence theory can, of course, always claim that since nuclear operators seem to be violating fundamental assumptions by refusing to respond in prescribed ways, their behavior is outside the scope of the theory and therefore does not constitute a fair test. The evidence that nuclear operators generally behaved in ways that violate the fundamental assumptions of the theory should nevertheless give theorists of deterrence pause. Theories that are consistently at variance with the behavior they assume are unlikely to have much traction over time.

Finally, this evidence creates challenging policy dilemmas. In a relationship where both parties have second-strike capability, the choices of nuclear operators undermine the strategy of nuclear deterrence insofar as deterrers seem unwilling to do what they are expected to do in the face of warnings of imminent attack. If deterrence theorists are correct, then dissemination of the knowledge of the way nuclear operators in the deterring state tend to respond could be destabilizing. For proponents of deterrence, this kind of knowledge could encourage would-be challengers to make risky choices and push against the frontier, taking comfort from the strength of the nuclear taboo both as psychological mechanism and social convention. On the other hand, for those who worry principally about miscalculated escalation in a world where nuclear powers are increasing, that deterrence theory, strategy, and practice is imperiled is of small concern against the comfort that the choices of nuclear operators can provide a brake against the use of nuclear weapons in an uncertain world.

NOTES

1. In a set of experiments, Tversky and Kahneman find a distinctive fourfold pattern of attitudes to risk: risk aversion for gains and risk acceptance for losses of high probability and risk seeking for gains and risk aversion for losses of low probability. Amos Tversky and Daniel Kahneman, "Advances in Prospect Theory: Cumulative Representation of Uncertainty," *Journal of Risk and Uncertainty* 5, no. 4 (1992): 297–323. Outcome probabilities also affect the strength of framing effects: bimodal choices between a certain outcome and a risky outcome produce greater effects than choices between two risky outcomes. Anton Kuhberger, "The Influence of Framing on Risky Decisions: A Meta-Analysis," *Organizational Behavior and Human Decision Processes* 75, no. 1 (1998): 23–55.

2. Thomas C. Schelling, *The Strategy of Conflict* (Cambridge, Mass.: Harvard University Press, 1960), 16–18, and *Arms and Influence* (New Haven, Conn.: Yale University Press, 1966), 37–38.

3. Jeffrey Lewis, "Our Nuclear Procedures Are Crazier than Trump," *Foreign Policy*, August 5, 2016, http://foreignpolicy.com/2016/08/05/our-nuclear-procedures-are-crazier-than-trump/.

4. Zbigniew Brzezinski, "A Conversation with Zbigniew Brzezinski," interview by Sam Feist, *Council on Foreign Relations*, March 30, 2012, https://www.youtube.com/watch?v=oTKOqH0mF9c, 8:L49–13:48. The "glitch" was the result of a training tape that had been inadvertently inserted into the computer running the early-warning programs. Geoffrey Forden, "False Alarms in the Nuclear Age," *NOVA*, October 6, 2001, http://www.pbs.org/wgbh/nova/military/nuclear-false-alkarms.html. In this case, operators did send the warning up the chain of command.

5. Center for Defense Information, "Accidental Nuclear War: A Rising Risk?" *Defense Monitor* 15, no. 7 (1986): 6. On June 30, 1980, at 2:26 a.m., computer screens at Strategic Air Command (SAC) in Nebraska lit up with a warning that two submarine-launched ballistic missiles were headed toward the United States. Eighteen seconds after the first signals, the displays showed additional missiles. The duty commander ordered pilots to their aircraft and told them to start their engines, then checked with NORAD in Colorado. Satellites and radars at NORAD showed no incoming missiles. After a short time, the warning display at SAC lit up again, as did the screens at the Pentagon's National Military Command Center. The duty officers in each location suspected the warning was an error. After a brief threat assessment conference at the Pentagon, the pilots were told to stand down. The false alarm was caused by the failure of a computer chip in one of NORAD's communication devices. Bruce Blair, president of the World Security Institute in Washington, D.C., describes this incident in the film *Countdown to Zero*, directed by Lucy Walker (Los Angeles, Calif.: Magnolia Pictures, 2010), DVD.

6. Paul Bracken, *The Command and Control of Nuclear Forces* (New Haven, Conn.: Yale University Press, 1983); Ashton B. Carter, "Assessing Command System Vulnerability," in *Managing Nuclear Operations*, ed. Ashton B. Carter, John D. Steinbruner, and Charles A. Zraket (Washington, D.C.: Brookings Institution Press, 1987), 555–610.

7. Morielle I. Lotan, "Strategic Dilemmas of WMD Operators," *Comparative Strategy* 34, no. 4 (2015): 345–66.

8. Ibid.

9. Ibid.; Peter D. Feaver, "Command and Control in Emerging Nuclear Nations," *International Security* 17, no. 3 (1993): 160–87; Peter D. Feaver, "Nuclear Command and Control in Crisis: Old Lessons from New History," in *Nuclear Weapons Security Crises: What Does History Teach?*, ed. Henry D. Sokolski and Bruno Tertrais (Carlisle, Pa.: Strategic Studies Institute, 2013), 205–27.

10. Lotan, "Strategic Dilemmas."

11. Scott Sagan, *The Limits of Safety* (Princeton, N.J.: Princeton University Press, 1993), 130.

12. Ibid., 189–90.

13. Ibid., 98–99.

14. Ibid., 189–90.

15. Evan Andrews, "5 Cold War Close Calls," *History Stories*, October 16, 2013, www.history.com/news/history-lists/5-cold-war-close-calls.

16. For a detailed analysis that draws on Russian sources, see Dmitry (Dima) Adamsky, "The 1983 Nuclear Crisis: Lessons for Deterrence Theory and Practice," *Journal of Strategic Studies* 36, no. 1 (2013): 4–41. On page 19, Adamsky paints a vivid picture: "With Perimetr [the reserve command system for retaliation under attack] under development, malfunctioning EW, unreliable C2, strategic menace from NATO conventional forces, and the possibility of decapitation promoted by U.S. strategy, the Soviet leadership's confidence in its ability to retaliate had been undermined."

17. Ibid.

18. Markus Wolf, *Man without a Face: The Autobiography of Communism's Greatest Spymaster* (New York: Random House 1997), 221–22.

19. The following account of this incident draws primarily on interviews that Stanislav Petrov gave to *Der Spiegel*, the *Washington Post*, *BBC Russia*, the *New York Times*, and *Time*. Direct quotes from Petrov are drawn from all these sources to create a detailed and coherent account. The first account of the incident was provided by Gen. Yuri Votintsev, the retired commander of Soviet missile defense, in an interview he gave to *Bild* (Мир услышал о Петрове год спустя, когда его бывший начальник, генерал Юрий Вотинцев, рассказал

об этом немецкому изданию Bild Оригинал новости ИноТВ, https://russian.rt.com/inotv /2017-09-19/Wirtualna-Polska-Petrov-spas-ot). In 1991, journalist Dmitri Likhanov wrote about Petrov's exploits on the basis of an interview with Votintsev, which was published in the weekly newspaper *Sovershenno sekretno* (Top secret), https://fishki.net/2390340–26-sentjabr ja-1983-godapodpolkovnik-stanislav-evgrafovich-petrov-predotvratil-jadernuju-vojnu.html. In 1993, Votintsev published his memoirs, in four issues of the journal *Voenno-istorichestkii zhurnal*, 1993, nos. 8, 9, 10 and 11.

Once the incident was disclosed, Petrov was honored by the United Nations and awarded several prizes. He was interviewed by the *Washington Post* (David Hoffman, "I Had a Funny Feeling in My Gut," *Washington Post*, February 10, 1999, A19, http://washingtonpost.com/wp -srv/inatl/longterm/coldwar/shatter021099.htm) and by *BBC Russia* (Pavel Aksenov, "Stanislav Petrov: The Man Who May Have Saved the World," Sept. 26, 2013, http://www.bbc.com /news/world-europe-24280831).

After Petrov's death in 2017, obituaries were published that drew on interviews that he had given to the *New York Times* (Sewell Chan, "Stanislav Petrov, Soviet Officer Who Helped Avert Nuclear War, Is Dead at 77," *New York Times*, September 19, 2017, https://www.nytimes.com /2017/09/18/world/europe/stanislav-petrov-nuclear-war-dead.html?_r=0) and *Time* (Simon Shuster, "Stanislav Petrov, the Russian Officer who Averted a Nuclear War, Feared History Repeating Itself," *Time*, September 19, 2017, http://time.com/4947879/stanislv-petrov-russia -nuckear-war-obituary/).

See also *Military Story*, "The Day Before: Stanislav Petrov and 1983 Soviet Nuclear False Alarm Incident," http://www.militarystory.org/the-day-before-stanislav-petrov-and-1983 -soviet-nuclear-false-alarm-incident/; Andrews, "5 Cold War Close Calls"; David Hoffmann, *The Dead Hand* (New York: Doubleday, 2009).

20. The film *Countdown to Zero* describes this incident.

21. Vipin Narang, "Posturing for Peace? Pakistan's Nuclear Postures and South Asian Stability," *International Security* 34, no. 3 (Winter 2009/10): 38–78.

22. Richard Ned Lebow and Janice Stein, *We All Lost the Cold War* (Princeton, N.J.: Princeton University Press, 1994).

23. For an excellent discussion of risk and uncertainty among decision makers responsible for the global financial system, see Stephen C. Nelson and Peter J. Katzenstein, "Uncertainty, Risk, and the Financial Crisis of 2006," *International Organization* 68, no. 2 (Spring 2014): 361–92.

24. Philip E. Tetlock, *Expert Political Judgment: How Good Is It? How Can We Know?* (Princeton, N.J.: Princeton University Press, 2005), 40.

25. Amos Tversky and Daniel Kahneman, "Availability: A Heuristic for Judging Frequency and Probability," *Cognitive Psychology* 5, no. 2 (1973): 207–32.

26. Robyn Dawes, "Judgment and Choice," in *Handbook of Social Psychology*, ed. Susan T. Fiske, Daniel T. Gilbert and Gardner Lindzey (New York: McGraw Hill, 1998), 497–548; Tetlock, *Expert Political Judgment*.

27. Tversky and Kahneman, "Availability"; Richard Nisbett and Lee Ross, *Human Inference: Strategies and Shortcomings of Social Judgment* (Englewood Cliffs, N.J.: Prentice-Hall, 1980); Daniel Kahneman, Paul Slovic, and Amos Tversky, eds. *Judgment under Uncertainty: Heuristics and Biases* (Cambridge: Cambridge University Press, 1982); Susan T. Fiske and Shelley E. Taylor, *Social Cognition* (Reading, Mass.: Addison Wesley, 1984); Robert Jervis, *Perception and Misperception in International Politics* (Princeton, N.J.: Princeton University Press, 1976); Detlof von Winterfeldt and Ward Edwards, *Decision Analysis and Behavioral Research* (New York: Cambridge University Press, 1986).

28. Tversky and Kahneman, "Availability"; Michael Ross and Fiore Sicoly, "Egocentric Biases in Availability and Attribution," *Journal of Personality and Social Psychology* 37, no. 3 (1979): 322–36; Shelley E. Taylor, "The Availability Bias in Social Perception and Interaction," in Kahneman, Slovic, and Tversky, *Judgment under Uncertainty*, 190–200.

29. Daniel Kahneman and Amos Tversky, "Subjective Probability: A Judgment of Representativeness," *Cognitive Psychology* 3, no. 3 (1972): 430–54; Daniel Kahneman and Amos Tverksy, "On the Psychology of Prediction," *Psychological Review* 80, no. 4 (1973): 237–51; Kahneman, Slovic, and Tversky, *Judgment under Uncertainty*, essays in part 2.

30. Fiske and Taylor, *Social Cognition*, 250–56, 268–75.

31. Amos Tversky and Daniel Kahneman, "Judgment under Uncertainty: Heuristics and Biases," *Science* 185, no. 4157 (1974): 1124–31.

32. Daniel Kahneman and Amos Tversky, "Prospect Theory: An Analysis of Decision under Risk," *Econometrica* 47, no. 2 (1979): 263–91; Daniel Kahneman and Amos Tversky, eds., *Choices, Values and Frames* (New York: Cambridge University Press, 2000); Tversky and Kahneman, "Advances in Prospect Theory."

33. Lotan provides evidence that in the two Soviet cases in 1962 and 1983, the Soviet operators paid a personal price as they were disgraced or reprimanded when their actions became known to their commanding officers after the fact. If the decision problem is framed as personal rather than collective (national), then it can be argued that the operators chose the risk-acceptant option but only if they assumed that they would survive the ensuing nuclear exchange. Lotan, "Strategic Dilemmas."

34. There is widespread theoretical dispute about the conceptualization of emotion. Political psychologists are sensitive to the complex siting of emotion at the interface of structure and action, material and psychological processes, and neurological and sociopolitical processes: "Emotion is a large set of differentiated, biologically-based complex[es] that are constituted, at the very least, by mutually transformative interactions among biological systems (e.g., cognition, physiology, psychology) and physical and sociocultural ones." Rose McDermott, "The Feeling of Rationality: The Meaning of Neuroscientific Advances for Political Science," *Perspectives on Politics* 2, no. 4 (2004): 692.

35. For the role of emotion in deterrence, see Jonathan Mercer, "Rationality and Psychology in International Politics," *International Organization* 59, no. 1 (2005): 77–106; Jonathan Mercer, "Emotional Beliefs," *International Organization* 64, no. 1 (2010): 1–31. On reputation and signaling, see Jonathan Mercer, *Reputation and International Politics* (Ithaca, N.Y.: Cornell University Press, 1996); Mercer, "Emotional Beliefs." On nuclear proliferation, see Jacques E. C. Hymans, "Theories of Proliferation," *Nonproliferation Review* 13, no. 3 (2006): 455–65.

36. Joseph LeDoux, *The Emotional Brain: The Mysterious Underpinnings of Emotional Life* (New York: Simon and Schuster, 1996); Piotr Winkielman and Kent C. Berridge, "Unconscious Emotion," *Current Directions in Psychological Science* 13, no. 3 (2004): 120–23.

37. "Dual-process" theories in psychology provide an account of how a phenomenon can occur as a result of two different processes, one implicit and the second explicit. See Lisa Feldman Barrett, Michele M. Tugade, and Randall W. Engle, "Individual Differences in Working Memory Capacity and Dual-Process Theories of the Mind," *Psychological Bulletin* 130, no. 4 (2004): 553–73; Daniel Kahneman, "A Perspective on Judgment and Choice," *American Psychologist* 58, no. 9 (2003): 697–720; Steven A. Sloman, "The Empirical Case for Two Systems of Reasoning," *Psychological Bulletin* 119, no. 1 (1996): 3–22; Ron Sun, *Duality of the Mind* (Mahwah, NJ: Lawrence Erlbaum, 2002). Implicit systems are automatic, fast, evolved early, use parallel processing, have high capacity, are not reflexive, and are effortless, while explicit systems are conscious, controlled, relatively slow, evolved late, use sequential processing, are

limited by attentional and working memory resources, and are effortful. See Kevin MacDonald, "Effortful Control, Explicit Processing, and the Regulation of Human Evolved Predispositions," *Psychological Review* 115, no. 4 (2008): 1012–31.

38. John A. Bargh, Shelly Chaiken, Paula Raymond, and Charles Hymes, "The Automatic Evaluation Effect: Unconditional Automatic Attitude Activation with a Pronunciation Task," *Journal of Experimental Social Psychology* 32, no. 1 (1996): 104–28; John A. Bargh and Tanya L. Chartrand, "The Unbearable Automacity of Being," *American Psychologist* 54, no. 7 (1999): 462–79.

39. Daniel Kahneman, *Thinking, Fast and Slow* (New York: Farrar, Strauss and Giroux, 2011).

40. Jennifer S. Lerner, Deborah A. Small, and George Loewenstein, "Heart Strings and Purse Strings: Carryover Effects on Economic Decisions," *Psychological Science* 15, no. 5 (2004): 337–41; Colin Camerer, George Loewenstein, and Drazen Prelec, "Neuroeconomics: How Neuroscience Can Inform Economics," *Journal of Economic Literature* 43, no. 1 (2005): 9–64.

41. In the wake of the global financial crisis in 2008–9, waves of panic selling depressed equities markets as sellers locked in their losses. Despite the best efforts of market gurus such as Warren Buffett in December 2008 to encourage people to see the sell-off as a buying opportunity, panic selling continued. It should come as no surprise that this kind of selling—far beyond what deleveraging requires—occurs after sudden and large drops in the equities markets that evoke panic through contagion. See Janice Gross Stein, "Fear, Greed, and Financial Decision Making," in *Psychology, Strategy, and Conflict: Perceptions of Insecurity in International Relations*, ed. James Davis (London: Routledge, 2012), 82–100.

42. George Loewenstein, Scott Rick, and Jonathan D. Cohen, "Neuroeconomics," *Annual Review of Psychology* 59 (2008): 647–72.

43. Again, the way operators frame the decision will depend on what they choose as their reference point. This conclusion assumes that their reference point is the status quo.

44. Loewenstein, Rick, and Cohen, "Neuroeconomics," 652.

45. Nelson and Katzenstein, "Uncertainty, Risk, and Financial Crisis," 362.

46. Nina Tannenwald, *The Nuclear Taboo: The United States and the Non-Use of Nuclear Weapons since 1945* (Cambridge: Cambridge University Press, 2007).

47. Robert Jervis long ago identified the contradictions in theory and strategy between the deterrence model and the spiral model. See Jervis, *Perception and Misperception*.

CHAPTER THREE

The Neurobiology of Deterrence
Lessons for U.S. and Chinese Doctrine

NICHOLAS WRIGHT

Deterring an adversary requires anticipating how they will decide to respond to our actions. Effective deterrence thus crucially depends on understanding human decision making. What are the accounts of others' decision making that governments use to make these forecasts of what an adversary will decide in the future? This question can be asked equally of China and the United States. One source of evidence is the doctrines they publish. As this chapter will show, U.S. and Chinese doctrine both explicitly contain accounts of how an adversary's decision making is expected to affect their behavior. Of course, using doctrine to understand real decision-making practice has limitations. For instance, doctrine may be overly general, out-of-date, or fail to capture important political aspects of decision making, but doctrine can provide one source of evidence about Chinese and U.S. accounts of others' decision making.[1] This matters because escalating conflict between these two nuclear-armed states has a far from zero probability.[2] In this chapter, I take insights from the behavioral sciences, grounded in neuroscience, and ask how these relate to the accounts of others' decision making described in U.S. and Chinese doctrine.

The chapter has five sections, followed by concluding observations. First, I discuss doctrine and introduce the specific examples of U.S. and Chinese doctrine examined in this chapter. Second, I ask what role psychological factors play in the concepts of deterrence contained in these doctrines. Third, I describe the modern, biologically based decision sciences that help better describe human decision making. In the context of this edited volume, this section describes how this biologically based approach fits within the broader context of behavioral economics. Fourth, I take a key aspect of decision making described by these decision sciences—neural prediction error—and ask how this relates to U.S. and Chinese doctrine. Fifth, I describe a second aspect of decision making—the rejection of unfairness—and again ask how this relates to U.S. and Chinese doctrine. Finally, I discuss more broadly not just whether this doctrine *does* reflect a more realistic understanding of human decision making but outline some criteria for whether it *should*. This concluding section also briefly notes some possible areas for further research.

U.S. AND CHINESE DOCTRINE AND CONCEPTS: CASE SELECTION AND SOURCES

I examine the strategic thought of the People's Republic of China (PRC) and the United States for four reasons. First, both countries are highly consequential actors, making them intrinsically important cases to consider. Second, there is a far from zero probability of future escalation between these actors, in which case the types of decision making discussed in their doctrines will interact. Understanding significant commonalities and differences may help anticipate potential sources of misperception. Third, the development of U.S. and Chinese strategic thinking followed relatively distinct trajectories. Unlike fellow East Asian countries Japan and South Korea,[3] the PRC's strategic thought was not shaped by intimate postwar security cooperation with the United States. Fourth, PRC and U.S. doctrine and strategic thought more broadly have both undergone rich analyses on which the current study can draw. Thus, overall both the PRC and the U.S. are highly significant actors with well-developed and potentially distinct bodies of strategic thought, providing two useful initial cases across which to examine cognitive findings.

Doctrine is a broad term. Barry Posen, for example, defines military doctrine as "the subcomponent of grand strategy that deals explicitly with military means" in which "grand strategy is a political-military, means-ends chain, a state's theory about how it can best 'cause' security for itself."[4] This chapter examines U.S. and Chinese military doctrine broadly defined and draws on specific texts produced by each country.

For the United States, the *NATO Glossary of Terms and Definitions* defines doctrine as "fundamental principles by which the military forces guide their actions in support of objectives."[5] Here, I particularly focus on two key U.S. documents. The first is the 2006 *Deterrence Operations Joint Operating Concept* (DO-JOC), which aims to guide and inform deterrence operations against state and nonstate adversaries.[6] The second is the 2012 *Joint Operational Access Concept* (JOAC), which would be particularly relevant for the types of scenarios likely in a near-term China-U.S. confrontation.[7]

Chinese doctrine is harder to examine as it is not as extensively presented on public websites. As the analyst Dennis Blasko writes, one can consider "'doctrine' to be a statement of how a military fights. The People's Liberation Army (PLA) has no single word for 'doctrine' and what is considered its warfighting doctrine is found in a variety of regulations and official documents, including teaching material used in its military education institutes."[8] I use two key

Chinese documents. First is *The Science of Military Strategy* (2005), produced by the Academy of Military Sciences in an English translation of a Chinese version published four years before for military education.[9] This five-hundred-page book covers many aspects of military strategy, including a chapter on deterrence. Second is *The Science of Second Artillery Campaigns* (2004),[10] produced in Chinese by the PLA press for internal use. It covers many aspects of strategy relevant to the People's Liberation Army Rocket Force (PLARF),[11] formerly known as the Second Artillery, which operates the missile forces whose use or threat of use would play a critical role in any Sino-U.S. escalation scenario.

THE PSYCHOLOGICAL DIMENSION IN U.S. AND CHINESE DOCTRINE ON DETERRENCE

In both U.S. and Chinese doctrine, deterrence has a fundamentally psychological component. In addition, doctrine in both countries considers the costs and benefits of potential outcomes for the adversary. This section discusses both these aspects.

In the U.S. case, from the 1990s until the past few years the Department of Defense (DoD) *Dictionary of Military and Associated Terms* stated that "deterrence is a *state of mind* brought about by the existence of a credible threat of unacceptable counteraction" (emphasis added); it now defines deterrence as "the prevention of action by the existence of a credible threat of unacceptable counteraction and/or *belief* that the cost of action outweighs the *perceived* benefits" (emphasis added).[12] This reflects an important strand of broader Western writing on deterrence. U.S. scholar Patrick M. Morgan, for example, states that "deterrence is undoubtedly a psychological phenomenon, for it involves convincing an opponent not to attack by threatening harm through retaliation."[13] The French analyst Bruno Tertrais similarly writes that "the fact that extended deterrence relies less on in-theatre means does not necessarily affect its credibility; deterrence is fundamentally a psychological process."[14]

The DO-JOC also prominently states that "the central idea of the DO JOC is to decisively influence the adversary's decision-making calculus."[15] Furthermore, as shown in figure 3.1, which I adapt from the core concept and illustration in the DO-JOC, the adversary's decision calculus is clearly shown as a decision between options (each of which has costs and benefits), and in which perception is key. The DO-JOC goes on to state that "an adversary's deterrence decision calculus focuses on their perception of three primary elements: The *benefits* of a course of action; The *costs* of a course of action; The *consequences of restraint*" (emphasis in original). Consideration of psychological aspects is also indicated in the DO-JOC bibliography, in which five of the thirty-five references that are not official DoD or White House documents explicitly focus on

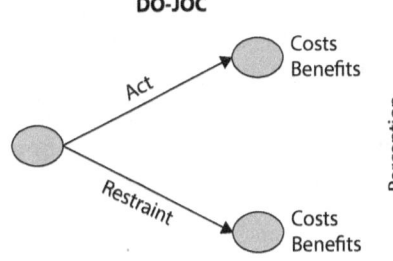

Figure 3.1. The Adversary's Decision Calculus in the U.S. *Deterrence Operations Joint Operating Concept*

psychology—including two discussions of prospect theory (a psychologically informed theory of economic choice in which, among many things, losses and gains are treated differently), Berejikian's cognitive theory of deterrence, and classic works by Robert Jervis and his colleagues.[16]

Similar to U.S. doctrine, Chinese doctrine also places psychology at the core of its thinking on deterrence. In chapter 9 in *The Science of Military Strategy*, titled "Strategic Deterrence," the authors write that "deterrence requires turning the strength and the determination of using strength into the information transmitting to the opponent, and to impact directly on his *mentality* in creating a *psychological pressure* to shock and awe the opponent" (emphasis added).[17] Elsewhere, this publication states, "There are three basic elements to carry out deterrence: First, appropriate military strength available; second, resolve and will to use force; and third, persuading the opponent to perceive such strength and resolve."[18] Note that this was translated into English by the Chinese Academy of Military Sciences; these are their own words, and while one may argue that the Chinese use the term *deterrence* slightly differently from the U.S. literature (e.g., to include coercive diplomacy more broadly), the broader point that their idea of deterrence has a psychological basis is clear.[19]

The Science of Second Artillery Campaigns also emphasizes the psychological dimension of deterrence. For instance, in its chapter on deterrence it describes how "the Second Artillery acts as an important long-range strike force, and its role in creating fear in an enemy's psychology cannot be underestimated."[20]

Chinese writing also accords with the concept that the adversary decides between actions based on costs and benefits associated with each, and it describes this as also being a type of psychological impact. For instance, the chapter on deterrence in *The Science of Second Artillery Campaigns* titles a subsection "A Clear Demonstration of Power to Deter the Escalation of a War" in which it writes that such a demonstration "causes the enemy psychological fear that there is no way for them to withstand a retaliatory strike, and make [sic] the enemy to abandon its adventurous activities. . . . The demonstration of power causes the enemy to dread the possible consequences of the actions it adopts or to dread that its gains will not equal its losses, thereby causing the enemy to change its plans for adventurous activities."[21] *The Science of Military Strategy* states similarly that "the essence of nuclear deterrence is to warn the opponent in advance... for the purpose of bringing about the opponent's dreadful mentality by his weighing the advantages against the disadvantages and the gain against the loss."[22] In its discussion of deterrence, this publication also notes that

> on the basis of the effect mechanism, deterrence is not simply the race of strength, more importantly it is a comparison of gains and losses. Only when the implementation of strategic deterrence brings about psychological shock on the opponent and he is aware of the outcome of his continuous confrontation to be the loss outweighing the gain, can he be forced to submit and compromise. Consequently, taking gains and losses of the enemy's interest into full account is extremely significant in deciding the objective and intensity of the strategic deterrence.[23]

In summary, both Chinese and U.S. accounts of deterrence contain important psychological dimensions. In the Chinese case, this also accords with other characterizations of such Chinese concepts.[24] Furthermore, Chinese and U.S. accounts also, at least in part, consider deterrence in terms of an account of the adversary's decision calculus, which includes the adversary's potential gains and losses from their alternative courses of action.

COMBINING NEUROSCIENCE, PSYCHOLOGY, AND THE SOCIAL SCIENCES TO UNDERSTAND DECISION MAKING

Before analyzing how specific psychological phenomena relate to U.S. and Chinese doctrine, it will help to note some general points about neuroscience, psychology, and the social sciences.[25] Three broad approaches have been particularly significant over the past three-quarters of a century in describing how individuals choose between alternative options based on the subjective values they place upon them. First, rational choice theory (RCT) accounts of decision making have dominated economics since the mid-twentieth century and more recently much of political science.[26] RCT's core concept is that an agent's choices are "rational" in that they are consistent. RCT models individual choice through accounts such as expected utility theory and interactions between actors through approaches such as game theory. However, despite providing some analytic traction, RCT does not capture many aspects of human choice.

Second, therefore, as a way to improve these models, a subfield called behavioral economics has aimed over the past four decades to "increase the explanatory power of economics by providing it with more realistic psychological foundations."[27] However, "it is important to emphasize that the behavioral economics approach extends rational choice and equilibrium models; it does not advocate abandoning these models entirely."[28] This combination of economics and psychology has, for example, sought to modify expected utility theory with prospect theory and game theory with behavioral game theory.[29] Again, however, it still does not capture many core aspects of decision making, so some of the most recent work has added insights from direct observations of the human brain made possible by advances in neuroscience. This third, biologically grounded account of choice is empirically based, can use but is not limited to the specific mathematical formalisms in behavioral economics and RCT, and is the approach taken in this chapter.

The biological study of decision making has a long tradition and since the turn of the millennium has been added to the combination of economics and psychology to provide an extra source of empirical evidence on decision making.[30] This new field, referred to by some as neuroeconomics, studies value-based decision making, which means decisions in which an agent chooses from alternatives based on the subjective values it places upon them.[31] This interdisciplinary approach has been made possible by noninvasive brain imaging technologies, in particular functional magnetic resonance imaging (fMRI), which measures changes in brain activity through monitoring tightly coupled changes in local blood flow, while individuals actually make decisions.[32] These new technologies permit rapid advances in our understanding of decision making because they work on a neural scale in the brain that enables us to link the vast existing neuroscientific literature from animals and humans directly to human behaviors previously described by psychology and economics. Why use biological evidence? This neuroscientific grounding helps us choose between competing explanations at the behavioral level, provides an additional independent source of evidence that increases the robustness of the conclusions, and enhances our prior belief about the generalizability of findings across cultures as these relate to international bargaining.[33] I describe the advantages further in the conclusions.

I now discuss two key aspects of human decision making described by this biologically-grounded work—neural prediction error and social motivations—and relate each to U.S. and Chinese doctrine.

THE IMPACT OF "PREDICTION ERRORS" ON DIPLOMATIC AND MILITARY SIGNALING

A core insight from neuroscience is that when we take an action, the impact it has on the adversary's decision making is crucially modulated by the action's associated "prediction error."[34] This prediction error is simply defined as the difference between what actually occurred and what the adversary expected. The bigger the associated prediction error, the bigger the psychological impact of the action.

	Event not expected	Event expected
Event occurs	a) Associated with prediction error	b) No prediction error
Event does not occur	(trivial case)	c) Associated with prediction error

Figure 3.2. Illustrating Prediction Errors

Differences in prediction error can lead to different impacts across diplomatic and military confrontations. A simple prediction error framework helps forecast an event's impact: the event can either occur or not occur and either be expected or not expected. There are four possible combinations of events and expectations, illustrated in figure 3.2. Strategic bombing illustrates the implications of different combinations of these effects.[35] First, an event occurs and was not expected, so it has a large associated prediction error (fig. 3.2, cell a). For example, World War I German air raids on London were small scale, but being so unexpected had a large psychological impact and caused panic. Second, an event occurs, but it was expected. For example, extrapolating from the World War I experience, influential interwar airpower theorists suggested powerful and recurrent bombing would psychologically paralyze an adversary causing rapid collapse. However, by World War II such recurrent bombing was well expected. For this reason, in the "Blitz" on London, recurrent bombing exerted far greater destructive power but had far less psychological impact than forecast (fig. 3.2, cell b). Third, an event is expected but does not occur, so this absence itself leads to large prediction error (fig. 3.2, cell c). For example, in the Vietnam War, U.S. campaigns bombed regularly and used pauses as a conciliatory signal. Here, the absence of expected bombing would be associated with a prediction error. The fourth possibility, where an event is neither expected nor occurs, has no prediction error or further implications and hence requires no additional discussion.

Prediction Errors: U.S. and Chinese Doctrine
A prediction error framework subsumes and explains core strategic concepts. For example, the psychological impact of strategic surprise is one instance of high prediction error. That is, an event has occurred but was not well predicted (fig. 3.2a). This aspect of prediction error, surprise, is central to U.S. doctrine. For instance, the U.S. JOAC, which covers U.S. doctrine critical to a potential

China-U.S. conventional limited war, prominently features surprise. It states that one goal should be to "*maximize surprise through deception, stealth, and ambiguity to complicate enemy targeting. Surprising the enemy is always a virtue in war, . . . and future commanders should spare no effort to achieve it by any available means*" (emphasis added).[36]

Other statements of U.S. doctrine also highlight surprise. For example, the Joint Publication 3-0, *Joint Operations*, published in 2017 and describing itself as "the keystone document in the joint operations series," also includes surprise as one of the twelve principles for joint operations.[37]

In contrast, the DO-JOC contains little on surprise, seizing the initiative, or shock. However, it notes that "the DO JOC offers a strategy and operational design for accomplishing the deterrence line of effort as part of the campaign framework for future joint operations: shape, deter, seize initiative, dominate, stabilize and enable civil authority."[38]

It is problematic, however, that other than embracing potential benefits from surprise, U.S. doctrine contains little on managing other aspects of prediction error. Since 1945, the United States has fought limited wars, not total wars, and this would very likely be so with nuclear-armed China. During limited confrontations, warfighting cannot be the only consideration. For example, in Vietnam the United States had to carefully design bombing campaigns to not unduly surprise China and the USSR.[39] Seeking only to maximize surprise loses the opportunity to use prediction errors as a tool in signaling to achieve an intended degree of impact on the adversary. Consider a Sino-U.S. escalation scenario: one might wish to enhance the impact of signals like moving a carrier fleet or alerting forces by conducting them abruptly—or reduce their impact by telegraphing them beforehand. Enhancing prediction error by using novel types of conventional forces, or by employing forces in geographically unexpected locations, might be desirable. But the key point is that the intended degree of impact should be a policy decision. Moreover, little suggests that current doctrine considers potentially undesired or inadvertent consequences from surprise on an adversary or observers, such as the potential to set off escalatory spirals by exerting larger than intended impacts on the adversary or third parties.

Managing prediction error, rather than simply maximizing it, can be incorporated into aforementioned areas of U.S. doctrine as it already has been in other aspects of security. For instance, when a population expects something and it is not delivered, this leads to a prediction error. Hence, managing expectations to prevent prediction error can be critical. This was recognized by the highly influential U.S. Army Field Manual 3-24, dealing with counterinsurgency operations, produced in 2006. It explicitly stressed the importance of managing expectations: "1-139. U.S. agencies trying to fan enthusiasm for their efforts should avoid making unrealistic promises. In some cultures, failure to deliver promised results is automatically interpreted as deliberate deception, rather than good intentions gone awry. In other cultures, exorbitant promises are normal and people do not expect them to be kept. Effective counterinsurgents understand local norms; they use locally tailored approaches to control expectations."[40]

Similar to, but in some ways going beyond the U.S. example, Chinese doctrine also stresses surprise, shock, and seizing the initiative. This includes the use of surprise in deterrence operations. For instance, *The Science of Military Strategy* chapter on deterrence states, "Only when the implementation of strategic deterrence brings about psychological shock on the opponent and he is aware of the outcome of his continuous confrontation to be the loss outweighing the gain, can he be forced to submit and compromise."[41]

The Science of Second Artillery Campaigns extensively discusses surprise, shock, and seizing the initiative, for example writing that "it is necessary to strike the enemy at the first opportunity, before the enemy has discovered our campaign intentions and actions, *surprise* the enemy, act before the enemy, strike rapidly, catch the enemy by *surprise*" (emphasis added).[42]

Examining *The Science of Second Artillery Campaigns* in more detail, it is important to note the link between deterrence and what they term conventional missile strike campaigns. This link is shown in three chapters that all discuss deterrence, and I discuss each chapter in turn: "Guiding Ideologies and Principles of Second Artillery Campaigns"; "Second Artillery Campaign Deterrence"; and "Second Artillery Conventional Missile Strike Campaign."

The chapter on "Guiding Ideologies" discusses the importance of active defense and seizing the initiative in its first section, I.A.[43] Here, it states:

> In future wars, our military will be guided by the strategic concept of "active defense," at the core of which is actively taking the initiative to annihilate the enemy, but which also requires positional combat (*lizubentu*; 立足本土) and employing counter strikes against the enemy (*houfazhiren*; 后发制人).... It is necessary to "stop the enemy at the first opportunity" (*xian ji zhi di*; 先机制敌) and then gain the initiative. The promulgation of Second Artillery campaign guiding ideologies must be conscious of active defense and seizing the initiative to strike enemy contents (*neirong*; 内容).[44]

It also discusses the integration of deterrence and conventional campaigns, stating that "the guiding ideology of Second Artillery campaigns is 'integrated deterrence and warfare and focused strikes' (*shezhan jiehe, zhongdian daji*; 摄战结合，重点打击)" and continuing that "'integrated deterrence and warfare' means that when preparing and executing Second Artillery campaigns, campaign deterrence activities and the realities of missile strike operations must be organically integrated to form overall operational capabilities."[45]

The chapter titled "Second Artillery Campaign Deterrence" focuses less on shock or seizing the initiative, although it does write that "the application of Second Artillery nuclear and conventional deterrence is the 'double edged sword' of campaign deterrence. Nuclear deterrence plays a huge shock-value role, but it is obviously restrained by international public opinion."[46] It qualifies maintaining the initiative with a step-by-step approach: "One must both be able to achieve the goals of deterrence and avoid as much as possible exacerbation of conflicts, and maintain the initiative in deterrence activities. From the perspective of campaign deterrence practices, the degree of strength for deterrence ranges from low to high and from weak to strong, escalating step-by-step."[47]

The chapter entitled "Second Artillery Conventional Missile Strike Campaign" again notes the link between conventional campaigns and deterrence. It begins by noting

> the basic missions of the Second Artillery missile strike campaign are: independent implementation of firepower strike against important targets in the enemy's strategic and campaign depths; assist the air force in seizing campaign air dominance; assist the navy in seizing campaign command of the sea; assist the army in seizing land operations' initiative; implement conventional deterrence.... Its objectives are to paralyze the enemy's command systems, weaken the enemy's military strength and its ability to continue operations, create psychological shock in the enemy and sway its operational resolve and halt the powerful enemy's military interventionist activities.[48]

This chapter also discusses the importance of surprise and "active defense," writing that: "The conventional missile strike campaign's operational guiding thought is 'strike the enemy at the first opportunity, and engage in focused strike, (*xianji zhidi, zhongdian tuji*; 先机制敌，重点突击).... To carry out this idea the first thing is to be grounded in offensive operation when it comes to campaign planning. Our military's strategic guideline is 'active defense.'" "Active defense is not simply only defense, there is offense within defense."[49] It adds that "the idea of 'strike the enemy at the first opportunity, engage in focused strike' emphasizes the synthesis of offense and defense, with offense assuming the main role, to strive to achieve the element of surprise in campaigns; stress earlier operations, strive to seize the initiative."[50]

To summarize this Chinese writing, there is a strong emphasis on shock and surprise, and there is an integration of deterrence with more offensive campaigns in part under the idea of "active defense." Active defense is widely held to form a key principle of Chinese doctrine more broadly, in which China can use offensive actions to achieve defensive goals.[51] The importance of surprise, shock, and seizing the initiative is supported by other analyses of Chinese doctrine. Writing about escalation management in Chinese doctrine, for example,

Lonnie Henley avers that "it is difficult to overstate how prominent the concept of the initiative is in Chinese writings.... Chinese war control theorists give little thought to the possibility that what China considers a resolute response that maintains the initiative, the opponent might misconstrue as alarming preparations for aggressive military action."[52] In another analysis of escalation in Chinese doctrine, Forrest Morgan et al. observe, "By far, the most prominent theme in Chinese writings about the military measures to contain war (as well as most other aspects of PLA operations) is the importance of seizing and retaining initiative.... A noticeable and worrisome omission is any recognition that the PLA's efforts to seize the initiative during a crisis could directly accelerate the outbreak of conflict by signaling imminent Chinese aggression."[53]

Thus, in summary, both the U.S. and Chinese doctrine described almost exclusively stress only maximizing surprise, which loses the opportunity to *manage* prediction errors as a tool in signaling to cause intended effects and avoid unintended effects. How might this work in practice? When analysts prepare potential options for a decision maker in their discussion of each option they should ask: "How unexpected will it be for the audience?" The analysis should describe each option's associated prediction error from the adversary's perspective and how that modulates its signaling impact.

HUMANS PAY HIGH COSTS TO REJECT UNFAIRNESS: THIS CAN LIMIT DETERRENCE

This section addresses the implications for deterrence of a second aspect of decision making. Considerable research shows that humans are prepared to reject unfairness at substantial cost to themselves, and this is rooted in our biology.[54] In a classic example called the ultimatum game, one individual gets an amount of money (e.g., ten dollars) and proposes a split with a second player (e.g., nine dollars for herself, one dollar for the second person). The other individual then decides whether to accept the offer (in which case both get the split as proposed) or reject the offer (in which case both players get nothing). Despite receiving an offer of free money, the second player rejects offers involving less than 25 percent of the money around half the time.[55] Even nonhuman primates reject unfairness. Capuchin monkeys performing a simple job reject payment of cucumbers (which they like) when for the same job a fellow monkey gets tasty red grapes (which they like better).[56] In essence, unfairness has a negative value that outweighs the positive value of the money (or cucumber) they would otherwise receive.

Neural activity reflects the precise degree of unfairness in social interactions, including in the game described above. Further, scientists are developing detailed knowledge of how this occurs within specific brain regions. Consider the insula cortex, where scanning of humans interacting socially shows that discrete parts of this region respond to unfairness in distinct ways. Greater fairness leads to higher neural activity in the middle part of the insula cortex, while in the front part greater *un*fairness leads to higher neural activity.[57] Later researchers went on to directly stimulate these regions in monkeys and their findings support this pattern, producing more friendly behaviors in the area that had higher activity for fairness in humans and producing disgust-related behaviors in the area related to unfairness.[58] The drive to reject unfairness is a powerful motivation in decision making, and it is often how nations end up in lose-lose situations.

The motivation to reject unfairness and the humiliation from unfair treatment can form a central part of national narratives and is reflected in national decision making. In a powerful Chinese narrative, "unequal treaties" imposed by external (mostly Western) powers in the nineteenth century unfairly exploited China's weakness, leading to a "century of humiliation."[59] This belief in earlier unfair treatment instills a sense of entitlement to recover and receive restitution for past losses. This played into the Chinese border clash with the Soviet Union in 1969, where scores died on both sides and nuclear threats were leveled.[60] China was motivated in part by the desire to revise one of the old unequal treaties with Russia, the 1860 Treaty of Peking, after the Soviets had four years before the border conflict refused a Chinese request to recognize the 1860 treaty as an unequal treaty. And the specific Chinese objection concerned how to split the uninhabited, useless islands in the river Ussuri between the two countries: the Soviets wanted them all, the Chinese an equal split. Propelled by the motivation to reject unfairness, China initiated the military confrontation, despite overwhelming Soviet nuclear and local conventional superiority.

Fairness: U.S. and Chinese Doctrine

How fairness affects deterrence is shown by considering the central concept in the DO-JOC. Figure 3.3 shows how in the DO-JOC the adversary chooses between two options (to act or show restraint) based on costs and benefits associated with each. Figure 3.3 also shows how in the ultimatum game the adversary chooses between two options (to reject or accept) based on the costs and benefits associated with each, but, crucially, correct forecasting of behavior must include the value attached to fairness that drives the other side to reject an unfair offer. Now consider the DO-JOC again, and see that when conducting a deterrence operation the social motivation of fairness may drive the other side to reject restraint, so deterrence fails. However, such social motivations do not figure in the DO-JOC except through the generic idea that perceptions in general are important. Neither does the JOAC contain such social motivations. They do appear in other U.S. doctrine; for instance legitimacy is one of the twelve principles for joint operations in Joint Publication 3-0, *Joint Operations*,

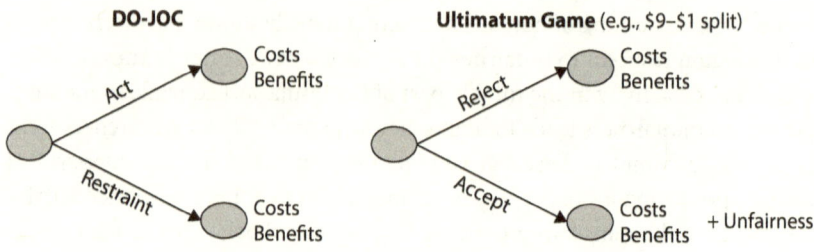

Figure 3.3. Fairness Can Limit Deterrence and Cause Escalation

although this is more within such contexts as peace operations, stabilization, or irregular warfare.[61]

However, in Chinese doctrine, something akin to this social motivation is explicitly discussed at the start of the first substantive chapter of *The Science of Military Strategy* (chapter 2, "Determinants of Strategy"). The authors write that "national interest is an aggregate of objectively physical requirements and spiritual requirements.... National interest is the cardinal basis to determine the alignment of the state's military strategy." They discuss the "essential components of Chinese national interest," which are (1) national territory, (2) national security, (3) national sovereignty, (4) national development, (5) national stability, and (6) national dignity. The last of these is most relevant here. Concerning it, they write, "National dignity means a state's deserved status and prestige.... As an 'intangible' national interest, national dignity generally is manifested by a state's deserved 'national prestige' and equality in international contacts.... Superficially loss of national dignity is an 'emotional' humiliation instead of 'material' damage, but the loss can gravely harm national security and development."[62]

Such a consideration also features prominently in *The Science of Military Strategy*'s chapter on "high-tech local wars that China may face in the future." Here it describes "the interests of China's national security and its objectives" and lists three: "1. Maintaining state sovereignty and territorial integrity," "2. Ensuring the economic development and prosperity of the nation," and "3. Safeguarding China's national dignity and status of equality and independence in international community."[63] In contrast, *The Science of Second Artillery Campaigns* has little on such a motivation, although the chapter on deterrence discusses exerting pressure through public opinion as a deterrence method and describes as a key element of this the need to "remain in line with the principle of being advantageous, justified and appropriate."[64]

The Science of Military Strategy also discusses crisis management. Here it describes five methods of crisis prevention and control, of which "[t]he fifth is to lay down regulations and set up supervision organizations. In laying down arms control regulations, fair, effective and scientific norms should be observed."[65] A Chinese stress on fairness and justice in crisis management has also been highlighted in a volume on Sino-U.S. crisis management by various Chinese and Western authors.[66]

This can be seen in a Chinese maxim on crisis management that several Chinese scholars argue Chinese leaders seem overall to follow in deciding when and how to use coercion or force in crises—*youli, youlli, youjie* ("On just grounds, to our advantage, with restraint").[67] This maxim can lead to situations where the Chinese understand their actions to be "on just grounds," even if preemptive or escalatory, but which to the other side may simply be seen as aggressive or risk taking. For example, Wang Jisi, Peking University's influential dean of the School of International Studies, describes how Mao Zedong formulated this maxim during the Sino-Japanese war and followed it subsequently to justify tactically offensive action, such as when China called the border war with India in 1962 and the one with Vietnam in 1979 "defensive counterattacks." In the 2001 Sino-U.S. crisis, in which a U.S. reconnaissance plane was forced to land on Hainan Island after colliding with a Chinese fighter, Wang argues that "probably basing its statements on the same reasoning, China during the EP-3 incident insisted from the beginning that 'all responsibilities lie on the U.S. side,' and China therefore presented a moral case in which the PLA was making a defensive move near Chinese coastal lines where the U.S. aircraft was on a mission of spying on China."[68]

Finally, one can also note further examples of such considerations of fairness in other areas of Chinese military thinking by Mao Zedong. For instance, Mao's famous injunctions known as the Three Rules of Discipline and Eight Points for Attention concerned successfully influencing populations in large part through building legitimacy. One of his eight points states, "Pay fairly for what you buy."[69]

In summary, unlike much of the U.S. doctrine described here, Chinese doctrine includes consideration of social motivations such as fairness, although of course the degree to which Chinese analysts or decision makers weight this when considering adversaries' decision calculi is another question.

DISCUSSION AND CONCLUSIONS

This preliminary analysis using concepts from neurobiology suggests three common points arising from U.S. and Chinese doctrine. First, there is a central psychological component to both U.S. and Chinese doctrine on deterrence. This may be more fully elaborated in the Chinese case, for example in the repeated discussion of psychology or mentality in the chapter on deterrence in *The Science of Military Strategy* and in *The Science of Second Artillery*

Campaigns. Interestingly, the U.S. doctrine emphasizes the importance of perception but rests on a less plausible account of human motivations, while the Chinese doctrine includes more plausible human motivations but downplays human error, perception, and misperception. Second, both U.S. and Chinese doctrine have an account of the adversary's decision making at the heart of deterrence, which for example includes the adversary's potential gains and losses associated with their possible actions. This account of an adversary's decision calculus is perhaps more explicit in the DO-JOC, which states this up front as its core concept.

Third, in both cases these accounts of the adversary's decision making could be made more realistic by incorporating aspects of human decision making such as prediction error and fairness, *if* these aspects of human decision making really affect decision making in international confrontations and are useful to add (an issue I take up next). With respect to prediction error, both U.S. and Chinese doctrine could usefully consider more than just maximizing surprise (one instance of prediction error) and should instead seek to *manage* prediction error as a tool to cause intended effects and avoid unintended effects such as escalation (for example, by placing greater weight on maintaining predictability when this would be beneficial[70]). With respect to fairness, U.S. doctrine in particular could include this social motivation as something that affects the other side's decision calculus.

However, the "if" above is critical: although these aspects of human decision making *could* be incorporated into thinking about deterrence, that does not mean they *should* be. Thus, I propose four considerations for whether they should be used, in the form of four questions for using neuroscience or biologically based insights in policy.[71] Then, lastly, I discuss areas for further research that could be useful.

(1) Are We Sure Enough of the Neuroscience?

A rapidly advancing field like neuroscience contains a plethora of findings. This is also the case in psychology, which contains innumerable, often contradictory, findings and theories. Furthermore, while it is little acknowledged by those seeking to use psychological, neuroscientific, or experimental economic findings in international relations, there are considerable concerns about the "replication crisis" in psychology where around half of experiments in well-controlled laboratory settings cannot be replicated.[72] This is also the case in many other scientific fields, such as cancer biology.[73] Thus, one should focus on robust findings. The importance of neural prediction error and fairness in choice meet this robustness criterion, as both are extremely widely replicated findings using multiple, mutually constraining methods.

(2) Does It Matter in the Real World?

Findings may be convincing in individuals in a lab, but what about the real world? Addressing this question can take two main approaches. First, for some phenomena or uses it may be possible to use experimental methods, such as randomized controlled trials or naturally occurring experiments. Good examples here include trials of interventions for conflict resolution between populations, for example, in Rwanda.[74] However, clearly this is not possible in key aspects of international relations relevant to deterrence, such as how to manage crises. As an alternative, second, one can examine historical cases. For example, as in the seminal work of Robert Jervis, one can ask if an aspect of decision making explains a variety of historical cases across contexts.[75] With respect to neural prediction error and fairness, it is beyond the scope of this chapter to test these phenomena in Chinese and U.S. cases, although some illustrations are noted above.[76]

(3) Even If It Is True in the Real World, Is It Worth Adding to the Policy Process?

Adding yet another consideration can carry a big opportunity cost. Here, for instance, instead of adding to the analytic burden, a prediction error framework can replace and simplify across a wide range of important phenomena, such as surprise, predictability, and expectation management.[77]

(4) What Does the Neuroscience Add That Behavioral Approaches (Psychology or Behavioral Economics) or Explanations Purely at the Level of Bureaucracies or the State System, Do Not Already Give Us?

There are two main answers to this question. First is the concept of "consilience," which is that we can be more confident of a particular explanation if it is supported by multiple, independent sources of evidence.[78] For example, we have greater confidence at the individual level if both psychological and neuroscientific evidence support an explanation. Equally, empirical evidence from the individual level can provide an additional source of empirical data to help explain phenomena at the state level. Second, a biological basis enhances our prior belief about the generalizability of findings between cultures and within cultures, which is important as the great bulk of psychology experiments are conducted on WEIRD undergraduates (Western, Educated, Industrialized, Rich, Democratic).[79] If we know prediction errors play an important role in decision making across many diverse species, including in humans, then it is much more likely that they play an important role across cultures. This also matters for generalizability within countries or cultures, for example as key decision makers may differ markedly from the general population.

Directions for Further Research

Finally, although this chapter analyzes two aspects of cognition and their place in U.S. and Chinese doctrine, further work may usefully extend this in three ways. First, as described above, is to examine these aspects of cognition in historical cases involving U.S. and/or Chinese coercion. Second would be to examine additional core findings from the biologically based account of human decision making. For instance, other significant social motivations include the human drive to cooperation.[80] International relations work arguing humans treat gains and losses differently often focuses on one particular axiomatic theory of choice—prospect theory—but biologically grounded approaches can provide simpler accounts that incorporate the key behavioral regularities related to losses and gains.[81]

Third, it would also be relevant to study the thinking of other significant countries such as Russia, India, Israel, the UK, or France. For instance, Russian or Soviet doctrine was extensively studied in the Cold War and has recently risen again to prominence particularly as it relates to the integration of "Grey Zone" activities between peace and war and between the conventional and nuclear dimensions of strategy.[82] One may ask how far Russian concepts of deterrence include significant psychological dimensions, as well as what accounts of others' decision making Russian doctrine uses to understand others' decision making in deterrence, coercion, and escalation. How Russian doctrine considers deliberate and inadvertent effects related to surprise and social motivations may help analysts understand how realistic such Russian accounts of others' decision making are. Identifying commonalities and differences between how Russian, Chinese, and U.S. accounts deal with these core aspects of human decision making may help anticipate sources of miscalculation and inadvertent escalation in confrontations between these states.

In conclusion, this chapter's preliminary analysis comparing a more realistic account of human choice to Chinese and U.S. doctrine suggests one might usefully add these considerations to doctrine. It also suggests the need for further analysis both against real-world international decisions and for practical operationalization.

NOTES

1. Numerous scholars have discussed the potential utility and pitfalls of analyzing doctrine. In the context of Chinese doctrine this includes, for example, Forrest E. Morgan, Karl P. Mueller, Evan S. Medeiros, Kevin L. Pollpeter, and Roger Cliff, *Dangerous Thresholds: Managing Escalation in the 21st Century* (Santa Monica, Calif.: RAND, 2008), ch. 3; Christopher P. Twomey, *The Military Lens: Doctrinal Difference and Deterrence Failure in Sino-American Relations* (Ithaca, N.Y.: Cornell University Press, 2010); Joe McReynolds, ed., *China's Evolving Military*

Strategy (Washington, D.C.: Brookings Institution Press, 2016); Andrew Scobell, *China's Use of Military Force: Beyond the Great Wall and the Long March* (New York: Cambridge University Press, 2003), 8–9 and ch. 3.

2. Avery Goldstein, "First Things First: The Pressing Danger of Crisis Instability in U.S.-China Relations," *International Security* 37, no. 4 (April 2013): 49–89.

3. I do not include Russia in this chapter's analysis, although as the conclusion notes, the study of Russian thinking may also be fruitful.

4. Barry R. Posen, *The Sources of Military Doctrine: France, Britain, and Germany between the World Wars*, Cornell Studies in Security Affairs (Ithaca, N.Y.: Cornell University Press, 1984), 13.

5. NATO, *AAP-6 Edition 2014: NATO Glossary of Terms and Definitions* (North Atlantic Treaty Organization, 2014), 2-D-9.

6. U.S. Department of Defense, *Deterrence Operations Joint Operating Concept* DO-JOC, Version 2.0 (Omaha, Neb.: U.S. Strategic Command, December 2006).

7. U.S. Department of Defense, *Joint Operational Access Concept* (JOAC), version 1.0, 2012, https://www.defense.gov/Portals/1/Documents/pubs/JOAC_Jan%202012_Signed.pdf. Part of a family of operational concepts, the JOAC has been described as "the main conceptual instrument for the Joint Force's response to A2AD [anti-access area denial] warfare." George M. Gross, "The New Generation of Operational Concepts," *Small Wars Journal*, 2016, http://smallwarsjournal.com/jrnl/art/the-new-generation-of-operational-concepts.

8. Dennis J. Blasko, *The Chinese Army Today: Tradition and Transformation for the 21st Century*, 2nd ed. (New York: Routledge, 2012), 255.

9. Guangqian Peng and Youzhi Yao, *The Science of Military Strategy* (Beijing: Military Science Publishing House, 2005). This volume is considered authoritative, although not constituting official doctrine, as discussed in McReynolds, *China's Evolving Military Strategy*. It should also be noted that a new edition of *Science of Military Strategy* was published in Chinese in 2013, although I have not focused on this here as there is continuity in the concepts of deterrence and "active defense" that are particularly relevant to this chapter. On continuity in these concepts, respectively, see Dennis J. Blasko, "China's Evolving Approach to Strategic Deterrence," and M. Taylor Fravel, "China's Changing Approach to Military Strategy: The Science of Military Strategy from 2001 and 2013," both in McReynolds, *China's Evolving Military Strategy*.

10. The Second Artillery Corps of the People's Liberation Army, *The Science of Second Artillery Campaigns* (Beijing: Press of the PLA, 2004).

11. The branch of the Chinese military that controls nuclear-armed missiles was known as the Second Artillery Force until December 31, 2015, when it was recommissioned as the PLARF (https://www.csis.org/analysis/pla-rocket-force-evolving-beyond-second-artillery-corps-sac-and-nuclear-dimension).

12. U.S. Department of Defense, *Department of Defense Dictionary of Military and Associated Terms*, Joint Pub 1–02. The earlier definition is present from the 1994 edition up to 2011 but not in 2016, http://www.jcs.mil/Portals/36/Documents/Doctrine/pubs/dictionary.pdf.

13. Patrick M. Morgan, "Saving Face for the Sake of Deterrence," in *Psychology and Deterrence*, ed. Robert Jervis, Richard Ned Lebow, and Janice Gross Stein (Baltimore: Johns Hopkins University Press, 1985), 125.

14. Bruno Tertrais, "Extended Deterrence: Alive and Changing," in *Weathering Change: The Future of Extended Nuclear Deterrence*, ed. Rory Medcalf, Lowy Institute for International Policy, 2011, https://archive.lowyinstitute.org/sites/default/files/pubfiles/Medcalf%2C_Weathering_change_1.pdf.

15. DoD, DO-JOC, 3

16. Prospect theory references include Barbara Farnham, *Avoiding Losses/Taking Risks: Prospect Theory and International Conflict* (Ann Arbor: University of Michigan Press, 1995); Jack S. Levy, "Prospect Theory, Rational Choice, and International Relations," *International Studies Quarterly* 41, no. 1 (1997): 87–112. On a cognitive theory of deterrence, see Jeffrey D. Berejikian, "A Cognitive Theory of Deterrence," *Journal of Peace Research* 39, no. 2 (2002): 165–83. Note that Berejikian's article also focuses on prospect theory. Classic references include Robert Jervis, *Perception and Misperception in International Politics* (Princeton, N.J.: Princeton University Press, 1976); Jervis, Lebow, and Stein, *Psychology and Deterrence*.

17. Peng and Yao, *Science of Military Strategy*, 214.

18. Ibid., 18

19. Li Bin, "China and Global Nuclear Arms Control and Disarmament," in *The War That Must Never Be Fought: Dilemmas of Nuclear Deterrence*, ed. George P. Shultz and James E. Goodby (Stanford, Calif.: Hoover Institution, 2015), 359; Blasko, "China's Evolving Approach to Strategic Deterrence."

20. Second Artillery Corps, *Science of Second Artillery Campaigns*, 270.

21. Ibid., 273.

22. Peng and Yao, *Science of Military Strategy*, 217.

23. Ibid., 225–26.

24. For example, Thomas J. Christensen writes that "it is fairly clear that deterrence, coercion, enemy psychology, and morale are key targets of many of the operations discussed in *Zhanyixue*" ("Coercive Contradictions: Zhanyixue, PLA Doctrine, and Taiwan Scenarios," in *China's Revolution in Doctrinal Affairs: Emerging Trends in the Operational Art of the Chinese People's Liberation Army*, ed. James C. Mulvenon and David Finkelstein (Alexandria, Va.: CNA, 2005), 307–28. Henry Kissinger, in *On China* (New York: Penguin, 2011), 133–35, observes that "Mao's actions in the Korean War require an understanding of how he viewed what, in Western strategy, would be called deterrence or even preemption and which, in Chinese thinking, combines the long-range, strategic, and psychological elements." Kissinger continues, "Mao's approach to preemption differed in the extraordinary attention he paid to psychological elements. His motivating force was less to inflict a decisive military first blow than to change the psychological balance, not so much to defeat the enemy as to alter his calculus of risks." Finally, he notes, "having restored the psychological equation, in Chinese eyes, genuine deterrence has been achieved."

25. This general subsection draws on Nicholas D. Wright, "The Biology of Cooperative Decision-Making: Neurobiology to International Relations," in *Handbook of International Negotiation*, ed. Mauro Galluccio (Cham, Switzerland: Springer International Publishing, 2015), 47–58.

26. John von Neumann and Oskar Morgenstern, *Theory of Games and Economic Behavior* (Princeton, N.J.: Princeton University Press, 1944).

27. Colin F. Camerer and George Loewenstein, "Behavioral Economics: Past, Present, Future," in *Advances in Behavioral Economics*, ed. Colin F. Camerer, George Loewenstein, and Matthew Rabin (Princeton, N.J.: Princeton University Press, 2004), 3–51.

28. Teck H. Ho, Noah Lim, and Colin F. Camerer, "Modeling the Psychology of Consumer and Firm Behavior with Behavioral Economics," *Journal of Marketing Research* 43, no. 3 (2006): 307–31.

29. Daniel Kahneman and Amos Tversky, "Prospect Theory: An Analysis of Decision under Risk," *Econometrica: Journal of the Econometric Society* (1979): 263–91. Colin F Camerer,

Behavioral Game Theory: Experiments in Strategic Interaction, vol. 9 (Princeton, N.J.: Princeton University Press, 2003).

30. Edward L. Thorndike, *Animal Intelligence: Experimental Studies* (New York: Macmillan, 1911); Nicholas J. Mackintosh, *Conditioning and Associative Learning* (New York: Clarendon Press, 1983).

31. Paul W. Glimcher, *Decisions, Uncertainty, and the Brain: The Science of Neuroeconomics*, 1st ed. (Cambridge, Mass.: Massachusetts Institute of Technology Press, 2004); Paul W. Glimcher and Aldo Rustichini, "Neuroeconomics: The Consilience of Brain and Decision," *Science* 306, no. 5695 (October 15, 2004): 447–52; Colin Camerer, George Loewenstein, and Drazen Prelec, "Neuroeconomics: How Neuroscience Can Inform Economics," *Journal of Economic Literature* 43, no. 1 (2005): 9–64.

32. Richard S. J. Frackowiak et al., eds., *Human Brain Function*, 2nd ed. (Amsterdam: Elsevier Academic Press, 2004).

33. In relation to choosing between competing explanations at the behavioral level, see John P O'Doherty, Alan Hampton, and Hackjin Kim, "Model-Based fMRI and Its Application to Reward Learning and Decision Making," *Annals of the New York Academy of Sciences* 1104 (May 2007): 35–53. For the value of independent sources of evidence, see Edward O. Wilson, *Consilience: The Unity of Knowledge* (London: Abacus, 1999).

34. This introductory subsection on prediction error draws on Nicholas D. Wright, "Neural Prediction Error Is Central to Diplomatic and Military Signalling," in *White Paper on Leveraging Neuroscientific and Neurotechnological (NeuroS&T) Developments with Focus on Influence and Deterrence in a Networked World*, ed. Hriar Cabayan, William Casebeer, Diane DiEuliis, James Giordano, and Nicholas D Wright (Washington, D.C.: U.S. DoD Joint Staff, 2014), 65–71. From simple tasks (see Yael Niv and Geoffrey Schoenbaum, "Dialogues on Prediction Errors," *Trends in Cognitive Sciences* 12, no. 7 [July 1, 2008]: 265–72), to more complex social interactions (see Timothy E. J. Behrens, Laurence T. Hunt, and Matthew F. S. Rushworth, "The Computation of Social Behavior," *Science* 324, no. 5931 [May 29, 2009]: 1160–64), it is central to how humans understand, learn, and decide about the world.

35. George H. Quester, "The Psychological Effects of Bombing on Civilian Populations: Wars of the Past," in *Psychological Dimensions of War*, ed. Betty Glad (Thousand Oaks, Calif.: SAGE Publications, 1990).

36. DoD, JOAC. This full quote is taken from 25 with the first sentence repeated on iii and 17.

37. U.S. Department of Defense, *Joint Publication 3-0: Joint Operations* (Washington, D.C.: Joint Chiefs of Staff, January 17, 2017), ix.

38. DoD, DO-JOC, 9.

39. Quester, "Psychological Effects of Bombing."

40. Headquarters, Department of the Army, *FM 3-24: Counterinsurgency*, U.S. Army Field Manual 3-24 (Washington, D.C.: Headquarters, Department of the Army, 2006), 1–25.

41. Peng and Yao, *Science of Military Strategy*, 225–26.

42. Second Artillery Corps, *Science of Second Artillery Campaigns*, 327.

43. Taylor Fravel describes active defense as follows: "The essence of active defense is that China adopts a strategically defensive posture, in which China 'will not fire the first shot' but will use offensive actions to achieve defensive goals. Other important elements of active defense include seeking to deter war, if possible, and mobilizing national support under the idea of 'People's War.'" Fravel, "China's Changing Approach," 52.

44. Second Artillery Corps, *Science of Second Artillery Campaigns*, 122–23.

45. Ibid., 125.
46. Ibid., 273.
47. Ibid., 280.
48. Ibid., 317–18.
49. Ibid., 323.
50. Ibid., 324.
51. Fravel, "China's Changing Approach," 52.
52. Lonnie D. Henley, "War Control: Chinese Concepts of Escalation Management," in *Shaping China's Security Environment: The Role of the People's Liberation Army*, ed. Andrew Scobell and Larry M. Wortzel (Carlisle, Pa.: U.S. Army War College, Strategic Studies Institute, 2006), 81–104.
53. Morgan et al., *Dangerous Thresholds*, 57.
54. This introductory subsection draws on Wright, "Biology of Cooperative Decision-Making."
55. Camerer, *Behavioral Game Theory*.
56. Sarah F. Brosnan and Frans B. M. de Waal, "Monkeys Reject Unequal Pay," *Nature* 425, no. 6955 (2003): 297–99.
57. Nicholas D. Wright, Mkael Symmonds, Stephen M. Fleming, and Raymond J. Dolan, "Neural Segregation of Objective and Contextual Aspects of Fairness," *Journal of Neuroscience* 31, no. 14 (April 6, 2011): 5244–52.
58. Fausto Caruana, Ahmad Jezzini, Beatrice Sbriscia-Fioretti, Giacomo Rizzolatti, and Vittorio Gallese, "Emotional and Social Behaviors Elicited by Electrical Stimulation of the Insula in the Macaque Monkey," *Current Biology* 21, no. 3 (February 2011): 195–99. Wright et al., "Neural Segregation."
59. Zheng Wang, *Never Forget National Humiliation: Historical Memory in Chinese Politics and Foreign Relations* (New York: Columbia University Press, 2012).
60. Michael S. Gerson, *The Sino-Soviet Border Conflict* (Washington, D.C.: Center for Naval Analyses, 2010).
61. U.S. Department of Defense, *Joint Publication 3-0: Joint Operations*. E.g., ix, xx, xxiii, I-2.
62. Peng and Yao, *Science of Military Strategy*, 39–44.
63. Ibid., ch. 23 and particularly 444–48.
64. Second Artillery Corps, *Science of Second Artillery Campaigns*, 284
65. Peng and Yao, *Science of Military Strategy*, 204.
66. Michael D. Swaine, Tousheng Zhang, and Danielle F. S. Cohen, *Managing Sino-American Crises: Case Studies and Analysis* (Washington, D.C.: Carnegie Endowment for International Peace, 2006).
67. Ibid., ch. 1, and interview by author.
68. Wang and Xu, in ibid., 141–42.
69. Stuart Schram, ed., *Mao's Road to Power: Revolutionary Writings, 1912–1949*, vol. 3 (Armonk: M. E. Sharpe, 1995), 283. Issued in the 1920s, these were also further promulgated later.
70. This is discussed further in Wright, "Neural Prediction Error Is Central."
71. These questions were discussed previously in Wright, "Biology of Cooperative Decision-Making."
72. Open Science Collaboration, "Estimating the Reproducibility of Psychological Science," *Science* 349, no. 6251 (August 28, 2015): aac4716-1-8.
73. C. Glenn Begley and Lee M. Ellis, "Drug Development: Raise Standards for Preclinical Cancer Research," *Nature* 483, no. 7391 (March 29, 2012): 531–33.

74. Elizabeth Levy Paluck and Donald P. Green, "Prejudice Reduction: What Works? A Review and Assessment of Research and Practice," *Annual Review of Psychology* 60 (2009): 339–67.

75. Jervis, *Perception and Misperception*.

76. See also Wright, "Biology of Cooperative Decision-Making."

77. Wright, "Neural Prediction Error Is Central."

78. Wilson, *Consilience*.

79. Joseph Henrich, Steven J. Heine, and Ara Norenzayan, "The Weirdest People in the World?" *Behavioral and Brain Sciences* 33, no. 2–3 (2010): 61–83.

80. Wright, "Biology of Cooperative Decision-Making."

81. Nicholas D. Wright, "Neurobiological and Emotional Influences: A Realistic Organic Account of Human Decision Making," in "The Science of Decision Making across the Span of Human Activity," Strategic Multilayer Assessment White Paper, ed. N. D. Wright and A. Astorino-Courtois (Washington, D.C.: DoD Joint Staff, 2015), 11–12. For example, many international relations scholars draw on the 1970s version of prospect theory, which is already complex enough to use, rather than the more complex later version considered standard by many behavioral economists: Amos Tversky and Daniel Kahneman, "Advances in Prospect Theory: Cumulative Representation of Uncertainty," *Journal of Risk and Uncertainty* 5, no. 4 (1992): 297–323.

82. N. D. Wright, *From Control to Influence: Cognition in the Grey Zone* (Birmingham, UK: Institute for Conflict, Cooperation and Security Report for the U.S. DoD Joint Staff, 2017), ch. 1.

CHAPTER FOUR

Apocalypse Now

Rational Choice before the Unthinkable

JEAN-PIERRE DUPUY

Contrary to common belief, especially among the military elite, the logic of mutually assured destruction (MAD) has not yet been fully understood, and this state of affairs matters today more than ever. Errol Morris, in his documentary *The Fog of War*, asks former U.S. defense secretary Robert McNamara what he thinks protected humanity from extinction during the Cold War, when the United States and the Soviet Union threatened each other with mutual annihilation. Deterrence? Not at all, McNamara replies: "We lucked out." Twenty-five or thirty times during this period, he notes, mankind came within an inch of apocalypse.[1] In this chapter, I will show that this response is self-contradictory. All those "near-misses" may have been the necessary condition for nuclear deterrence to work.

Contrary to what many critics of rational choice theory (RCT) contend, RCT can still be helpful in addressing such problems as the efficiency and even ethics of nuclear deterrence. To be sure, RCT in its present state is undermined by a series of paradoxes (prisoner's dilemma, chain-store paradox, Newcomb's problem, backward induction paradox, etc.) that make many reject it in favor of weaker conceptions of rationality (such as bounded rationality, etc.). I will show that the way out leads elsewhere. The problem is less the kind of rationality that the agents exhibit than the conception of time that they harbor. The efficiency and rationality of nuclear deterrence can be supported by another metaphysics of temporality than the one implicitly chosen by economists, game theorists, and all kinds of planners. I dub it "projected time" and contrast it with the latter, which I name "occurring time."

The following text is an exercise in applied metaphysics. Metaphysics seems to be at the antipodes of behavioral science. However, following the lead of epistemologists Karl Popper and, before him, Emile Meyerson, I believe that no science exists which does not rest on a "metaphysical research program," a set of presuppositions about the structure of the world that are neither testable nor "falsifiable" empirically, but which nonetheless play an essential role in the progress of science.[2] If behavioral economics fares much better than mainstream economics in the apprehension of the logic of nuclear deterrence, it is because it has shown that "projected time," far from being the invention of metaphysicians detached from reality, is the conception of time most of us entertain. In an appendix to this chapter, I discuss psychology experiments that support this claim. These experiments link the discussion in this chapter to behavioral economics; they provide empirical support for the following metaphysical analysis.

TWO METAPHYSICS OF TEMPORALITY

My starting point is the age-old problem of the compatibility between determinism and free will in its modern version fleshed out by such philosophers as David K. Lewis and Robert Stalnaker.[3] Lewis uses the term *soft determinism* as a label for "the doctrine that sometimes one freely does what one is predetermined to do; and that in such a case one is able to act otherwise though past history and the laws of nature determine that one will not act otherwise." He then defines *compatibilism* as "the doctrine that soft determinism may be true."[4]

Let us call C the state of the world at a time t_1. We have:

    A1:   C was the case at t_1

Consider a subject S whose action x at $t_2 > t_1$ is determined by the laws that govern his world according to:

    A2:   If C was the case at t_1, then S does x at t_2

From A1 and A2 we derive by *modus ponens*:

    A3:   S does x at t_2

Can x be a free although predetermined act? To defend soft determinism, it is always useful to start from the argument(s) put forward by those who deny it. The so-called incompatibilist thesis uses an operator $\Box$, which, applied to a proposition p, asserts that p is true in all possible worlds: it is necessary. More specific to our problem, we will call $\Box^S_t$ the operator of necessity such that:

    $\Box^S_t$ (p) means: p is true and S is not free at t to perform an act such that, if S were to perform it, p would be false.

The incompatibilist argument can be written as follows:

    N1: $\Box^S_{t_2}$ (C was the case at t_1)
    N2: $\Box^S_{t_2}$ (If C was the case at t_1, then S does x at t_2).

Thus, by *modus ponens*,[5]

    N3: $\Box^S_{t_2}$ (S does x at t_2).

N1 expresses the principle of the fixity of the past. N2 says that the laws that determine the subject's actions remain the same in all possible worlds. The conclusion N3 states that S does actually do x at t_2, but S does not act freely since it is not in his or her power to act otherwise.

Can this argument be refuted? Depending on the nature of the problem, there are two possibilities, neither of which has greater a priori legitimacy than the other:

> (a) We could accept N1, in which case we would have to reject N2. The past is fixed, and the subject, supposedly able to act otherwise, has the power to invalidate the fixity of the temporal chain which links C to x. The nature of this power must be made very clear. As Lewis puts it, we must distinguish between two versions:
> - *Strong version*: "I am able to break a law."
> - *Weak version*: "I am able to do something such that, if I did it, a law would be broken."[6]

Obviously, there is no way that *in our world* the subject could act so that the link between C and x would be violated: this would be contrary to hypothesis A2, which indeed remains valid. The strong version is eliminated but not the weak one. To paraphrase Lewis, the way in which I was determined not to do anything other than x "was not the sort of way that counts as inability."[7] The power that this sort of ability represents is called "counterfactual."[8]

> (b) Conversely, we could accept N2, in which case we would have to reject N1. This time the temporal chain A2 is held to be fixed (that is, true in all possible worlds). To maintain that the agent's action, x, is free although determined by the past and the laws that govern the world, we have to grant the agent a power to invalidate the past. This power obviously cannot be causal. Here too we must distinguish between:
> - a *strong version*: "I am able to change the past," which is "utterly incredible," to use Lewis's terms,
> - and a *weak one*: "I am able to do something such that, if I did it, the past would have been different from what it was in the actual world."

The Calvinist theologian and analytic metaphysician Alvin Plantinga, who defends the weak version, has logically dubbed this kind of ability "counterfactual power over the past."[9]

Although, as I said, the two ways of grounding compatibilism have an a priori equal legitimacy, contemporary philosophers such as David K. Lewis or Robert Stalnaker, probably because of their respective stints in the domain of orthodox RCT, have focused almost exclusively on the former, which preserves the fixity of the past.[10] This leads to the metaphysics of occurring time.

Elsewhere, I have explored thoroughly the second approach, that is, projected time,[11] and in this chapter show that it solves elegantly the paradoxes of nuclear deterrence.

WHY MAD IS NOT SUPPOSED TO WORK

Throughout the Cold War, two arguments were made that seemed to show that nuclear deterrence in the form of MAD could not be effective.[12] The first argument has to do with the noncredible character of the deterrent threat under such circumstances: if the party threatening a simultaneously lethal and suicidal response to aggression that endangers its "vital interests" is assumed to be at least minimally rational, calling its bluff—say, by means of a first strike that destroys a part of its territory—ensures that it will not carry out its threat. What chief of state having in the aftermath of a first strike only a devastated nation to defend would run the risk, by launching a retaliatory strike out of a desire for vengeance, of putting an end to the human race? In a world of sovereign states endowed with this minimal degree of rationality, the nuclear threat has no credibility whatever. Jonathan Schell summarizes this argument beautifully:

> Since in nuclear-deterrence theory the whole purpose of having a retaliatory capacity is to deter a first strike, one must ask what reason would remain to launch the retaliation once the first strike had actually arrived. It seems that the logic of the deterrence strategy is dissolved by the very event—the first strike—that it is meant to prevent. Once the action begins, the whole doctrine is *self-canceling*. It would seem that the doctrine is based on a monumental logical mistake: one cannot credibly deter a first strike with a second strike whose raison d'être dissolves the moment the first strike arrives.[13]

Another, quite different argument was put forward that likewise pointed to the incoherence of the prevailing strategic doctrine. To be effective, nuclear deterrence must be absolutely effective. Not even a single failure can be allowed, since the first bomb to be dropped would already be one too many. But if nuclear deterrence is absolutely effective, it cannot be effective. As a practical matter, deterrence works only if it is not 100 percent effective. One thinks, for example, of the criminal justice system: violations of the law must occur and be punished if citizens are to be convinced that crime does not pay. But in the case of nuclear deterrence, the first transgression is fatal.[14]

WHY EXISTENTIAL DETERRENCE MIGHT BE THE SOLUTION

Belatedly, it came to be understood that in order for deterrence to have a chance of succeeding, it was absolutely necessary to abandon the notion of deterrent *intention*. In principle, the mere *existence* of two deadly arsenals pointed at each other, without the least threat of their use being made or even implied, is enough to keep the warheads locked away in their silos.

This solution came with a name: *existential deterrence* (ED). The intention or threat to retaliate and launch a counterattack that will lead to the apocalypse is the problem. Let us get rid of the intention. As two major philosophers put it, "the existence of a nuclear retaliatory capability suffices for deterrence, regardless of a nation's will, intentions, or pronouncements about nuclear weapons use"[15]; or: "It is our military capacities that matter, not our intentions or incentives or declarations."[16] If deterrence is existential, it is because the existence of the weapons alone deters.

There are two arguments that show why ED may work. One has to do with the "vertical" dimension that links the individual agents to the ensemble they make up; the other is couched in terms that belong to the horizontal axis, traditionally the axis of time. All things considered, these two arguments are one and the same expressed from two different vantage points.

The kind of rationality at work here is not a calculating rationality, but rather the kind of rationality in which the agent contemplates the abyss and simply decides never to get too close to the edge. As David K. Lewis puts it: "You don't tangle with tigers—it's that simple."[17] In other terms, the game is no longer played between two adversaries. It takes on an altogether different form. Neither is in a position to deter the other in a credible way. *However, both want and need to be deterred*. The way out of this impasse is brilliant. It is a matter of creating jointly a fictitious entity that will deter both at the same time. The game is now played between one actor, humankind, whose survival is at stake, and its double, namely its own violence exteriorized in the form of fate. The fictitious and fictional "tiger" we had better not tangle with is nothing other than the violence that is in us but that we project outside of us: it is as if we were threatened by an exceedingly dangerous entity, external to us, whose intentions toward us are not evil but whose power of destruction is infinitely superior to all the earthquakes or tsunamis that nature has in store for us. Günther Anders and Hannah Arendt were right: we are living under a new regime of evil—*an evil without harmful intent*.

The second argument can be introduced by another revelatory quote, this time by Bernard Brodie: "It is a curious paradox of our time that one of the foremost factors making deterrence really work and work well is the lurking fear that in some massive confrontation crisis it may fail. Under these circumstances one does not tempt fate."

"Fate and the Tiger": let it be said in passing how significant it is to see rational scholars like Lewis and Brodie resort to such apparently magical thinking to make their point. A first interpretation of Brodie's statement is as follows. The probability of error is what makes deterrence effective. But error, failure, or mistake, here, is not strategic. It has nothing to do with the notion that a nation, by irrationally running unacceptable risks, can limit a war and achieve advantage by inducing restraint in the opponent. Thomas Schelling popularized this idea—known as the "rationality of irrationality" theory—in his landmark *Strategy of Conflict*, published in 1960.[18] Here, by contrast, the key notion is *"fate."* The error is *inscribed* in the future, whatever that means. This is the point I want to elaborate on.

TWO VERSIONS OF THE BACKWARD INDUCTION PARADOX (BIP): THE INEFFICIENCY OF PROMISES AND THREATS

Consider what game theorists call an assurance game. Informally analyzed by Hobbes, Hume, and Kant, it may be described more technically by using the type of formal model familiar from game theory. In the game shown in figure 4.1, Pierre and Marie each decide whether to cooperate or not (a move labeled defection), but the game is played sequentially with Pierre moving first. In principle, a mutually advantageous exchange between Pierre and Marie is possible that will lead them from their present state—the vector (0, 0), the first element of which represents Pierre's utility (or some other index supposed to order preferences), and the second Marie's utility—to a state (+1, +1), which each of them prefers. But if, for one reason or another, the exchange depends on Pierre making the first move at time 1 *(C)*, there is a risk that Marie will fail to cooperate, keeping what Pierre gives her without giving him anything in return. In that case, by defecting *(D)* at time 2, Marie would wind up with +2, leaving Pierre with −1.

Backward induction convinces us that the exchange cannot take place, even though it would improve the situation of each party. Let us look first at the last

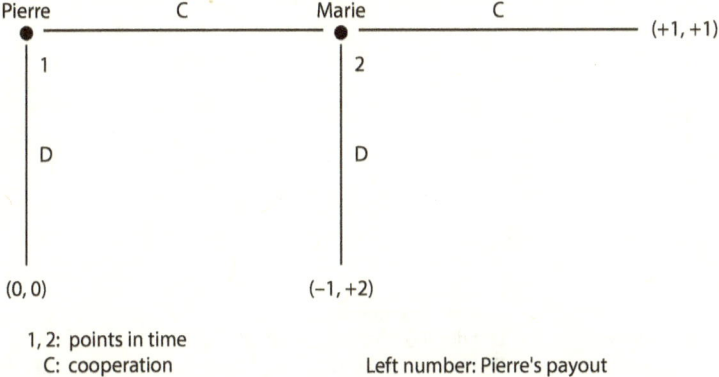

Figure 4.1. An Assurance Game Played over Time

step, that is at time 2, when it is Marie's turn to decide whether to cooperate or to defect. It is rational for her to defect since she obtains +2, as against +1 if she cooperates. Pierre, on the other hand, at time 1, has a choice between making the first move (in which case he anticipates that Marie will not reciprocate and that he will end up with –1), and making no move, which is to say *D* (in which case his situation is unchanged, since he still has 0). Therefore, he makes no move, and the exchange does not take place.

One is tempted to say that this mutually disadvantageous outcome could be avoided by resorting to the institution of promising. Marie, since she stands to gain as much from cooperating as Pierre, should promise him at time 0, before the game begins, that she will cooperate at 2 if he will cooperate at 1. But this is a futile hope! Marie knows perfectly well that when the time comes, which is to say time 2, she will be better off not keeping her promise. Pierre, reading her mind, knows this too. Even if Marie swears to him on a stack of Bibles, her promise is not *credible*. Pierre therefore makes no move. This is the form assumed by the BIP in the present case.

Rational choice theorists (as well as "enlightened capitalists") try to wriggle out of this difficulty by making ethics into a sort of deus ex machina. Sometimes they call it "confidence," sometimes "trust"—a kind of magic wand that brings about what rationality alone is powerless to achieve. Thus, it is imagined that Marie, by breaking her promise to Pierre and doing what rationality tells her to do, will suffer pangs of conscience. But this amounts to divorcing ethics from rationality, right from the start. There must be a better way forward.

Consider likewise the game shown in figure 4.2, which formalizes the situation known as MAD. Alter contemplates attacking Ego. If Alter actually does attack, Ego has a choice between yielding—in which case he loses, for example,

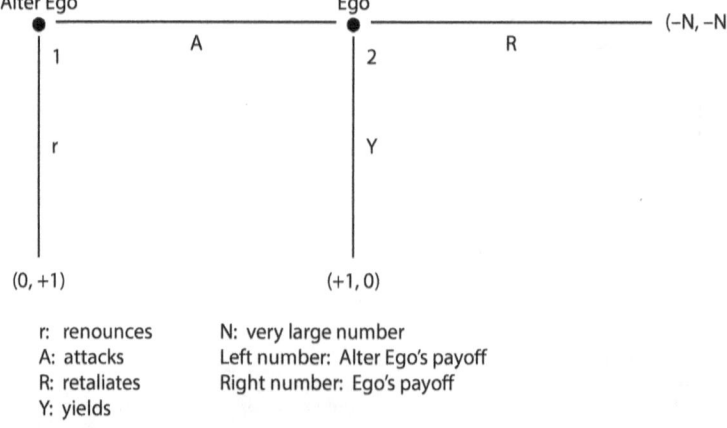

Figure 4.2. A Mutual Assured Destruction Game

some part of his territory or zone of influence—and counterattacking—in which case the escalation of violence spells disaster for both belligerents.

This diagram illustrates a zero-sum game played on the edge of the abyss. Backward induction leads us to conclude that the deterrent threat "if you, Alter, attack me, I, Ego, will launch a counterattack that will annihilate both of us" is not credible. Finding himself at 2, Ego, after having been attacked by Alter, will find it prudent to do Y. Alter therefore attacks at 1 and Ego yields at 2. This problem, the noncredibility of the threat on which nuclear deterrence rests, makes up the better part of the strategic literature on the subject as we already saw.

THE METAPHYSICS OF TIME: OCCURRING TIME AND PROJECTED TIME

Backward induction is the usual form of reasoning when we deal with a strategic problem with a finite horizon. It corresponds to the metaphysics of occurring time, in which time bifurcates into a series of successive branches, the actual world constituting one path among these. It is structured like a decision tree (see fig. 4.3).

In prior work, I have attempted to demonstrate the coherence of an alternative metaphysics of temporality, one adapted to the obstacle that the noncredible character of catastrophes represents. I have dubbed this alternative metaphysics "projected time," and it takes the form of a loop, in which past and future reciprocally determine each other (see fig. 4.4). In projected time, the future is taken to be fixed, which means that any event that is not part of the present or the future is an impossible event. It immediately follows that in projected time, prudence can never take the form of prevention. Prevention assumes that the undesirable event that one prevents is an unrealized possibility. The event must

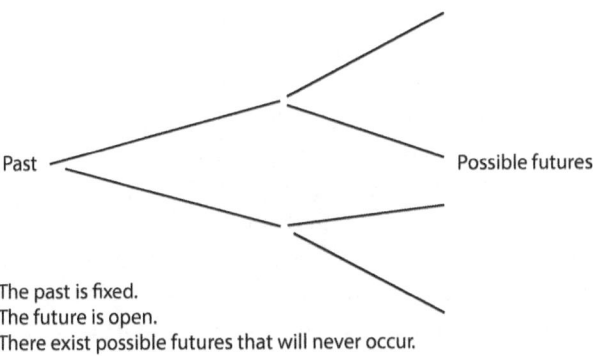

Past   Possible futures

The past is fixed.
The future is open.
There exist possible futures that will never occur.

Figure 4.3. Occurring Time

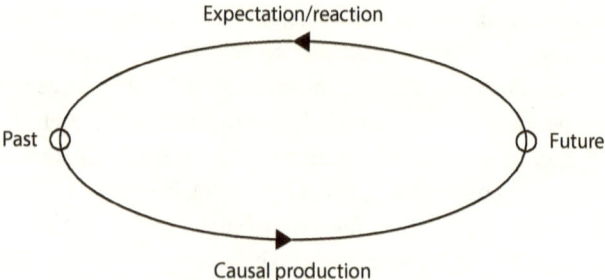

The future is fixed, i.e. necessary.
The past is open. The future can act on it *counterfactually*.
The past and the future *must* come together in a closed loop: the future is the *fixed point* of the loop.

Figure 4.4. Projected Time

be possible for us to have a reason to act; but if our action is effective, it will not take place. This is unthinkable within the framework of projected time.

To foretell the future in projected time, it is necessary to seek the loop's *fixed point*, where an expectation (on the part of the past with regard to the future) and a causal production (of the future by the past) coincide. A quasi-perfect illustration of this structure was the French postwar economic planning whose aim was, as one might put it hypothetically, "to achieve by concerted deliberation and study an image of the future that is sufficiently optimistic to be desirable and sufficiently credible to give rise to actions that will bring about its own realization."

Counterfactual Power over the Past

The metaphysics of projected time makes the future the cornerstone of our relationship to temporality. Its ambition is to formalize what Hans Jonas called *Ethik für die Zukunft*, meaning not a future ethics but an ethics *for* the future, for the sake of the future, that is to say, the future must become the major object of our concern.[19] The major stumbling block of our current, implicit metaphysics of temporality, formalized by what I call occurring time, turns out to be our conception of the *future as unreal*. From our belief in free will—we might act otherwise—we derive the conclusion that the future is *not real*, in the philosophical sense: "future contingents," that is, propositions about actions taken by a free agent in the future, are held to have no truth value. They are neither true nor false. If the future is not real, it is not something that we can have cognizance of. If the future is not real, it is not something that projects its shadow onto the present. Even when we know that a catastrophe is about to happen, we do not believe it: we do not believe what we know. If the future is not real, there is nothing in it that we should fear or hope for.

The former French economic planning is just one illustration among many of what might be called *coordination by means of the future*. It entails that agents all take the same future as being fixed. No matter what an agent does, he assumes that his action will have no counterfactual effect on the future, even though it is causally responsible, in part, for bringing it about. If he were to have acted differently from how he in fact did, in other words, the future *would have been* the same.

This future is a fixed point, a common point of reference for everyone. But this fixed point is an *endogenous* fixed point, since it is causally produced by the actions of individual agents. It is immediately apparent that, in order for this to work, the loop connecting past and future must be a *closed* loop. This means that the reactions to a future that is held to be fixed must be able to causally produce this same future.

Coordination by means of the future therefore combines freedom of individual choice with something that can only be called predestination. This is not the place to explain how I have tried to ground this form of compatibilism.[20] I shall content myself with saying simply that there is in fact nothing aberrant about reasoning as though one were able to choose one's own destiny; able, that is, to choose the very thing that, in the past, determines one's fate. Let me give an example from my own personal experience. My Brazilian daughter, who lives and works in Brazil, was on board Air France flight 447 from Rio de Janeiro to Paris on May 31, 2009. Had she delayed her flight by a day she would have been counted among the victims when that same flight crashed the following day. At least this is what I said to myself when finally—I was traveling myself at the time—I learned of the catastrophe and heard that my daughter had arrived in Paris safe and sound the day before. Perhaps I was wrong. Seeking to relieve my anxiety, my daughter said to me: "But Dad, if I'd flown the next day the crash wouldn't have occurred that day!" By that she meant that she had been born under a lucky star: in all the possible worlds in which she might have been on an Air France flight between Rio and Paris, no accident would have occurred. My daughter thereby endowed herself with a power of acting, through her present choice, on the chain of past events that led to the crash of an airplane. This power, altogether improbable if it were a matter of causality, becomes perfectly plausible if it is interpreted as a *counterfactual power over the past*.[21] Accordingly, the metaphysical principle that the past must be regarded as fixed, which is to say as counterfactually independent of present actions, is invalid. The fixity of the future entails the open-endedness of the past.

Counterfactual Power over the Past Solves the Promise Paradox but Not, at Least Not Immediately, the Deterrence Paradox

There exist situations in which the *counterfactual* power an agent possesses over the past *causally* prohibits him from acting in a certain way. That is the essence of the BIP. Therein resides also its solution in projected time.

In the Assurance Game, the metaphysics of projected time leads us to reason as follows. Were Marie to play at 2 *and* to defect at 2, the counterfactual past, that is, Pierre's move at 1, would have been "Pierre defects at 1," which would have falsified the premise "Marie plays at 2." The two premises lead to a contradiction and therefore one logically entails the negation of the other. We then get: If Marie were to play at 2, she would cooperate at 2. As a consequence, Pierre cooperates at 1 and the mutually advantageous exchange between Pierre and Marie takes place.

Can a similar argument based on projected time salvage the effectiveness of deterrence? The argument from prevention with which I began gives cause for doubt. Could it be that the response R (known after Clausewitz as "escalation to the extreme") constitutes the fixed point of the loop between past and future that defines the metaphysics of projected time? Alter's anticipation at 1 of Ego's choice at 2 to do R would prevent Ego from deciding at 2, since Alter would then refrain from attacking. R is not part of the future, *therefore* (this logical derivation only makes sense in projected time) it is impossible. Ego's threat ("I will launch R if you attack me") is undermined from the start. The loop is joined together at a fixed point only if Ego yields and Alter attacks. The conclusion is therefore the same as the one arrived at by backward induction: deterrence is ineffective. And yet, the reason why deterrence is ineffective in projected time is no longer the noncredibility of the threat but the self-refuting character of perfectly successful deterrence, that is, the second argument against the effectiveness of deterrence mentioned above. To repeat: if nuclear deterrence is effective, then R will not occur, therefore R is impossible, therefore nuclear deterrence is ineffective.

This analysis has the merit of showing that the two arguments to the effect that nuclear deterrence is ineffective are supported by two incompatible metaphysics of temporality: occurring time and projected time.

THE ESSENTIAL ROLE OF INDETERMINACY

Suppose we stand the formula of French economic planning I mentioned earlier on its head so that now it is a question instead of "achieving by concerted deliberation and study an image of the future that is sufficiently pessimistic to be repulsive and sufficiently credible to give rise to actions that will prevent it from being realized." Immediately, we run up against a paradox. As one of the detectives of the future in Spielberg's film *Minority Report*—inspired by a marvelous short story of the same name by Philip K. Dick, itself a variation on Voltaire's devastating anti-Leibnizian tale *Zadig*—says, "It's not the future if you stop it."[22] How can the concept of coordination by means of the future be applied to a case in which agreement is reached about a future that is not a future at all, since it is a matter of acting in such a way that this future does not occur?[23] What form does the endogenous fixed point assume in this case?

In order for the expected catastrophe to exert a deterrent effect on the present, it is necessary that the catastrophe be part of the future—written down, as it were, on the great scroll of history. But if this is the case, we are doomed. It is necessary, then, that both the occurrence of the catastrophe *and* its nonoccurrence be part of the future. What does this *and* mean if it is not a contradiction? The answer is to be found in the philosophy of quantum information. As long as the box containing Schrödinger's unfortunate cat remains unopened, we must say that it is *both* dead and alive, or more precisely, that the living state and the dead state coexist in a relation of *superposition*. Opening the box puts an end not to what is too often called "uncertainty" but to what in German is called *Unbestimmtheit*, which should be translated as "indeterminacy." For the prospect of future catastrophe to have a deterrent effect, it is similarly necessary that coordination be achieved with reference to *a future that is at once fixed and indeterminate*. The endogenous fixed point is the superimposition in it of catastrophe and noncatastrophe.

This vindicates Bernard Brodie's quotation above and illuminates Robert McNamara's blind spot. Were the several dozens of "near-misses" during the Cold War failures of deterrence? Quite the opposite: it is precisely these unscheduled expeditions to the edge of the black hole that gave the threat of nuclear annihilation its dissuasive force. "We lucked out," McNamara says. Quite true, but in a very profound sense it was this repeated flirting with apocalypse that saved humanity. Those "errors" were the condition of possibility of the efficacy of nuclear deterrence. Accidents are needed to precipitate an apocalyptic destiny. Yet unlike fate, an accident is not inevitable: it *can* not occur.

Appendix

COGNITIVE PSYCHOLOGY VINDICATES PROJECTED TIME

In the late 1960s, a quantum physicist named William Newcomb invented a formidable paradox that has been argued over ever since and never satisfactorily resolved. It is a true paradox, one that takes us straight to the heart of perhaps the most perplexing enigma of all: how human beings can act freely in a world that is nonetheless causally determined through and through by blind, subjectless processes.

Imagine an agent who is presented with two boxes. One of them is transparent and visibly contains a thousand dollars; the other is opaque, and, he is told, may contain either a million dollars or nothing at all. The agent is then given a choice between two strategies:

S1) Taking what is in the opaque box alone; and
S2) Taking what is in both boxes.

At the moment when the choice is explained to the agent, a being who has the power to predict the agent's choices will already have placed a million dollars in the opaque box *if and only if* he has predicted that the agent will choose S1. The agent knows this, and what is more, he has total confidence in the predictive abilities of the predictor. What should he do?

One's first reaction is to say that the agent should choose S1. The predictor will have predicted this choice, and so the agent will have a million dollars. If he were to choose S2 he would have only a thousand dollars—the thousand dollars he sees in the transparent box, while the opaque box would remain empty. The paradox arises from the fact that another way of looking at the matter seems equally persuasive, although it leads to the opposite conclusion. When the agent makes his choice, *either there are or there are not* a million dollars in the opaque box: in taking what is in both boxes, he stands to win a thousand dollars more in either case than if he were to take only what is in the opaque box. S2 is therefore what game theorists call a dominant strategy.

Cognitive psychologists have conducted laboratory experiments showing that the broad stratum of "ordinary people"—roughly 75 percent of the subjects tested—make the choice S1, in violation of the strategic dominance principle.[24] Each of them can claim one million dollars. The remarkable thing is that virtually all professional philosophers, game theorists, and other experts in so-called rational choice choose S2 on the ground that it is the dominant strategy. Each of them can claim a thousand dollars—but also, as a sort of consolation prize, the certainty of being right.

They may be right, but their reward is risibly small by comparison with the amount won by all those ordinary people who, contrary to reason (as the experts define it), *deliberately refuse* to see the obviousness of the dominant strategy. One is tempted to say that Newcomb's problem is worded in such a way that it rewards agents who act irrationally—in which case it would be rational to act irrationally. But this would make no sense unless there were some other criterion of economic rationality than simply maximizing one's gains over a range of possible choices. The difficulty cannot be escaped so easily. What makes Newcomb's problem seem so intractable is that it pits reason against itself.

I believe it is possible to solve analytically Newcomb's problem thanks to Alvin Plantinga's concept of counterfactual power over the past.[25] What matters here is that cognitive psychology has shown that most of us spontaneously endow ourselves with this kind of power. The solution presented in the chapter regarding how nuclear war can be avoided is hence compatible with experimental findings from behavioral economics.

NOTES

1. *The Fog of War: Eleven Lessons from the Life of Robert S. McNamara*, directed by Errol Morris (New York: Sony Pictures Classics, 2003).
2. Émile Meyerson, *De l'explication dans les sciences* (Paris: Payot, 1927).
3. David K. Lewis, *On the Plurality of Worlds* (Oxford: Blackwell Publishers, 1986); Robert Stalnaker, *Ifs: Conditionals, Belief, Decision, Chance, and Time* (Dordrecht: D. Reidel, 1981). The discussion in this chapter utilizes the following standard definitions: given an adequate definition of a possible world, *possible* refers to that which is true in at least one possible world, *necessary* that which is true in all possible worlds, *impossible* that which is untrue in all possible worlds, and *contingent* that which is possible without being necessary.
4. David K. Lewis, "Are We Free to Break the Laws?" *Theoria* 47, no. 3 (1981): 112.
5. Whether *modus ponens* remains valid under the operator of necessity could be questioned.
6. Lewis, "Are We Free," 113.
7. Ibid., 112.
8. In comparing an actual world and another possible world, we make use of a linguistic and metaphysical device known as a *counterfactual conditional proposition*. A conditional proposition of the "if *p* then *q*" type may be indicative ("if it rains tomorrow, I will not go to work") or counterfactual ("if I were wealthier than I am, I would buy a Lamborghini"). The term "counterfactual" refers here to the presence of an antecedent ("if I were wealthier") that is contrary to fact (alas, I am not wealthier than I am). The truth status of these two types of conditionals is not at all the same, however. To take a classic example, the proposition "if Shakespeare did not write *Troilus and Cressida*, someone else did" is indubitably true since the play exists and so it must have had an author. By contrast, to assert the truth of the counterfactual proposition "if Shakespeare had not written *Troilus and Cressida*, someone else would have," is highly problematic—at least for those who believe that only the Bard could have produced a masterpiece of this order.

Counterfactual propositions concern possible worlds, worlds that exist somewhere near our world—neighbors, in a sense, of the actual world, which after all is the only one we know firsthand. However, we cannot do without such propositions in our thinking and reasoning about the past and the future, for example when something important happens that might not have occurred or, conversely, when something does not happen that, if it had occurred, would have changed our life and the world, for better or for worse.

9. Alvin Plantinga, "On Ockham's Way Out," *Faith and Philosophy* 3, no. 3 (1986): 235–69.
10. My mentor Maurice Allais, one of the founders of neoclassical economics and for a long time the only French Nobel laureate in that discipline, used to say, "When it comes to rationality, the fundamental maxim is: *only the future matters.*" Obviously, he did not mean that the past is not important. What Allais's maxim asserts is that the past will always be what it was and, specifically, our present decision cannot change it.
11. For some of my previous publications addressing the two metaphysics of temporality, see note 25.

12. See the excellent synthesis of the debate by Steven P. Lee, *Morality, Prudence, and Nuclear Weapons* (Cambridge: Cambridge University Press, 1996).

13. Jonathan Schell, *The Fate of the Earth* (New York: Knopf, 1982), 307.

14. The most telling sign that *in a sense* nuclear deterrence did not work is that it did nothing to prevent an unrestrained and potentially catastrophic arms buildup. If indeed it did work, nuclear deterrence ought to have been the great equalizer. As in Hobbes's state of nature, the weakest nation—measured by the number of nuclear warheads it possesses—is on exactly the same level as the strongest, since it can always inflict "unacceptable" losses, for example by deliberately targeting the enemy's cities. France enunciated a doctrine ("deterrence of the strong by the weak") to this effect. Deterrence is therefore a game that can be played—indeed, that must be able to be played—with very few armaments on each side.

15. Gregory Kavka, *Moral Paradoxes of Nuclear Deterrence* (Cambridge: Cambridge University Press, 1987), 48.

16. David K. Lewis, "Finite Counterforce," in *Nuclear Deterrence and Moral Restraint*, ed. Henry Shue (Cambridge: Cambridge University Press, 1989), 67.

17. Ibid., 68.

18. Thomas C. Schelling, *The Strategy of Conflict* (Cambridge, Mass.: Harvard University Press, 1960).

19. Hans Jonas, *The Imperative of Responsibility: In Search of an Ethics for the Technological Age* (Chicago: University of Chicago Press, 1984).

20. For more on how I have grounded this form of compatibilism see, Jean-Pierre Dupuy, *Economy and the Future: A Crisis of Faith* (East Lansing: Michigan State University Press, 2014).

21. Plantinga, "On Ockham's Way Out."

22. *Minority Report*, directed by Steven Spielberg (Century City, Calif.: Twentieth Century Fox, 2002).

23. This is the paradox described by Hans Jonas: "The prophecy of doom is made to avert its coming, and it would be the height of injustice later to deride the 'alarmists' because 'it did not turn out to be so bad after all'—to have been wrong may be their merit." See *Imperative of Responsibility*, 120.

24. Notably Amos Tversky, who performed this test on his students at Stanford. See Eldar Shafir and Amos Tversky, "Thinking through Uncertainty: Nonconsequential Reasoning and Choice," *Cognitive Psychology* 24, no. 4 (1992): 449–74.

25. See Jean-Pierre Dupuy, "Philosophical Foundations of a New Concept of Equilibrium in the Social Sciences: Projected Equilibrium," *Philosophical Studies* 100 (2000): 323–45; Jean-Pierre Dupuy, "Two Temporalities, Two Rationalities: A New Look at Newcomb's Paradox," in *Economics and Cognitive Science*, ed. P. Bourgine and B. Walliser (Oxford: Pergamon, 1992), 191–220; Jean-Pierre Dupuy, "Common Knowledge, Common Sense," *Theory and Decision* 27 (1989): 37–62; Jean-Pierre Dupuy, ed., *Self-deception and Paradoxes of Rationality* (Palo Alto, Calif.: C. S. L. I. Publications, Stanford University, 1998).

CHAPTER FIVE

Sanctions, Sequences, and Statecraft

Insights from Behavioral Economics

ETEL SOLINGEN

The process of extending positive or negative inducements to change the behavior of a state pursuing nuclear weapons is ridden with risk and uncertainty.[1] How actors make decisions under conditions of uncertainty, or may or may not behave in that context, is one of the main foci of research within behavioral economics, making the subject of nuclear proliferation amenable to its insights. The strategic interaction between senders of inducements aimed at persuading states to abandon nuclear designs on the one hand, and the targets of those inducements on the other, is one fraught with possibilities for flawed interpretations of their respective intentions and behavior. Nor is external analysis of that interaction by experts free of this potential for systematic bias and inadequate readings of actors' behavior.

In this chapter, I discuss four major problems in studies of inducements that assume full rationality. First is the common fallacy of assuming an "evident" (monolithic) aggregate state-level preference. Jervis identified an additional cognitive bias, often overlaid on the assumption of states as monoliths, leading each side in a bargaining process to assume that their interlocutors are more unified than they really are.[2] A second concern is the tendency, particularly but not uniquely in quantitative studies of sanctions, to pronounce sanctions as having "worked" or "not worked," in dichotomous fashion, ignoring the nuanced and nonlinear nature of outcomes. This often leads to a conventional pronouncement that "sanctions don't work" or work only very rarely. A third, related problem is the failure to understand the complexity of causal mechanisms through which positive and negative inducements operate.[3] The casualty of this failure is a neglect of the intricate, interim, and indirect effects that might lead to a different assessment of how, and whether, inducements may or may not work. A fourth weakness lies in ignoring how, when, and if senders and targets "learn" and from whom. The result of this omission is a failure—which can affect both sending states and outside analysts—to recognize how target states may update bargaining positions throughout the course of inducements processes. None of these problems are easy to tackle, perhaps explaining why undiluted rationalistic frameworks in the analysis of inducements find it convenient to circumvent them altogether. But those omissions can potentially entail high costs, detracting from a proper understanding of statecraft.

This chapter relies on recent and ongoing efforts to persuade states to abandon nuclear weapons ambitions to illuminate how these problems affect our understanding of sanctions, statecraft, and nuclear proliferation. The first section presents one solution to the problem of disaggregating state preferences in target states and an approach to better identification of relevant actors, building on domestic distributional considerations. The second section explores the elusiveness of estimating *final* outcomes (those at some presumed end of the inducements process). Such estimations often hinge on the eyes of analytical beholders who differ in their prior predisposition toward positive or negative inducements. The third section elaborates the complexity introduced by causal mechanisms operating concomitantly, each yielding intricate, interim, and indirect effects. The fourth introduces the relevance of understanding what kinds of "learning," if any, guides bargaining positions in the process under scrutiny. The final section highlights additional considerations from behavioral economics that might be brought to bear to attain a deeper understanding of how, when, and why external inducements may or may not work.

THE DEMAND SIDE OF NUCLEAR WEAPONS: AN OBSERVED REGULARITY MODIFIED BY PROSPECT THEORY

Theories of nuclear proliferation often refer to the factors that may motivate states to seek nuclear arms as the demand side. I here use the phrase *supply side* to refer to the available range of positive and negative inducements that external actors can rely on to dissuade would-be proliferators from pursuing nuclear weapons, including the supply of coercion, persuasion, and other elements of statecraft.[4] Excessive reliance on the assumption that states are coherent actors has handicapped both our understanding of the demand side for nuclear weapons as well as of the supply of external inducements to dissuade states from acquiring them. In both cases, the unitary actor assumption regarding target states has precluded a proper appreciation of the complexity entailed in mapping those states' responses to inducements.[5]

Much work in recent decades has challenged the notion that states behave inexorably according to some vague and unspecified function of their relative international power, a flawed heuristic at best, and one afflicted with too many empirical anomalies at worst.[6] The rather recent relaxation of the unitary actor assumption in some quarters leads naturally to proper attention to domestic distributional effects of external inducements and of their differential impact on diverse constituencies in target states. I begin with a brief discussion of a framework explaining the demand side (who wants nuclear weapons and why, and who does not). Without a proper understanding of a chief driver on the demand side, supply-side tools (policy and statecraft) are bound to be inefficient.

There are many ways to slice the domestic landscape influencing nuclear decisions. One particular finding suggests that a state's nuclear choices are highly related to the nature of its dominant political-economy model.[7] Accordingly, among states entertaining the possibility of nuclear weapons since the 1960s, leaders who rejected the global economy as a driver of industrialization have been more prone to develop such weapons than those advocating economic growth through global integration. The underlying foundations for exploring *cui bono* and *cui malo* from different nuclear choices builds on the premise that political leaders build supportive coalitions to gain and survive in power. They accordingly craft favored models of political survival across constituencies with preferences bearing on political economy and national security. Given their favored model, leaders and ruling coalitions vary in their tolerance for the relative political and economic (including opportunity) costs that their nuclear policies might entail.

Inward-looking leaders emphasizing economic nationalism, sometimes dressed in rigid religious or ethnic identities, have cast ambiguous nuclear programs as tools of modernization and symbols of defiance against perceived dominant global political and economic orders. From Juan Perón and Gamal Nasser to Saddam Hussein, the Kim dynasty, Muammar Qaddafi, and radical strongholds in Iran's Islamic Revolutionary Guard Corps (IRGC), nuclear policies have been nested in broader economic nationalism and critiques of the global political economy and its associated international regimes. Leaders advancing inward-looking models have shielded favored constituencies including internationally uncompetitive industries, military-industrial enterprises, and associated state bureaucracies. Nuclear weapons programs have provided ideal technological allies for inward-looking leaders because they enable vast scientific, technological, industrial, and bureaucratic complexes, which are often beyond formal budgetary oversight. These complexes were portrayed as putatively leading to actual or imaginary outputs—referred to as a "self-reliant program," "independent program," "parallel program," or simply "the bomb," depending on the degree of secrecy about its ultimate objectives—that played out as powerful sources of myths germane to inward-looking models.[8]

By contrast, leaders relying on economic growth through internationalization have largely shied away from nuclear weapons, seeking instead political and economic stability to reduce uncertainty and maximize access to foreign markets, resources, capital, investments, aid, and technology. Such access requires expanding private economic activities, contracting military expenditures, progressively reducing trade and investment barriers, and abiding by international institutions that validate and promote those choices. A policy of nuclear assertion or ambiguity is much less synergistic with those choices, leading internationalizers to downgrade the value of nuclear weapons out of concern that pursuit of the bomb would sap the domestic economy, strengthen domestic opponents of global integration, place valuable external resources in jeopardy, have international reputational effects detrimental to their preferred objectives, and contribute to regional tensions and instability. Yoshida Shigeru, Park Chun Hee, Lee Kwan Yew, and their successors, as well as others who also faced severe security dilemmas, nonetheless chose to forego nuclear weapons.[9]

These two models of political survival are only ideal types and entail only proclivities or probabilistic tendencies rather than lawlike generalizations; real types can be more eclectic or hybrid. Yet, most cases of nuclear aspirants since the conclusion of the Non-Proliferation Treaty (NPT) in 1968 seem to validate the association between approaches to the global economy and nuclear policies. Of all nuclear aspirants under regimes that shunned integration in the global economy, not one endorsed denuclearization—fully and effectively—while such regimes remained in control. Only regimes that relied on integration in the global economy to advance their political survival undertook effective commitments to denuclearize, including South Korea, Brazil, Argentina, Japan, Egypt under Sadat, South Africa, Taiwan, and Libya in 2003, among others. Their nuclear decisions were nested in a broader attempted shift toward internationalization in economics and security, even if ultimately internationalizing efforts did not always come to fruition. Where internationalizers became stronger politically, the departure from nuclear claims was maintained even as the security context deteriorated, as in the Korean peninsula and the Taiwan Straits, at various points. Where internationalizers were weaker, as in Iran for much of the time since 1979, they were more politically constrained in curbing nuclear weapon programs.

However, this central propensity is only probabilistic, bounded, and subject to potential deviations rather than an inevitable or deterministic outcome. It is bounded in several ways, but most pertinent to a collection on behavioral economics and nuclear proliferation, it appears bounded by temporal sequences in the acquisition of nuclear weapons in ways that trample other logics. Disincentives related to internationalization may operate more forcefully where nuclear programs have not yet yielded weapons at the time major decisions were taken (Japan, South Korea, Taiwan, Argentina, Brazil, Spain, and others). Those same disincentives, however, may weigh less once nuclear thresholds have been crossed, a condition that weaves prospect theory into the framework. For example, China developed nuclear weapons during the "first nuclear age" (the 1950s), decades prior to its decisions to integrate into the global economy, and it tested them in 1964. North Korea, as well, developed nuclear weapons well before any consideration of genuine integration into the global economy, and its interest in the latter is still not at all certain as of mid-2018. Prospect theoretic insights suggest that it might be costlier politically to eliminate existing weapons than it is to abandon earlier steps in that direction.[10]

As prospect theory suggests, politicians, negotiators, and publics may value what they already have (the "endowment effect") more than they do potential future gains; they are more averse to losses, such as would be incurred by giving up something already possessed. Hence, under otherwise similar circumstances, they may accept higher costs and risks associated with retaining existing nuclear weapons than they would if they were only entertaining potential acquisition. Giving up an existing capability would almost certainly be framed as a loss, whereas renouncing a program at an earlier stage could be framed as a potential means for facilitating access to the global economy. The disincentives stemming from an internationalizing strategy may thus be stronger at deliberative or incipient stages of nuclear weapons consideration than once these weapons have been acquired. Denuclearization may arguably be more difficult when nuclearization *precedes* the inception of internationalizing models. Eliminating operational weapons may be politically costlier than eliminating an incipient or stalled program—all else being equal—if popular sentiment in fact reflects endowment effects. But since all else is usually not equal, one must also consider whether a particular state's regional environment is dominated by inward-looking or internationalizing models. The latter may reinforce incentives to forego nuclear weapons programs far more significantly than the former. Internationalizers interpret the intentions of fellow internationalizing neighbors more benignly than those of inward-looking ones, either because of cognitive or emotional considerations. The dominance of one model or another throughout a region, in other words, can reinforce or dilute the strength of endowment effects.

Prospect theoretic insights reinforce rational concerns with audience costs (e.g., potential removal from office) that might accrue from giving up actual weapons. An existing weapon's "endowment" can make audience costs higher not merely in democratic contexts. After all, the NPT-recognized nuclear weapon states, both democratic and nondemocratic, have not yet renounced those weapons, indeed declining to join the 2017 treaty to ban nuclear weapons approved at the UN by 122 states. That position may suggest some combination of endowment effects and audience costs effects at work. Most importantly, however, endowment effects can operate independently of relative power or pure "security" considerations.

Presumed anomalies—states that gave up actual nuclear weapons—are of interest here. South Africa abandoned such weapons in tandem with internationalizing efforts to extricate the country from diplomatic isolation. This case was a successful instance of sanctions that both stigmatized the regime and blocked beneficial economic exchange with the rest of the world. Would-be internationalizers overcame the endowment effect by associating nuclear weapons with the inward-looking Apartheid regime that they sought to replace. Post-Soviet leaders in the Ukraine, Kazakhstan, and Belarus overcame endowment effects by connecting nuclear weapons to a Soviet inheritance that never allowed them control over such weapons in any event. Further research on these cases would require recreating the temporal context that enabled leaders to relinquish nuclear weapons in the 1990s, not an easy feat methodologically particularly considering cognitive distortions (such as hindsight bias) that may arise from looking at such episodes through contemporary lenses informed by knowledge not available to actors at the time. Later Russian aggression has led at least some Ukrainians to reassess their renunciation of nuclear weapons through the 1994 Budapest Agreements. Putin would have not invaded them, they argue, had Ukraine retained a nuclear deterrent, a counterfactual proposition that may or may not gain some validity with in-depth research able to control for such bias.[11]

Partial anomalies do not challenge the basic prospect theoretic contention that many more states abandoned nuclear weapons–related programs than gave up nuclear weapons themselves. Prospect theory, temporal sequences, timing, and audience costs considerations suggest that backing down from (even implicit) commitments to acquire full nuclear capabilities may be easier for leaders in states that have yet to weaponize, as presumably remained the case with Iran under the Joint Comprehensive Plan of Action (JCPOA). However, stronger inward-looking constituencies at home and in the neighborhood may neutralize that tendency, making it harder to renounce a weapons-related program. Iran's Ahmadinejad made commitments to uranium enrichment a central—if not the most central—feature of his hold on power, celebrating enrichment and ancillary paraphernalia as ritual objects and sacred symbols in public parades.

Insights from prospect theory and audience costs can also illuminate why renouncing commitments might be more difficult, but not impossible, even prior to the acquisition of actual weapons, once certain thresholds, such as weapons-grade enrichment, nuclear tests, expelling inspectors, and renouncing the NPT, have been crossed. Where powerful internationalizing constituencies exist, leaders can overcome such effects, particularly when they are able to associate nuclear designs with a regime they seek to replace, as in South Africa. Neither Iran nor North Korea, however, seems close to such circumstances. North Korea has not only tested nuclear weapons several times but has also rejected China-style or Vietnam-style reforms for decades, favoring an inward-looking "military first" economy in practice. That policy (*songun*) increased North Korea's distance from a more favorable context for voluntary denuclearization. However, its replacement with *byungjin* (parallel emphasis on both the economy and weapons) first, and potentially with an "economy first" policy in the future, might bring it closer to compromises. It is too early to tell at the time of this writing whether Kim Jong Un will indeed move in that direction, but an economy-first approach would go a long way to explain some of his recent outreach to the United States and South Korea. As of June 2018, any conclusions that a robust economy-first policy is already in place or that it underpins major concessions are premature. Indeed, the endowment effect could make North Korea's price tag for relinquishing nuclear weapons especially high.

CALIBRATING THE INSTRUMENTS: SYSTEMATIC BIAS TOWARD POSITIVE OR NEGATIVE INDUCEMENTS

Many disagreements over putative outcomes of inducement episodes or processes stem from competing interpretations of the empirical record. This variance in estimating the results of external inducements, positive and negative, can be traced, among other things, to systematic cognitive bias in the form of "excessive coherence."[12] This bias arises from efforts to fit incomplete or contradictory information into a coherent narrative, where the chosen narrative will likely reflect a person's prior beliefs. Such bias leads both real-world actors and analysts to consider only, or primarily, evidence compatible with strongly held beliefs or ideological commitments.[13] Outcomes are interpreted as rational estimates in terms that validate a preferred course of action while invoking evidence congenial to a favored viewpoint. For example, those favoring positive inducements often emphasize the negative effects of sanctions, characterizing them as too harsh; prone to undermine civil society, democracy, and human rights; and unable to make targets more pliable.[14] This school often also stipulates that positive inducements are very rarely extended despite competing studies that found such inducements to have been proffered at much higher rates for all cases of nonproliferation since the 1990s.[15]

Even North Korea, with its dense track record of deception, was the beneficiary of a long list of positive inducements including the 1994 Agreed Framework, U.S. security assurances, oil provision, a promise of a sequenced process of normalization, the Six Party talks' 2005 Joint Statement of Principles, and the 2008 removal of North Korea from the U.S. list of state sponsors of terrorism, among others. And with what results? The easing of sanctions elicited some short-term positive responses, but subsequent North Korean behavior included a retraction of commitments, continued illicit activities including exports of missiles and sensitive technologies to rogue states (including a secret reactor to Syria), several nuclear tests since 2006, ballistic missile tests lobbed over neighbors' territory, construction of new state-of-the-art enrichment facilities to "diversify" its technical path to weapons, and expansion of fissile material stockpiles.[16] One way to sustain the case for positive inducements, even against this background, is to argue that positive inducements were either too little, too late, or both. For instance, some argue that U.S. extension of negative security guarantees to North Korea in the 2005 Joint Statement was not bold enough.[17] Such assessments may reflect some degree of excessive coherence bias since we cannot know ultimately whether even more positive inducements would have yielded better results.

The "sanctions don't work" camp gathers an awkward alliance of hard-liners, who favor more muscular approaches than economic sanctions alone, and soft-liners, who favor positive inducements. Legions of pundits, including some scholars, joined the "sanctions don't work" chorus in the context of years of negotiations with Iran by the EU along with the five permanent members of the UN Security Council plus Germany (the EU/P5+1). Yet, few publicly retracted such statements once an unprecedented Iranian disposition to enter direct conversations with the United States led to the 2013 interim agreement.[18]

Rather than conceding that sanctions may have played a significant role in the election of Hassan Rouhani and in his team's receptivity to negotiations, the "sanctions don't work" camp resorted to two main strategies of argumentation. Some focused on lack of evidence that Iran had indeed abandoned its presumed ultimate desired outcome: nuclear weapons. Others contested the causal weight of sanctions on Rouhani's election. Advocates of positive inducements had assigned hefty causal effects to the extension of diplomatic and trade relations to former president Khatami. These may indeed have been the right form of inducement under those circumstances, but such arguments also downplay major contextual qualifications. Khatami's receptivity to positive inducements—compatible with a would-be internationalizing strategy—ultimately failed when his openness to a more outward-looking approach was overwhelmed by a much stronger inward-looking camp. Advocating positive inducements *under all circumstances* thus raises the possibility of at least two biases: excessive coherence and treating states as monolithic entities both contextually and over time.

Similar forms of systematic bias can afflict actors and analysts predisposed to endorse sanctions as more effective tools of statecraft than positive inducements. Many regarded too many positive inducements to have been proffered to Iran to no avail, breeding moral hazard and deceit. A common argument invoked by those who doubt the value of positive inducements is to point to a statement by then Supreme National Security Council secretary Hassan Rouhani to a hardened inward-looking domestic audience. In 2005, Rouhani conceded that positive inducements extended by France, Germany, and the U.K. (the EU-3) while Khatami was in power had achieved brilliant results for Iran, enabling it to advance its nuclear program while increasing oil and gas contracts with India,

China, the UAE, and others.[19] While this was indeed the case, skeptics of positive inducements sometimes overlook the fact that Khatami and his allies were under domestic assault by inward-looking radicals. Indeed, the latter went as far as assassinating some Khatami supporters under mysterious circumstances.[20] Whether or not positive inducements under the Clinton administration could bear fruit was less a function of any inherent flaw in U.S. policy than of the unfolding domestic balance of power between factions *within* Iran.

Alas, such balance can be more easily gauged empirically after the fact, particularly in nontransparent authoritarian contexts. Yet, given the state of knowledge at the time, the extension of positive inducements may have been the correct policy under the circumstances, when incomplete information could not allow certainty about their ability (or inability) to elicit concessions. These conditions characterized negotiations with Iran subsequently as well. Opponents of positive inducements also invoked the presumed failure of President Obama's effort to reinvigorate a diplomatic breakthrough under much of Ahmadinejad's tenure, when Iran consistently rejected EU/P5+1 offers while new undeclared facilities kept popping up.

Yet the Obama administration's olive branch, reinforced by Ahmadinejad's domestic economic debacle, bore preliminary fruit when direct secret U.S.-Iranian negotiations were launched in 2013 in Oman. Advocates of sanctions, however, sidelined the administration's openness to positive inducements, pointing instead to the stronger sanctions regime that emerged with the EU's boycott of Iranian oil as a more crucial driver of both Rouhani's election and a new disposition to enter negotiations.[21] The Obama administration's positive inducements, Iran's domestic economic difficulties toward the end of Ahmadinejad's rule, and enhanced European sanctions may have all lined up to favor negotiations, a more complex causal landscape than excessive coherence accounts of either sort can accommodate.

Those with strong commitments to sanctions as a favored form of external inducement frequently dismiss counterarguments by suggesting that it is not sanctions per se but their putative puny size that may fail to yield results. This is the mirror image of the too little, too late positive inducements account. Sanctions hawks too summon supportive findings to buttress their claims: that the higher the cost of sanctions to targets, the higher the probability of success, and that comprehensive sanctions are more effective than targeted ones. Iraq (pre-2003) and Libya, for instance, are invoked as referents for the kind of comprehensive sanctions that thwarted progress toward nuclear weapons. Unilateral U.S. or multilateral but mild UN sanctions could not, in this view, bring Iran to the negotiating table.[22] Instead, according to this view, it took truly "biting" comprehensive financial sanctions and the EU oil boycott to finally bring about the kind of deterioration of the Iranian economy that yielded the desired political results.

These conditions might well explain the election of Rouhani in 2013, which positive-inducement variants of excessive coherence often fail to recognize. Yet, this latter camp can point to similarly comprehensive sanctions on oil-poor North Korea, which make it more difficult to argue that "toothless sanctions" accounted for North Korea's failure to comply—more difficult but not impossible, since proponents of hard and comprehensive sanctions can invoke China's role in diluting the effect of sanctions.[23] The bite of sanctions did increase as China's evolving approach to North Korea later incorporated a partial, intermittent oil embargo, which affected the North Korean military significantly, and eventually even stronger measures under 2018 UNSC resolutions.[24]

The point here is not to settle this debate but to sensitize analysts to informational biases that sometimes make it hard to reach *balanced* assessments of the effects of positive or negative inducements. Additional factors increase informational biases. For instance, leaders targeted by either form of inducement have strong incentives to invalidate accurate interpretations of those effects. They may forcefully challenge the view that sanctions played any role in their behavior, which would signal weakness at home and abroad, especially as inward-looking leaders may be engulfed in an outbidding race with other inward-looking competitors. Most of Ahmadinejad's tenure is an instance of such defiance; he denied the effect of sanctions, labeling them a "used handkerchief" fit for the dustbin.[25]

Nor do leaders under similar conditions have any incentive to praise positive inducements by external actors who, after all, are the same actors the regime consistently characterizes in the vilest terms. Kim Jong Un provides plentiful examples of harshly offensive characterizations of external interlocutors, including of Presidents Obama and Trump, and various inward-looking Iranian leaders do not fall too short. Positive inducements can also be perceived as redolent of side-payments and can easily be used by inward-looking competitors at home to the detriment of those who accept them. Proponents of positive inducements often ignore these twists that foil their preferred tools of statecraft. Whatever the actual reasons for Kim Jung Un's assassination of his uncle Jang Sung-taek, the alleged acceptance of external "bribes" provided the seemingly perfect justification, given the *juche* ideology of self-reliance.

The litany of incentives and cognitive biases that obscure the real effect of inducements—positive or negative—should encourage ample caution in interpreting official statements. Careful examination of the latter can illuminate evident (but failed) efforts to conceal their actual impact, as seen in many statements by Khamenei and Ahmadinejad. Domestic reformist challengers may or may not have a more accurate estimation of the costs of sanctions. They may also have rational incentives to heighten those costs, which they can use, in turn, to question the very policy triggering sanctions. They may, in other words, suffer from excessive coherence bias as well. Wielding the costs of sanctions as a motive for concessions can also be a political Achilles heel for regime opponents, enhancing their vulnerability to accusations of treason.[26]

In sum, excessive coherence hinders appropriate evaluation of the instruments of nonproliferation statecraft. Cognitive pressure for consistency leaves little room for the possibility that events do not conform to strongly held beliefs. Such pressure is resistant to rationalistic understandings that even covering laws need not apply to individual occurrences.[27] Avoiding imputation of too much causality to either form of inducement entails a delicate calibration that enables getting the mix of inducements, in Goldilocks fashion, "just right."

Some guidelines for avoiding excessive coherence include awareness of the following five considerations: (1) Positive and negative inducements are generally complementary rather than mutually exclusive. (2) "Grand bargains" may include both very attractive and very unpleasant inducements, transcending the "too little of either" debate. (3) Whether inducements of either type are too little or too much hinges on who benefits and who is hurt by different options, which is why frameworks attentive to domestic distributional effects can be helpful. (4) The same behavior can generate conflicting interpretations. When targets reject positive inducements, it is often impossible to distinguish whether they do that because of the presumed small size of such inducements or because they are inherently opportunists forever seeking more concessions. Haggard and Noland have noted this dilemma in the case of North Korea but negotiations with Iran brought it back to the fore.[28] Finally, (5) We should beware of polling enterprises with a specific point of view that heightens excessive coherence of any sort, particularly when surveys are conducted in countries that hinder the expression of true preferences. Such surveys were deficient in foreseeing the 1989 revolutions, the "Arab Spring," and other important upheavals in no small part because of rigid commitments to strongly held beliefs.[29]

CAUSAL MECHANISMS AND COMPLEXITY: INTRICATE, INTERIM, AND INDIRECT EFFECTS

All forms of excessive coherence in the interpretation of inducement cases fail to come to terms with the complexity of causal mechanisms through which sanctions operate and with stages along that causal sequence.[30] Simply evaluating the final outcome (did they abandon the nukes or not?) falls short of understanding interim effects that might have led in a different direction. A given inducement may have worked in the short term only to be derailed by extraneous causal drivers. Ignoring that initial effect could conceal the potential for the same inducement to lead to a different final outcome under alternative circumstances. Intricate, interim, and indirect effects introduce greater complexity, but ignoring them undermines a proper assessment of the effects of positive and negative inducements. Their consideration is often resisted by even highly trained, boundedly rational analytical satisficers bent on keeping the number of variables, and informational demands, at relatively low levels. As Tetlock and Lebow argue, analysts committed to strongly held beliefs—which by definition are prone to cognitive closure—lean on parsimonious interpretations of evidence that invoke as few causal constructs as possible and prefer deterministic accounts that downplay probabilistic qualifiers.[31] The sources of this kind of cognitive bias differ from, but can also exacerbate, tendencies discussed in earlier sections, such as excessive reliance on the assumption that states are coherent actors and excessive coherence regarding the effects of inducements of either type.

Assessing intricate, interim, and indirect effects of different inducements is far more exacting than are analyses of sanctions focusing on a minimal number of drivers and final outcomes for several reasons. First, a preference for deterministic interpretations and observed outcomes militates against the use of close-call counterfactuals. The latter force attention to possible scenarios where relatively minor rewrites of history could have led to a different final outcome. For instance, the result of the 2013 elections in Iran was not the one anticipated by Khamenei.[32] Had Khamenei intervened to thwart that outcome—as he did in 2009—positive inducements may have arguably found far less receptivity among those hard-liners that Khamenei presumably would have handpicked. One may quarrel whether this is indeed a minimal counterfactual rewrite of history, but advocates of parsimony often avoid even minimal rewrites, even where they might be available.

Second, detailed process tracing often introduces greater complexity regarding the connections among causal drivers, the identification of definitive beginning and end conditions, and the recognition of cognitive biases along the process. Greater complexity thus prompts a much broader and conditional set of questions regarding the effectiveness of sanctions. When faced with more difficult assessments entailing interim and indirect effects, there is a cognitive tendency to default to an easier question that is rarely a perfect substitute for the more crucial one.[33] For instance, prior to the JCPOA, the default question—can Iran accept the ultimate bargain offered by the P5+1 process?—hinged on a much more complex set of questions that transcended monolithic interpretations of Iran's objectives as a unified state.[34] Would Rouhani's team persuade Khamenei of the merits of a specific agreement, and if so, in exchange for what concessions, and if not, to what effects for the different elements in Iran's leadership? Would such effects split segments of the Revolutionary Guards who might detect mostly benefits or mostly costs in that agreement? Did Khamenei genuinely favor an open economy that might accrue from successful negotiations or a "resistance economy" that would thrive in the absence of an agreement?[35]

These and other questions were the most difficult ones to answer—particularly because the negotiating team (and perhaps even Khamenei himself) may not have known most answers for some time—yet, they were the crucial ones to ask.

Third, a given causal mechanism may have different effects in different spatial and temporal contexts. Detailed process tracing is better positioned to capture such variability over time and space. Comprehensive sanctions on all imports of refined oil products may not be as effective under certain conditions, as when domestic publics rally around the regime to condemn external intervention. Under different circumstances, such as the aftermath of rigged elections or heightened repression, such measures may gain broader popular acceptability as means to weaken the regime. Some indeed sensed greater receptivity to targeted sanctions against the repressive apparatus including the IRGC after 2009, particularly among democracy activists.[36] Nincic instead regards positive inducements to be especially effective when the regime's domestic position is insecure, as in the aftermath of the 2009 elections (the worst possible timing from the standpoint of signaling utter disregard for human rights).[37]

Finally, even if analysts can avail themselves of a final outcome of a negotiating process, decisions to give up nuclear weapons are rarely seen as definitive as they were in the South African case. Such decisions are often incremental, incomplete, nonlinear, and require forceful confrontation with evidence of deceit and concealment, accompanied by unimpeded access for verification purposes, as was the case in Iraq and Libya.[38] Unrestricted inspections and strong verification mechanisms are thus barriers not simply against rational incentives to defect but also against a complex set of contingencies and biases of interpretation, to which I turn now.

LEARNING AND UNLEARNING

Another pervasive source of uncertainty involves challenges to accurate estimations of what are the "right" lessons from past experiences for current negotiations. The lessons from past failures of compliance with international legal commitments or with prior nuclear agreements are particularly pertinent in this context. As an astute expert commented in his congressional testimony on negotiations with Iran regarding historical analogy, a historian's caution seems pertinent: "Our present state of knowledge is one of mitigated ignorance. In such situations, the honest enquirer always has one consolation—his blunders may be as instructive as his successes."[39] Another senior U.S. intelligence official, reflecting on Iran's record of pursuing covert nuclear facilities, offers a common view: "We have not seen much lately, . . . but over the past 10 years, we've uncovered three covert programs in Iran, and there's no reason to think there's not a fourth out there."[40]

This view was shared not only by skeptics of the JCPOA but also by some strong supporters of an agreement that incorporates intense scrutiny of Iran's past nuclear behavior. Pointing to Iran's record of deception and its unwillingness to provide a complete and correct declaration of all its nuclear related activities, Tobey avers that "anytime, anywhere" inspections will be as ineffective as "an Easter egg hunt" if they are not backed by an orderly declaration and verification process. If experience was a guide, he added, June 2015 was the high-water mark of international pressure on effective verification, and Iran's unwillingness to disclose the "possible military dimensions" of its nuclear program did not bode well for a postagreement future when such pressures would have dissipated. In sum, he argued, "sacrificing knowledge of past and possibly present actions for a future agreement would signal to Tehran at the outset that verification and compliance will not be serious priorities."[41]

At the other end were proponents of an agreement that reflected scarce, if any, concern with lessons from the past. Extracting such lessons is a process ridden with cognitive biases described earlier, including the search for closure and parsimony reflecting the impact of excessive coherence and assumptions of states as monoliths, singular causal mechanisms, and linear and definitive outcomes. As Kahneman notes, "overconfidence is fed by the illusionary certainty of hindsight."[42] So how should past transgressions be considered? If such transgressions are equivalent to Bayesian base rates—revealing a certain probability of future noncompliance—ignoring them would be not merely a failure of Bayesian reasoning, a cognitive flaw, but could also lead to a colossal bargaining failure.[43]

Yet taking such a base rate at face value, as if it reflected Iran's preference as a monolithic entity, could also overstate the probability of future noncompliance. More accurate identification of the dominant domestic faction under which transgressions took place—a "causal base rate," reflecting the factors discussed in the first section of this chapter—might lead to improved updates of priors. Even then, openness to new information might reveal that actors associated with previous instances of noncompliance might have also evolved into more credible partners, a lesson especially pertinent to the Korean peninsula negotiations. Yet the P5+1 group can never discard the possibility that even seemingly credible partners who appear to have learned the right lessons from the past may cave under pressure from domestic opponents.[44]

Lessons from the past also inform Iranian negotiators and their opponents. Iran's hard-liners interpret the P5+1 process as one more instance of external coercion going back to the British- and U.S.-backed 1953 ousting of Iranian prime minister Mohammad Mossadegh, a concern reinforced by their ambivalence about Russian and Chinese designs vis-à-vis Iran.[45] The Trump administration has contributed to fueling this perception. This across-the-board suspicion of external actors is used skillfully to perpetuate an inward-looking strategy that was skeptical even of the most conciliatory P5+1 positions under the Obama administration. The Rouhani team may have been more prone to learn other lessons from previous, if half-hearted, attempts at reconciliation under the Clinton administration, given Rouhani's own role as a nuclear negotiator under Khatami. Rouhani's team urged the P5+1, however obliquely, to strike a deal that strengthened them against their opponents, a compelling argument prima facie. Yet, not all agree this was the best lesson to be learned.

In a rational world, extracting significant concessions from external negotiating partners—which Rouhani acknowledged was his negotiating strategy in the 1990s—should have buttressed the domestic position of Khatami's moderate camp back then. As it turned out, that was not the outcome; Khatami was replaced by ever more intractable hard-liners. Rouhani's contemporary team inferred that extracting robust concessions was merely a necessary, but in the end an insufficient, condition for staying in power and that only positive results from a complete removal of sanctions would ultimately cement favorable political results for Rouhani's faction. The intervening years since the signing of the JCPOA, especially after the Trump administration pulled the United States out of the deal, have only enhanced uncertainty on all sides about the proper lessons to be learned and from whom.

Turning to a state that acts as a sender of inducements, China's own transformation offered a model that others have tried to emulate. China's internationalizing shift reveals a learning process that left Mao's policy of support for any state's sovereign right to develop nuclear weapons behind for a more conventional nonproliferation posture. Sanctions were once deemed serious violations of noninterference under Mao's "Five Principles of Peaceful Coexistence," which challenged "hegemonistic" Soviet and Western dictates, much as Iran's (and Chinese) hard-liners do today. By 2003, officials still described China's position on nuclear proliferation as one that consistently opposed sanctions and coercion. Yet, China began endorsing UNSC resolutions sanctioning North Korea and Iran and has done so on multiple occasions since 2006.[46]

Those sanctions were less biting than others would have preferred, but Rouhani himself appears to have understood the change in China's adherence to them. In his 2005 statement, Rouhani argued that China could not be counted on to defend Iran's nuclear behavior:

> Most of the activities that we had not reported to the IAEA had already been reported to the IAEA by other countries that had worked with us and that were party to those activities, such as China. We had certain projects with China in the past that, according to the regulations, we had to report to the IAEA and had not

done so.... China, for instance, has hundreds of billions of dollars' worth of trade with the West, with Europe, and is not ready to jeopardize all that for our [Iran's] sake.... The powerful countries are all against [our nuclear fuel cycle activities].[47]

In 2012, China indeed reduced by half its purchases from Iran and urged Iran consistently to cooperate with the International Atomic Energy Agency (IAEA). Then-premier Wen Jiabao, expressing strong criticism of Iran's nuclear defiance, stated in Qatar that China "adamantly opposes Iran developing and possessing nuclear weapons" and warned Iran against closing the Strait of Hormuz, an action that would be regarded as "aggression against most of the world's nations."[48]

China also got tougher on North Korea over time. China supported limited sanctions on North Korea following its 2006 first nuclear test, but after the second test in 2009, China endorsed UNSC resolution 1874 calling on states to "inspect and destroy all banned cargo," imposing financial sanctions, asset freezes, and targeted travel bans (a rare concession), and blocking trade in nuclear and missile components. Only after it returned to the NPT, Chinese officials argued, would North Korea enjoy the right to peaceful use of nuclear energy. Meanwhile, China would "implement the resolution earnestly."[49] China has endorsed even stronger resolutions since, but increased instability in North Korea has led to uneven implementation. China's leadership appears to have learned that positive inducements alone have not only not achieved desired results in North Korea but have indeed undermined their authority within China itself.

CONCLUSIONS

The strategic interaction between senders and targets of inducements to abandon nuclear designs is one fraught with potential for biased and flawed interpretations of both past learning and current intentions and behavior. Applying some insights from behavioral economics reveals some of the sources of systematic bias and excessive reliance on assumptions of full rationality. Interlocutors rarely represent monolithic preferences, which analysts often derive from vague estimations of what drives aggregate state behavior. Parties to negotiations are rarely as unified, or as divided, as their interlocutors may assume. External inducements have distributional costs on senders and targets that are not always easy to estimate a priori. Prospect-theoretic effects often modify expectations from models assuming stable, unchanging preferences across time, space, and circumstances. Inducements can have a wider—and certainly nonlinear—range of effects than the standard dichotomous outcomes (they worked; they didn't work) that observers often expect. Inducements operate through multiple causal mechanisms that add far more complexity and contingency. Neglect of intricate, interim, and indirect effects may lead to inaccurate assessment of outcomes and of inducements that might have worked in an alternative sequence of events. Excessive coherence bias is rampant not only among actors but analysts as well, affecting the ability to assess what lessons might have been learned from experience.

Improved knowledge about these and other systematic deviations from rationality does not guarantee that we can anticipate outcomes with any more certainty. It can, however, increase our awareness of thought repertoires at all stages of the bargaining process, help frame bargaining positions, and ultimately improve our understanding of statecraft geared to prevent the further proliferation of nuclear weapons.

NOTES

1. Positive inducements are benefits or rewards extended to target states to persuade them to eschew nuclear weapons. Security assurances are one form of positive inducements; see Jeffrey W. Knopf, ed., *Security Assurances and Nuclear Nonproliferation* (Stanford, Calif.: Stanford University Press, 2012). Sanctions are negative inducements designed to punish or deny benefits to target states to dissuade them from acquiring nuclear weapons; see Etel Solingen, ed., *Sanctions, Statecraft, and Nuclear Proliferation* (Cambridge: Cambridge University Press, 2012). References to inducements henceforth imply both positive and negative ones unless otherwise specified. For an excellent study of sanctions in nonproliferation, see Nicholas L. Miller, "The Secret Success of Nonproliferation Sanctions," *International Organization* 68, no. 4 (Fall 2014): 913–44.

2. Robert Jervis, *Perception and Misperception in International Politics* (Princeton, N.J.: Princeton University Press, 1976), ch. 8.

3. Robert Jervis, "The Future of World Politics: Will It Resemble the Past?" *International Security* 16, no. 3 (Winter 1991/92): 39–73.

4. The supply side is also used to refer to the availability of materials and technology needed to build nuclear arms, but the focus in this chapter is on the supply of external inducements, both positive and negative.

5. An example is the presumed uncontroversial "knowledge" that "external threats against Iran" were the leading reason for Iranian interest in a possible nuclear weapon (see, for instance, Paul Pillar, "Correspondence: Nuclear Negotiations with Iran," *International Security* 38, no. 1 [2013]: 174–92). This statement ignores a much longer trajectory in Iran's pursuit of nuclear weapons, fueled by far more diverse causal drivers and reflecting different proclivities by different actors.

6. John Vasquez, *The Power of Power Politics: From Classical Realism to Neotraditionalism* (Cambridge: Cambridge University Press, 1998); Jeffrey W. Legro and Andrew Moravcsik, "Is Anyone Still a Realist?" *International Security* 24, no. 2 (1999): 5–55.

7. Etel Solingen, *Nuclear Logics: Contrasting Paths in East Asia and the Middle East* (Princeton, N.J.: Princeton University Press, 2007).

8. Ibid.

9. Ibid.

10. Daniel Kahneman and Amos Tversky, "Prospect Theory: An Analysis of Decision under Risk," *Econometrica* 47, no. 2 (1979): 263–91; Robert Jervis, "Political Implications of Loss Aversion," in *Avoiding Losses/Taking Risks: Prospect Theory in International Politics*,

ed. B. Farnham (Ann Arbor: University of Michigan Press, 1994), 23–40; Rose McDermott, *Risk-Taking in International Politics: Prospect Theory in American Foreign Policy* (Ann Arbor: University of Michigan Press, 1998); Rose McDermott, "Prospect Theory in Political Science: Gains and Losses from the First Decade," *Political Psychology* 25, no. 2 (2004): 289–312; Jonathan Mercer, "Rationality and Psychology in International Politics," *International Organization* 59, no. 1 (2005): 77–106.

11. On the use of counterfactuals to probe nonlinear causation, see Richard Ned Lebow, *Forbidden Fruit: Counterfactuals and International Relations* (Princeton, N.J.: Princeton University Press, 2010).

12. Daniel Kahneman, *Thinking, Fast and Slow* (New York: Farrar, Straus and Giroux, 2011), 74–76, 82–85.

13. This is analogous to "belief-system overkill"; see Jervis, *Perception and Misperception*, 129.

14. See examples in Solingen, *Sanctions, Statecraft, and Nuclear Proliferation*.

15. Celia Reynolds and Wilfred T. Wan, "Empirical Trends in Sanctions and Positive Inducements in Nonproliferation," in Solingen, *Sanctions, Statecraft, and Nuclear Nonproliferation*, 56–122.

16. Stephen Haggard and Marcus Noland, "Economic Crime and Punishment in North Korea," *Political Science Quarterly* 127, no. 4 (2012): 659–83.

17. This is akin to a counterfactual claim: "Had more positive inducements been offered, the result would have been what we predicted." As Tetlock and Lebow have argued, "the more credence observers place in relevant covering laws, and the stronger their cognitive-stylistic preferences for explanatory closure, the more likely they are to be guided by those covering laws in judging what could have been, and the less likely they are to make judgments of historical contingency on a case-by-case basis." Philip Tetlock and Richard Ned Lebow, "Poking Counterfactual Holes in Covering Laws: Cognitive Styles and Historical Reasoning," *American Political Science Review* 95, no. 4 (2001): 830.

18. Estimates in 2015 suggest that sanctions had cost Iran over $160 billion in oil revenues since 2012, contributing—along with the decline in oil prices—to a 9 percent GDP decline by March 2014 (a GDP 15–20 percent smaller than Iran's pre-2012 growth trajectory would have yielded). See Institute of International Finance (IIF) estimates, December 7, 2014, https://en.zamanalwsl.net/news/7852.html; and Jacob J. Lew, "Remarks of Treasury Secretary Jacob J. Lew to the Washington Institute," Washington, D.C., April 29, 2015, http://www.washingtoninstitute.org/policy-analysis/view/remarks-of-treasury-secretary-jacob-j.-lew. Iran's currency also lost over 60 percent of its value against the U.S. dollar in this time period.

19. William Tobey, "Lessons Learned from Past Negotiations to Prevent Nuclear Proliferation," testimony before the Senate Foreign Relations Committee, U.S. Capitol, Washington D.C., June 24, 2015, http://belfercenter.ksg.harvard.edu/files/Tobey_Lessons%20Learned%20from%20Past%20Negotiations%20to%20Prevent%20Nuclear%20Proliferation.pdf.

20. Muhammad Sahimi, "The Chain Murders: Killing Dissidents and Intellectuals, 1988–1998," January 5, 2011, *Frontline*, PBS, https://www.pbs.org/wgbh/pages/frontline/tehranbureau/2011/01/the-chain-murders-killing-dissidents-and-intellectuals-1988-1998.html.

21. Jessica Mathews argued that "for the first time in the long nuclear standoff, Iran is paying a price for its pursuit of nuclear weapons." "The World in 2013," Carnegie Endowment for International Peace, November 29, 2012, http://carnegieendowment.org/globalten/?fa=50178.

22. Solingen, *Sanctions, Statecraft, and Nonproliferation*.

23. Haggard and Noland, "Economic Crime and Punishment."

24. On the oil boycott, see "Chinese Oil Embargo Paralyzes North Korean Army," *Chosum Ilbo*, June 30, 2015.

25. BBC News, "Ahmadinejad: New UN Iran Sanctions 'Fit for Dustbin,'" June 10, 2010, http://www.bbc.co.uk/news/10280356.

26. Economist Saeed Laylaz, a credible Iranian analyst who acknowledged the costs of sanctions and who also served as advisor to reformers Khatami and Mousavi, was arrested by Ahmadinejad and banned from publishing the business daily *Sarmayeh*. Laylaz had declared Iran as "the most financially corrupt country in the history of the Middle East." Arash Karami, "Iranian Economist: I Can't Recollect Such 'Corruption and Plunder,'" *Iran Pulse*, February 7, 2014, http://iranpulse.al-monitor.com/index.php/2014/02/3852/iranian-economist-i-cant-recollect-such-corruption-and-plunder.

27. Philip E. Tetlock, *Expert Political Judgment: How Good Is It? How Can We Know?* (Princeton, N.J.: Princeton University Press, 2005).

28. Haggard and Noland, "Economic Crime and Punishment."

29. A number of pre-2011 polls on the Arab world asked questions about external actors (the United States, Iran, Israel) and failed to identify the primacy of domestic drivers of discontent that led to the 2011 upheavals. See Timur Kuran, "Now out of Never: The Element of Surprise in the East European Revolution of 1989," *World Politics* 44, no. 1 (1991): 7–48. For an important exception, see Amaney Jamal and Mark Tessler, "Attitudes in the Arab World," *Journal of Democracy* 19, no. 1 (2008) 97–110.

30. Daniel W. Drezner, "An Analytically Eclectic Approach to Sanctions and Nonproliferation," in Solingen, *Sanctions, Statecraft, and Nuclear Proliferation*, 154–73.

31. Tetlock and Lebow, "Poking Counterfactual Holes," 830.

32. Khamenei was regarded as a hard-liner aligned with the commander of the Revolutionary Guards Mohammed Jafari and the head of the elite al-Quds Force General Qassem Suleimani.

33. Kahneman, *Thinking, Fast and Slow*, ch. 9.

34. In *Perception and Misperception*, Jervis notes the biased assumption that interlocutors are more unified than they really are. The opposite bias of assuming far more division on the other side than may be the case may also be in play.

35. Press TV, "Resistance Economy, Long-Term Strategy for Iran: Leader," March 11, 2014, http://www.presstv.com/detail/2014/03/11/354217/resistance-economy-longterm-strategy.

36. Abbas Milani and Karim Sadjadpour, "Testimony to House Committee on Foreign Affairs, Iran: Recent Developments and Implications for U.S. Policy," 111th Cong., 1st sess., (2009), 81–83, http://foreignaffairs.house.gov/111/51254.pdf; Nazenin Ansari and Jonathan Paris, "The Message from the Streets of Tehran," *New York Times*, November 6, 2009.

37. Miroslav Nincic, *The Logic of Positive Engagement* (Ithaca, N.Y.: Cornell University Press, 2012).

38. Tobey, "Lessons Learned from Past Negotiations."

39. Ibid.

40. David E. Sanger, "Obama Sees an Iran Deal That Could Avoid Congress," *New York Times*, October 19, 2014.

41. Tobey, "Lessons Learned from Past Negotiations." See also the open letter sent by former advisors to the Obama administration, including former chief adviser on nuclear policy Gary Samore, described in David E. Sanger, "Ex-Advisers Warn Obama that Iran Nuclear Deal 'May Fall Short' of Standards," *New York Times*, June 24, 2015.

42. Kahneman, *Thinking, Fast and Slow*, 14.

43. Ibid., 169.

44. An informed Iranian expert suggested that "we are either witnessing an Iranian president seeking room to pursue his own moderate inclinations on foreign-policy issues in the face of an inflexible, and suspicious, supreme leader, or the Iranian leadership is being pushed in one direction, and then another, by rapidly shifting winds." Haleh Esfandiari, "Interpreting Iran's Mixed Messages," Wilson Center, Middle East Program, September 24, 2014, http://pages.wilsoncenter.org/index.php/email/emailWebview?mkt_tok=3RkMMJWWfF9wsRouv6%2FIZKXonjHpfsX56u0vWq6ylMI%2F0ER3fOvrPUfGjI4ATcBjMK%2BTFAwTG5toziV8R7LEJcltzMAQXRXh.

45. For a view that the role of external forces in 1953 was far smaller than Iranian hardliners posit, see Robert Jervis, "Foreign Affairs Focus: Robert Jervis on Nuclear Diplomacy," March 12, 2014, https://www.foreignaffairs.com/videos/2014-03-12/foreign-affairs-focus-robert-jervis-nuclear-diplomacy.

46. On the evolution of China's policy on sanctions on nonproliferation, see Etel Solingen, "Three Scenes of Sovereignty and Power," in *Back to Basics: Rethinking Power in the Contemporary World*, ed. Martha Finnemore and Judith Goldstein (New York: Oxford University Press, 2013), 105–38.

47. Speech to the Supreme Cultural Revolution Council, "Beyond the Challenges Facing Iran and the IAEA Concerning the Nuclear Dossier," Rahbord (in Persian), September 30, 2005, 7–38, Iran Watch, November 1, 2004, https://www.iranwatch.org/library/government/iran/ministry-foreign-affairs/beyond-challenges-facing-iran-and-iaea-concerning-nuclear-dossier.

48. Michael Wines, "China Leader Warns Iran Not to Make Nuclear Arms," *New York Times*, January 21, 2012, 8. Yin Gang, a Middle East expert at the Chinese Academy of Social Sciences, argued that "the Iranians have disappointed China time after time with their nuclear program. . . . If Iran continues with its nuclear program in this manner, they should not expect China to acquiesce," *Los Angeles Times*, April 2, 2010, A3.

49. United Nations, "Security Council, Acting Unanimously, Condemns in Strongest Terms Democratic People's Republic of Korea Nuclear Test, Toughens Sanctions," June 12, 2009, http://www.un.org/News/Press/docs/2009/sc9679.doc.htm; NTI, Global Security Newswire, "U.S. Says North Korean Blast 'Probably' Nuclear," June 16, 2009.

CHAPTER SIX

Justice and the Nonproliferation Regime

HARALD MÜLLER

Among the most momentous findings of behavioral economics is the rehabilitation of the time-honored but long discredited philosophical and religious view of the human being as endowed with a moral sense, notably a sense of fairness or justice. The most heralded tool to explore this proposition—but by no means the only one—was the ultimatum game. In this game (which is described in detail in in the introduction and chapter 4), one player proposes a split of some money; if the other player accepts, both receive the proposed split, but if she rejects they both get nothing. Experiments with this game, which simulates human decision making in distributional conflicts, proved that the behavior of players deviated significantly and systematically from predictions on the basis of the standard behavior of the "economic man" model; specifically, players reject highly unequal splits even though this leaves them with a lower payout than they would receive from saying "yes." On this basis, Fehr and Schmidt developed an innovative "Theory of Fairness, Competition, and Cooperation." They showed that fairness, which serves as a way of assessing justice and is a key feature of cooperative behavior, was not only part and parcel of the economic behavior of real-world subjects but a necessary condition for competition to function as a welfare-enhancing mechanism.[1]

In addition to experimental work such as tests using the ultimatum game, neuroscientific research has corroborated and provided a biological basis for findings about the central role of justice in human affairs. Fehr, for instance, confirmed his theory by measuring brain processes that occur during distributive choices.[2] This research reveals an innate sense of fairness by measuring positive (feelings of happiness) and negative (feelings of disgust) reactions to experiences of fairness and injustice, respectively.[3]

The other branch of science that has contributed to this body of theory was evolutionary game theory. The work of Brian Skyrms, first written 1996 and considerably amended in 2014, shows how cooperative behavior, notably in terms of fairness/justice, could prevail in the history of the evolutionary "competition for fitness" over more selfish strategies.[4]

The work by Fehr and Skyrms, inter alia, follows the proposition—counterintuitive as it was in the age of "economic man" and the "selfish gene"—that if prosocial behavior is a behavioral fact, then it must be a result of the evolution of humankind, which selected genetic and cultural traits that afford human beings the capacity to work together socially, including, in particular, a "sense of fairness" and behavior that is at least partially guided by this sense.[5] If this is so, then empirical disciplines beyond behavioral economics should have found indications for this proposition. And indeed, twenty years of progress in neuroscience, evolutionary biology, primate research, and behavioral economics have delivered empirical findings that converge on an insight that amounts to a revolution in the social sciences: issues of fairness and justice exert a heavy impact on human decision making and social behavior.

New scientific insights, not the least in some "hard sciences," undermine the images of humans as governed solely by a narrow type of selfishness. Evolutionary biologists, primate researchers, and anthropologists have explained the competitive advantages of species living in social communities, which result from fairness rules concerning the distribution of food and the punishment for unruly behavior.[6] Such rules were found both in groups of our next relatives, the primates, and early human societies. These modes of behavior reflect justice- and fairness-guided motivations. Neuroscientists have clarified the biochemical processes connected with experiences that are perceived as just or unjust and identified the regions of the brain where these processes originate.[7] These findings help us to understand that our everyday experiences of both the satisfaction of being treated justly as well as the frustration of suffering perceived injustice are connected to strong emotions such as disgust or anger, in the latter case stimulating even violent reactions. Sociologists have confirmed the finding of behavioral economists in many experiments showing that persons in games simulating distributive conflict and dilemmas deviate from the model of utility maximizing behavior in favor of rules of fair distribution.[8] Developmental psychologists have found the capacity for fair behavior already exists in early childhood and have followed the unfolding of this trait throughout the growth of the child's and adolescent's psychic capacity.[9]

This chapter explores the role of justice concerns—and the resulting disputes and conflicts—on the stability of the nuclear nonproliferation regime and the dynamics of its normative development. The nonproliferation regime is a quintessentially unequal order given the two-tier structure of nuclear weapon states (NWS) and nonnuclear weapon states (NNWS) as enshrined in the nuclear Non-Proliferation Treaty (NPT). For this reason the regime suffers from justice frustration that renders it harder and harder to make any progress.

Following Nancy Fraser's typology, I distinguish between three dimensions of justice that might lead to conflict.[10] Distributive justice concerns the allocation of (material and immaterial) values and goods among actors. Procedural justice issues are related to the decision-making structures in the regime. Recognition justice—the most fundamental dimension—concerns who is recognized by the others as an actor of equal standing, as a carrier of entitlements with the authority to make justice claims in the first place.

Starting with an analysis of how the unequal structure of the nonproliferation regime is bound to produce disputes about justice issues, the analysis illustrates this point by examining the cases of disarmament, export controls/peaceful uses, and nuclear security (part of which have been entrusted to extra-NPT institutions). The analysis will show how intimately related the justice issue is to the most troubling causes of confrontation among parties, and how it creates showstoppers for well-minded and quite reasonable suggestions for regime improvement. The chapter draws on the proceedings of extra-NPT institutions in addition to NPT Review Conferences.

The chapter then summarizes how justice disputes affect regime stability and constructive normative development in light of new challenges; it also points to the interesting and somehow surprising insight that conflicts over justice have been used occasionally to create constructive solutions that have made the regime better and have overcome blockage and stalemate. The conclusions review the main findings and suggest some roads for future research. Throughout the chapter, I draw heavily on a book that I coedited with Carmen Wunderlich for the empirics. I also rely on a study we prepared jointly for the Swedish Radiation Safety Authority and on an article coauthored with Marco Fey and Aviv Melamud.[11]

JUSTICE AND POLITICS: THE AMBIVALENT RELATION

We are accustomed to think that politics, notably high politics that deal with conflicts of interest, peace, and war, are fundamentally distinct from ethical and moral considerations to which justice issues belong. We are equally accustomed under rationalist hegemony to think of this realm as the fiefdom of cool strategic calculation, remote from emotions. But if the sense of justice is part of both our genetic and our cultural inheritance, then it is utterly implausible that politics, as a central area of human activity, could be isolated from its influence. In the end, this is an empirical question, and some studies, which I will note below, have started to document the empirical evidence for the role of justice concerns in world politics.

Justice "goes political" by channeling the desires and demands of actors through the "justice motive," a concept that was first developed by sociologist Melvin Lerner. Translating the ancient principle of *suum cuique* (to each his own) into modern language, Lerner sees the justice needs of an actor satisfied if this actor has realized his or her entitlement. The actor develops a subjective understanding of his/her entitlements against the background of culture and lifeworld and in comparison with other actors. When the actor's situation and the claims to which the actor believes he or she is entitled are in contradiction, that is when reality falls short of fulfilling anticipated entitlements; this triggers the justice motive, the drive to reduce this discrepancy.[12] The justice motive can work at the individual and the collective level; for example, the nationalistic claim to get back lost territory that putatively belonged to one's nation in ancient times has been a driver of domestic and international conflict and has motivated and mobilized huge masses of humans from the beginning of history until our time.

Once we stop the futile quest for a theory of justice acceptable to everybody and recognize the subjective core of the justice motive, we will not be surprised by empirical findings that show the deep ambivalences toward the pursuit of justice in politics: When justice claims—where moral demands and ordinary interests mix up in ways frequently unnoticed by claimants—are accepted and fulfilled in a given grouping, rules gain legitimacy, and peace is given a chance. Where they remain unsatisfied and frustrated, order experiences heavy stress and violence looms.

Justice claims in politics are thus bound to have one of two outcomes. On the one hand, the settlement of disputes becomes possible, and solutions have a chance of lasting if they satisfy the justice claims of all relevant actors or are perceived by them as reasonably just when the outcomes for all parties are compared.[13] On the other hand, incompatible justice claims or contradictory justice principles applied to a specific case may lead to enduring disputes and stimulate strong emotions that make the rational management of the conflict difficult or impossible and motivate parties to resort to violent behavior.[14]

Two factors give rise to this ambiguity. First, our disposition for justice is not impartial or symmetrical. We react most strongly as far as our own individual justice claims are concerned. We are considerably engaged when those of our in-group are involved. And we have the capability, still measurable, but also definitely weaker than the two preceding situations, to develop empathy with the justice claims of strangers (including out-groups).[15] It is this latter capability on which the pacifying potential of justice rests. It is the former two capabilities that drive its potential for conflict.

Second, our basic genetic disposition for the sense of justice does not determine the content with which we fill the term *justice*.[16] This filling happens during the long socialization process to which humans are subjected and differs between cultures. As a consequence, there are vastly different ideas in the world—and in the heads and souls of humans—about what justice means and how to implement it. The claim for justice is a universal phenomenon; the understanding of what justice means is not.

The impact of this dichotomy on politics is of particular salience because of the emotions involved. There is a growing understanding in political science and international relations that politics is not precisely the exchange of coolly calculated strategic moves that the rationalist ideal type postulates. Rather, emotions, based on basic functions of our brain, are an integral part of all our processes of cognition, evaluation, and decision.[17] As stated earlier, justice issues trigger strong positive and negative emotions, depending on whether an outcome is experienced as one of justice or injustice. These emotions can make friendship deeper and reconciliation easier or, alternatively, make agreement more difficult and violent conflict more likely.

THE IMPACT OF JUSTICE CONCERNS ON INTERNATIONAL RELATIONS: PIONEERING WORK

Even though the concept of justice was present at the dawn of systematic political thinking, the realist/rationalist school of thought has prevented it from obtaining its rightful place in the discipline of international relations, with a few remarkable exceptions. David Welch, Bill Zartman, Cecilia Albin, Dan Druckman, and Richard Ned Lebow stand out as the pioneers of this approach.

The impact of justice concerns on war and peace was confirmed by the pioneering study of David Welch on justice and the origins of major war, which applied Lerner's concept of the justice motive.[18] Path breaking in both theoretical and empirical terms, Welch's study found justice claims as part of the causal mechanism leading to war in the majority of his cases (that his book did not trigger a major research program on the issue documents the strength of rationalist hegemony).[19] Shifting the focus from the impact of perceived injustice to that of just outcomes, Bill Zartman identified agreement on a "justice formula," on which the parties to a conflict agree and which will guide devising solutions at the microlevel, as a precondition for successful conflict settlement.[20] Among the important findings in a series of studies by Cecilia Albin and Dan Druckman is the insight that peace agreements that include a comprehensive set of justice principles have tended to last longer than agreements lacking this feature.[21]

From a different angle, Ned Lebow reconstructed the connection between justice, society, and international relations: he offered an original rereading of the Greek classics by Thucydides, Plato, and Aristotle.[22] Their understanding of a multilayer human soul in which the idea of what belongs to each individual and social class is rooted in the desire for "standing"—closely related to Nancy Fraser's concept of "recognition justice"—made justice a central focus of human interaction in society, politics, and international relations (then largely relations between sovereign cities).

These pioneers did enough work to make engaging with justice issues in international politics a promising endeavor. The field of security should be a hard case for this approach, as this has been the realm of the realist paradigm more than any other competing theory. Nevertheless, security issues have been the subject of the pioneering studies from the beginning. An important example was Cecilia Albin's study on justice in international negotiations, which included the first inquiry of the justice problematic concerning the NPT. She showed the strong impact that justice concerns had during the negotiations that produced this treaty and how the disputes present between different groups and their justice concerns shaped the undertakings laid down in the NPT, constituting frontlines for intergroup conflict until today.[23]

JUSTICE CONFLICTS IN THE NONPROLIFERATION REGIME

The inherent inequality in the nuclear nonproliferation regime, which feeds misgivings about justice, has been discussed many times over, but most of the time, the connection to the overarching theme of justice is not made. There are a few remarkable exceptions, most of them rather recently. Harald Müller followed Albin's work (see above) by identifying justice disputes as the main driver behind well-known conflicts within the regime, notably (but not exclusively) between the nonaligned movement (NAM) countries and the NWS.[24] Nina Tannenwald arrived independently at the same conclusions.[25] Müller et al. then drew attention to parallels and differences among justice disputes in the three weapons of mass destruction (WMD) regimes and showed that the impact on the regimes' capability to address new challenges was not determined by the mere presence of justice conflicts but depended on their form and the way actors handled them.[26] Finally, Fey, Melamud, and Müller demonstrated how justice claims impacted the early skepticism of West Germany toward the NPT and what it took to overcome this impact to change Germany from a reluctant to a proactive member of the NPT community.[27]

Nuclear Disarmament

Justice conflicts in the regime start with the key contradiction between nuclear deterrence and nuclear disarmament. Within the small group of NWS, there are two frontlines. The first one runs between the United States on the one hand and Russia and China on the other hand and concerns the notion of "equal security." It pits the U.S. drive for absolute superiority or "full spectrum dominance" against Chinese and Russian attempts to curb national missile defense, treat offensive long-range conventional strike options ("prompt global strike") as equivalent with offensive nuclear capability, and prevent the deployment of weapons in outer space that could impact the nuclear balance. The second one is located between the two "nuclear superpowers"—the United States and Russia—and the other three NWS, which hold smaller nuclear arsenals. Here, the issue is at what point the smaller three should join the big two in disarmament negotiations. While the first conflict is fed by notions of equality as establishing equal entitlements, the second one points to inequality as justifying different treatment in favor of the weaker parties.

The most disruptive, persistent, and consequential conflict has been the one between the NWS and the NNWS on nuclear disarmament. This dispute centers on whether nonproliferation or disarmament is of more weight in the fabric of the NPT.[28] This issue is pivotal as it concerns the basically unequal structure of the NPT. The justice content of the issue concerns the perceived immorality of a situation in which a small group of states could annihilate any possible adversary and probably destroy whole regions and even the world as a whole, while the rest have to hope haplessly that the goodwill and reason of the states possessing nuclear weapons will prevent this fatal event from ever happening. The profound unfairness of this dependency that NNWS had not chosen, and of a self-appointed "stewardship" of the NWS that the NNWS had never voluntarily transferred to them, can only be removed by all states becoming equal through nuclear disarmament; this is the justice objective of Article VI of the NPT, which contains the essential obligation of nuclear disarmament and which was inserted into the initial American-Soviet draft on the insistence of NNWS.[29] It is worth considering what justice dimension is at stake in the disarmament controversy. One could assume that this is a *distributive* justice conflict in which the highly valued good of security is at stake, and the problem is the unequal distribution of this good between NWS and NNWS.

This interpretation grasps certainly a part of the disarmament dispute, but there may be more to it; the bifurcation of the world in those possessing absolute destructive power and those being completely dependent on them constitutes two drastically unequal groups of actors. This creates problems of identity and status. There were unsuccessful attempts to neutralize the problem through legally binding security guarantees that would grant assistance to NNWS in case of a nuclear threat and oblige the NWS to abstain from such threats and, of course, from making good on them. Present security assurances fall short of NNWS demands.[30] This bifurcation, then, is combined with the frustrating perception that the NWS are engaged not in nuclear disarmament but rather in the functional adaptation of their nuclear arsenals to a changed security situation, which is incidentally compatible with quantitative reductions but is not at all carried out with the objective of moving toward a nuclear-weapon-free world. Even worse, in the last few years the indications have multiplied that we are moving back into a new nuclear arms race, this time involving more than just two states. If this interpretation—which is widely held among NNWS—is valid, it means a categorical refusal of eliminating the status inequality by NWS. With these elements, we have the structure of a *recognition* conflict in which the small, privileged group rejects recognizing the rest in the capacity in which the rest wants to be recognized, as fully equal actors on the world stage. Since recognition conflicts are the justice conflicts that are most emotionally loaded and thus of most potential consequence, we should expect visible and strong manoeuvres by the disadvantaged parties to create an even position, as I will discuss below.

Since the NPT entered into force, NNWS have generally demanded meaningful steps toward a world without nuclear weapons. Different states do so with differences in emphasis and determination. Those allied to NWS are only moderately outspoken in their disarmament rhetoric, as they themselves rely on extended deterrence for their security. Neutral countries from the industrialized world usually try to find ways to push the disarmament agenda forward but try to avoid uttering demands that the NWS will refuse outright as too utopian and radical. Most NAM states take very principled positions and stick to specific demands, such as negotiating a nuclear weapons convention or agreeing on a binding timetable for reaching a nuclear-weapon-free world, which are known to be unacceptable to the NWS.[31]

One of the most momentous developments in recent years has been the alliance between "northern" neutrals and "southern" NAM states to pursue a treaty to ban nuclear weapons, a purpose that succeeded in 2017 when more than 120 states in the UN General Assembly approved a treaty text against the express preference of the NWS and their allies.[32] The impetus for the movement comes from the frustration triggered by the inequality embedded in the NPT. Today, it is not just the slow pace of disarmament that drives NNWS emotions from frustration to resentment to hostility toward the NWS and their allies. It is the feeling of being the victim to an offense constituted by two NWS attitudes: first, the cavalier refusal to honor commitments made during successful NPT reviews (e.g., to negotiate and bring into force a Comprehensive Nuclear-Test-Ban Treaty and a Fissile Material Cut-off Treaty); second, the claim of the NWS that nuclear disarmament is their exclusive turf and that the have-nots have no seat at the table.[33] Both types of behavior suggest that the NWS keep nuclear weapons not for security needs but because they believe in a privileged status derived from nuclear weapons possession.

The ban negotiations enabled the NNWS to show agency instead of passivity. The treaty effort grew out of the Humanitarian Initiative (HI). Promoted by most NNWS and several NGOs increasingly concerned about the humanitarian consequences of nuclear war, the HI became a vehicle for them to act determinedly to leave passivity behind. That the NWS abstained from most HI conferences and eventually from the ban negotiations convinced the majority that they had established a process of self-empowerment that put the NWS at the receiving end for the first time.

Nonproliferation and Peaceful Uses

If nuclear disarmament stands by itself as one source of dispute—at least at first glance (but as I will discuss below it can be connected to other issues through "justice linkage")—the two other pillars of the NPT, nonproliferation and peaceful uses of nuclear energy, are closely coupled in the second major justice discourse. The name of the NPT reflects the priority afforded to nonproliferation by the United States and Russia. For a majority of parties—and this has long included even close allies of the United States—the three pillars must be given equal weight, and nonproliferation measures must be calibrated so as not to impede unduly the opportunity for NNWS to enjoy the peaceful uses of nuclear energy.

Particularly because the NWS are accorded the (supposedly temporary) privilege of vastly superior weaponry, they should not draw from this privilege additional (unfair) advantages concerning peaceful uses.[34] This justice demand, based on the well-established justice principle of equal opportunity, was strongly emphasized by a group of industrialized countries including Japan, Germany, Belgium, and Switzerland, among others, during the first twenty years of the NPT's existence. It led to at times acerbic disputes within the NPT process (namely during review conferences) and outside of it (e.g., during the evaluation of fuel cycle alternatives in the international fuel cycle evaluation (INFCE) process of the late 1970s). The said industrialized countries defended their right to develop the full fuel cycle and to take their own sovereign decisions on nuclear trade with a vigor that was not so dissimilar from the Iranian obstinacy during the years before agreement was achieved in 2015 (though without a parallel to the Iranian noncompliance record). They suspected that their nuclear-armed allies were aiming at a competitive advantage for their nuclear industries, unfairly disadvantaging the companies of their nonnuclear weapons friends. The latter ones reacted by opposing stricter policies in the areas of nuclear exports and nuclear safeguards as well as constraints on fuel cycle development.[35]

The controversy lost acrimony and salience after the revelations of Iraq's clandestine nuclear weapons program but was still visible and audible during the reform of the Nuclear Suppliers Group (NSG) guidelines in the early 1990s, the negotiations on the Additional Protocol in the IAEA in the mid-1990s, and deliberations on multinational fuel cycle arrangements in the first decade of this century.[36] And it must be emphasized that while the discourse between the United States and its allies on these issues became more constructive, the positions expressed earlier by the latter states were increasingly taken over by NAM countries interested in nuclear energy, where the nonproliferation versus peaceful uses trade-off was not connected to equal opportunity but to the justice principles of need and compensation for injustice suffered in the colonial past. This interpretation is actually quite in line with the language of Article IV of the NPT, which emphasizes the needs and entitlements of developing countries by declaring the peaceful uses of nuclear energy an "inalienable right" of all members and which obliges members to cooperate in these peaceful uses and to make particular efforts in that regard in favor of the developing countries.

Universalism and the Injustice of Unequal Standards
By its basic objectives and ambitions, the NPT aims at universal membership. However, universality has not only not been achieved, it is unlikely to be achieved in the foreseeable future. Even though the NPT is the most universal multilateral arms control treaty ever, four countries—India, Pakistan, Israel, and North Korea—appear committed to staying out, and they all possess nuclear weapons and are presently determined to keep them.[37]

The fact that reality falls short of the goal of universality creates tensions, all the more so for the NPT parties that live in a nuclear-armed neighborhood involving one or more of the holdouts. This tension is strongest in the Middle East, where nuclear inequality adds to Arab frustration at the continued conflict regarding Palestine; the present state of this conflict, characterized by occupation and settlements, is perceived by Arab majorities as a profound injustice. Arabs (plus Iranians) feel also that regional states other than Israel are treated differently when they are under suspicion regarding nuclear ambitions (e.g., Iraq, Libya, Syria, Iran).[38]

The accusation that nonparties are treated better than NNWS party to the NPT, directed against the depositories or against the global north at large, has a long tradition. Indeed, in the first twenty years of the NPT, nonparties were frequently recipients of major, and at times sensitive, exports while most developing countries, at this time party to the NPT, had not progressed far enough in their development to even consider significant nuclear imports.[39] The situation was precarious as some of the recipients of nuclear imports were suspected (or even known) to have highly ambiguous intentions, including developing a "hedging" or even an open military option.

The situation changed when major nonparties with significant nuclear activities joined the NPT in the late 1980s and 1990s (such as Argentina, Brazil, Chile, Algeria, South Africa, Spain), and exporters party to the NPT agreed on new rules, which included "full-scope (comprehensive) safeguards," excluding nuclear transfers to nonparties. This change did not silence Arab suspicions about clandestine nuclear cooperation with Israel by a couple of Western countries but put the issue on the backburner for about fifteen years.

The conclusion of a nuclear agreement between the George W. Bush administration and India that treated the latter country like a NWS party to the NPT, and the ensuing change of rules in favor of India by the NSG, created bad feelings in quite a few NPT NNWS, including some NSG members, and reinforced such NAM feelings toward the NSG.[40] This should not come as surprise, as the apparent favoritism, which benefited a state that had defied the objectives of the NPT and not undergone the sacrifice that 185 NPT parties had undertaken, constituted a fairly obvious act of injustice, one that was initiated by a NWS without any consultation with anybody. The process enhances misgivings along the recognition justice front. And while India is important and powerful enough that smaller states have decided not to engage in continuous confrontation over the issue, the lasting impact on the "mood" among parties should not be underrated.

Procedural Justice

After distributive and recognition justice, procedural justice is the third and by no means minor dimension of the justice problematic. As with distributive justice, there is no universally agreed justice standard about who should participate in decisions and how, and again, we have to investigate how actors feel about that issue in order to understand the political dynamics that related justice claims engender. There can be a general presumption that actors desire to be in the decision game once the decisions will touch them.

In the context of the nonproliferation regime, we can distinguish between four levels of decisions that are taken not at the national level but internationally with the participation of several states or groups of states. The broadest participation we observe is in NPT Review Conferences (RevCons), where parties deliberate on how the NPT works, how it should work in the future, and what measures should be taken to make it work better. These decisions are all-inclusive. All NPT parties have the opportunity to participate, and decisions are customarily taken by consensus, even though there is the theoretical possibility, opened by the rules of procedure, to vote on a resolution with the same voting modalities that apply in the UN General Assembly.

Decisions on verification and other nonproliferation measures, and many decisions on peaceful uses, are taken in the IAEA with the inclusive General Conference and the exclusive (thirty-five-member) Board of Governors as the relevant organs. Decisions on compliance/noncompliance, on sanctions that are within the authority of the IAEA in case of noncompliance, and on referring a case of noncompliance to the United Nations Security Council (UNSC) are all made by the Board of Governors.

Noncompliance and enforcement policy that goes beyond the IAEA—the most crucial and critical cases—is within the authority of the UNSC. It cannot be different: in matters as crucial for global security as the proliferation of weapons of mass destruction, serious sanctions and even the use of force are possibilities, and only the UNSC can make such decisions under the legal rules of the UN Charter. Finally, decisions concerning rules for nuclear and nuclear-related dual-use trade are discussed and made by the NSG.

Naturally, all—or nearly all—inclusive decision-making bodies pose little problem for procedural justice. However, among the bodies enumerated above, most are of limited membership; this feature opens immediately the problem of exclusion. In addition, the exclusion problem falls more heavily on the global south than on the global north. In the UNSC and the IAEA Board of Governors, industrialized countries are overrepresented and thus exert disproportional influence. The NSG is almost an all northern club, with its "southern" membership constituting less than 10 percent of the total.

This constellation has created considerable resentment, notably regarding the roles of the UNSC and the NSG. In the case of the NSG, procedural justice concerns come on top of the misgivings about the distributive consequences related to associated burdens and access to peaceful uses.[41] The demand to negotiate universal rules for nuclear trade, a standard NAM request, is a direct response to the perceived injustice inherent in nuclear trade decision making.[42]

In the case of the UNSC, bad feelings emerge from the paradox that the erstwhile proliferators possess the authority to punish, if necessary by force, those who try to follow their example. Proposals to establish additional procedures beyond those prescribed by Article X of the NPT in case of withdrawal from the NPT fell on deaf ears because the UNSC would have to be eventually tasked with the more consequential decisions in that scenario, and the developing countries did not want to concede anything beyond the status quo. For the same reason, despite some attempts during RevCons, no endorsement of the role of the UNSC in the nuclear nonproliferation regime has been adopted by review conferences.[43] Canadian efforts to establish some mechanism in which the whole NPT membership would be empowered to engage in cases of noncompliance and withdrawal met the opposition of the NWS, which prefer to keep this brief in their own hands as permanent members of the UNSC.

JUSTICE LINKAGE

Justice linkage is a strategy by which weaker parties condition specific changes preferred by stronger parties, which they themselves regard as problematic on justice grounds, with changes in other areas that would rectify injustices of particular importance. The strategy reflects the classical bargaining move of "issue linkage" under the particular objective to improve the acceptance chances for one's own justice claims. In recent years, the NPT regime has witnessed such strategies by the NAM countries.[44]

Disarmament, Nonproliferation, and Peaceful Uses

The NAM countries have pulled together the three "pillars" of the NPT—disarmament, nonproliferation, and peaceful uses—in a way that blocked all progress in nonproliferation that would have brought new burdens to NNWS, including, particularly, new constraints on peaceful uses, as long as no tangible progress on nuclear disarmament was made. This strategy led to a freeze in progress on three issues.[45]

First, the strongly improved safeguards system enshrined in the Additional Protocol (AP) in 1997 fell victim to this strategy.[46] While a majority of NAM countries were willing to endorse it as voluntary measure, there was strong opposition to calling it the "state of the art standard for verification" and even stronger objections to making it binding. Representative of many moderate NAM members (of which quite a few had adopted the AP voluntarily), Brazil made it explicitly clear on several occasions that no new binding measure on nonproliferation was welcome as long as nuclear disarmament was not going forward. Reiterating this long-standing position, during general debate at the 2015 Review Conference, the Brazilian representative declared that "attempts to reinforce commitments on non-proliferation without previous concrete progress on nuclear disarmament could only further erode the Treaty regime."[47]

Second, the repeated attempts by industrialized countries (not only the NWS) to get recognition for the work of the NSG and to make its guidelines the accepted standard for export controls of all NPT parties did not succeed. Many NAM states see the NSG as a rich man's cartel designed to deprive developing countries of their right to access to civilian nuclear technology. This distrust, in addition to the justice linkage with disarmament, adds to the aversion of many to accept export controls as a legitimate and necessary instrument for effective nonproliferation. Against some expectation, not even the practice of implementing UNSC Resolution 1540, which had made NSG-equivalent export controls the obligation of all UN members, has helped to change this negative attitude.[48]

Third, proposals for multilateral nuclear fuel guarantees (MFG) and for multilateral nuclear fuel cycle arrangements (MNA), both designed to reduce incentives for the building of national capacities for uranium enrichment and spent fuel reprocessing, met considerable antipathies in the developing world. Unfortunately, the offers uniformly originated with industrialized countries (or their industries), while the addressees were uniformly developing countries (even though only Iran and Brazil had any specific activities related to the offers). In addition to the justice linkage problematic, there were issue-specific justice concerns that also motivated resistance. Fuel cycle activities fall squarely under the Article IV NPT formulation of the "inalienable right to enjoy the peaceful uses of nuclear energy" (which does not indicate, of course, whether to pursue them is a good idea or not). Policies to dissuade countries from making use of this right, then, are meant to talk them out of an entitlement, which is, from a justice perspective, highly sensitive, all the more so in the NPT environment that is already tilted towards inequality.

To make things worse, President George W. Bush, following the instinct of his administration for unilateralist behavior, had declared it the policy of the United States to deny fuel cycle technology to states that did not already possess it, thereby promising to add pressure and sanctions to the use of persuasion in order to deprive states of what the NAM regarded as their perfectly justified right. At the end of the MFG/MNA campaign, another basic inequality would have been established in addition to the NWS/NNWS divide, namely a bifurcation between fuel cycle technology owners and have-nots. Trust was completely lost during the debate concerning Bush's position.[49] In one of the few serious efforts to come up with a solution to the justice gap, the IAEA MNA Group of Experts pointed out that a principle of "no new national technology holders" could be established only as a universal norm that would be applied equally to all; this would require present technology holders to submit their respective national technologies and facilities to multinational control or even ownership.[50] Not surprisingly, this suggestion was not picked up by present technology holders. All the projects were dealt with as offers to sovereign states that would decide on the basis of their national interest, and consequently, multilateral fuel-supply ideas scored only very limited success. In the NPT context, the proposals were noted without explicit endorsement.

Justice Conflicts in the Nonproliferation Regime and Nuclear Security

A more recent issue that is close to, but still distinct from, the nuclear nonproliferation regime is nuclear security. In this field, concerns and considerations that originated in the realm of nonproliferation policies were applied and expanded to serve the essential objective of preventing nonstate actors from obtaining nuclear weapons, materials, or technologies.[51] In principle, nuclear security should be in the interest of all states as, contrary to state actors interested in these weapons, the type of terrorist that would try to acquire and potentially use nuclear devices or weapons could probably not be deterred. Thus, deterrence provides no reliable fallback position in the area of nuclear security. In an effort to jumpstart progress in this area, in 2010 U.S. president Barack Obama hosted the first of a series of Nuclear Security Summits.

The presumption that nuclear security is in the interest of all and would thus attract broad practical and normative support is borne out by reality only to a limited degree. While the United Kingdom and the United States considered attaching nuclear security to the nuclear nonproliferation regime as a "fourth pillar," they eventually decided not to try. The reason was the strong aversion of many countries to add still another area to the NPT setting, which might weaken the relative weight of peaceful uses and nuclear disarmament and, like nonproliferation, might be abused to invent new burdens for NNWS and new impediments for developing countries to earn the supposed sweet fruits of the peaceful uses of nuclear energy. As a consequence, the 2010 NPT RevCon touched upon nuclear security and experienced a most interesting controversial discussion of the Nuclear Security Summits, when Iran and a few friends tried to condemn the summits but met a series of statements by NAM peers, who called the summits a good thing.[52] But the RevCon did not endorse the notion of nuclear security as a "fourth pillar."[53]

In order to understand the related political mechanics of support and opposition better, a group of researchers at Peace Research Institute Frankfurt undertook a comparative study of different initiatives connected to nuclear security.[54] We analyzed the NSG, the Proliferation Security Initiative, the G8 Global Partnership against the Spread of Weapons and Materials of Mass Destruction, the Global Threat Reduction Initiative, the Global Initiative to Combat Nuclear Terrorism, and the Nuclear Security Summits. We compared mission, membership (with a view to exclusivity), structure/organization (looking for rather flat and flexible against rather hierarchical and rigid organization), decision-making structures (with a focus on binding/nonbinding), outreach, confrontational versus cooperative instruments, and relations to the NPT. We were interested in two outcome parameters, relative efficiency and acceptance.

We found that more inclusive, flexible initiatives with rather remote relations to the NPT, emphasizing cooperative rather than coercive measures, caused less opposition and showed at least as much, if not more, goal attainment (efficiency) than those with opposite attributes. Among cooperative measures, capacity building stands out as an instrument with the double advantage of buying enhanced support and legitimacy for the initiative as well as enhancing its success because enhanced capacity to act enables weaker participants to achieve better the initiative's objectives.[55] This finding supports those of Albin/Druckman and Zartman, which were discussed previously, that justice-informed agreements tend to work more efficiently.

Consequences for Regime Stability and Dynamics

As a rule of thumb, international regimes in the security field as well as smaller, more specific initiatives are in a better position to achieve their mission when there is unity and agreement in the membership rather than many conflicts, bad feelings, or hostility. This proposition applies already when unity and agreement are disturbed by traditional conflicts of interest. Negative consequences can be expected to be larger, and remedies will take more effort and face more difficulties, when regime conflicts are charged with justice claims. Emotions will run higher, parties will probably be more tenacious in the defense of their positions, and compromises will require the overcoming of deep attachments and some compensation for the failure to achieve the status of justice, which, after all, would be preferable to any alternative in the eye of the beholder.[56]

NORM DEVELOPMENT AND STAGNATION IN THE NPT

In the following I rely on empirics from NPT RevCons that managed to bridge existing gaps and from the nuclear security initiatives already presented. In the NPT, it has proved possible at times—and over time—to mitigate and find pragmatic solutions to some of the justice conflicts analyzed above, thereby enabling the regime to adapt some of its features to new or changed challenges. In some nuclear security initiatives, participants found measures to mitigate the justice problems in specific ways by addressing some of the inequalities at the heart of these problems and also by providing for working mechanisms that deprived procedural problems of their exacerbating impact on distributive cleavages.

Disarmament: What Does Article VI Mean?

Among the perpetual complaints against the NPT is the obvious—and unjust—difference between the undertakings of the NNWS, which are specific and precise, and those of the NWS, which are vague and fail to require any specific action steps. More than anything, this applies to the language used in Article VI.

Disarmament issues have been the most powerful showstopper for NPT RevCons. Those of 1980, 1990, 2005, and 2015 failed completely or partially on this issue, and the review part of 1995 ended in disagreement because of disarmament as well; this failure, however, was not essential because the (successfully achieved) extension of the NPT was the much more consequential subject of this conference.

The 1995 conference, however, marked the start of another development that, further pursued in 2000 and 2010, has enabled the parties to the NPT to specify to a considerable degree what they understand as the meaning of Article VI. In 1995, the conference adopted a set of "Principles and Objectives," including some on nuclear disarmament. They specified with some precision what the parties, at that time, saw as priorities for disarmament (a comprehensive test-ban treaty, the beginning of negotiations on a treaty to prohibit the production of fissile material for weapons, and further systematic reductions in nuclear arsenals). In 2000, the conference detailed "13 steps," including transparency, irreversibility of disarmament, and the inclusion of nonstrategic nuclear weapons in the disarmament process. In 2010, nuclear disarmament steps such as constraints on new types of warheads and "systematic reporting" by the nuclear weapon states were part of the agreed-upon "Action Plan," containing altogether sixty-four steps in all three "pillars."

As a result of this process, there exists a catalogue today that tells those who want to know what the NWS should do; I would also argue that it has established a norm of accountability of the NWS to their fellow NPT parties on how they implement their disarmament obligation. While this process has not eliminated the inherent asymmetries of the NPT, it has served to reduce the imbalance of rights and obligations. If there is still very strong dissatisfaction, it results from vastly insufficient implementation, rather than inherent and structural asymmetries of entitlements and duties. As noted, this fact caused the movement resulting in the 2017 Ban Treaty on nuclear weapons.

The said process of norm specification became possible through the particular procedure chosen to work out compromises. In each case it was smaller groups with a global representation, in which NWS, industrialized NNWS, and leading NAM delegations participated. In 1995, this group was brought together by the conference president. In 2000, it was a series of private talks by the New Agenda Coalition (Egypt, Brazil, Ireland, New Zealand, Mexico, South Africa, and Sweden) and the NWS, which, in the course of their talks, co-opted additional players for better representation. In 2010, it was semiprivate talks, to a degree mandated by the conference president, under the chairmanship of Egypt, and with even broader representation (different from 2000, Iran was in the room this time). In all cases, the informal mandate for negotiations was to bridge the justice gap by addressing the existing grievances, and in all cases, the format of negotiations attempted to meet procedural justice criteria by way of sufficient representation.

Mitigating the Intra-Northern Conflict on Nonproliferation and Peaceful Uses

A second, briefer example of the constructive use of cleavages was the justice-based quarrel within the northern world on verification, peaceful uses, fuel cycle policies, and nuclear exports. Rather than digging themselves deeply into the ditches, industrialized countries looked for ways to reduce or eliminate the problem of competitive disadvantage for NNWS's nuclear industries and the constraints arising from external pressure on the ability of countries to choose freely their national nuclear policies. The solution was, by and large, the development of common rules that applied to all, notably in the field of export controls, and a decision to make relevant parts of the Additional Protocol applicable to NWS (some call this method the "equal misery principle"). The justice gap did not disappear but was essentially narrowed. The new rules were the result of negotiations in which those previously at the receiving end got to participate on an equal footing. New norms were emerging that strengthened the nonproliferation regime but mitigated the old justice conflict among industrialized countries.[57] However, as collateral damage, parts of the agreement exacerbated those with the nonaligned world, which remained excluded from the process.

The Justice Linkage and Stagnation

If the intra-northern justice cleavage turned out to be a driver for successful norm development, the same is not true for the justice linkage effort characterizing the relationship among the three pillars. One could have expected that actors could just apply the model for specifying disarmament steps to nonproliferation and peaceful uses in order to come to a balanced set of further developed norms, but this did not happen. One reason may be that disarmament norm development was not followed up with sufficient implementation by the NWS. Another reason might have been the feeling that NNWS had already delivered compliance many times over and NWS had not even seriously started reciprocating this practice. In the end, further progress on nonproliferation measures largely stagnated by the late 1990s, and new proposals failed with the refusal by southern countries to add anything more to the NNWS homework book for the time being.

Needless to say, huge dreams for free technology transfer or gracious aid to establish nuclear energy programs in developing countries did not come true; developed countries preferred leaving nuclear energy development to the market and the private sector. The total picture thus included the following: first, useful, if marginal, norm development for disarmament; second, considerable norm development for nonproliferation, most of which was frozen at the level of proposals that states could adopt voluntarily but had no obligation to do; and third, many pious exhortations in the sectors of nuclear security, again without checks, reviews, or assessments other than on a voluntary basis.[58] One could speculate that the differences in the justice gap along the North/North axis and the North/South axis were causal for the moderate progress in the first and the lack thereof in the second case. Finally, on universality, tenacious efforts by Egypt managed to establish a commitment norm for the depositaries to engage in making the Middle East nuclear weapon free only to face lackluster readiness by the United States—the only depositary with some clout with regard to Israel—to implement this norm. This frustration of Egypt contributed to the failures of the 2005 and 2015 NPT Reviews.

Nuclear Security: Bridging the Gap

Now, it makes sense to revisit the nuclear security sector and to interpret our findings there in the light of our justice discussion. In the NPT context, nuclear security is tainted by the perceptual pattern derived from the disarmament/

nonproliferation/peaceful uses linkage. In this context, then, it is interpreted as another ruse to divert resources and attention from the NAM-preferred pillars on disarmament and peaceful uses and to use the subject as a pretense to request new constraints on what developing countries might be permitted to do in civilian nuclear energy. Outside of this context—when there is no talk about a fourth pillar of the NPT but a focus instead on practical steps taken to make nuclear activities in developing (and other poor) countries more safe, more secure, more sophisticated, and more efficient—the valuation of related initiatives remains apparently untainted by the NPT connection. To the contrary, the feeling that nuclear security might be in the best interest of all participating states seems to prevail, which is different from the NPT context where at times one could gain the impression that nonproliferation measures are a favor done by the rest to the NWS or the northern world at large rather than an enhancement of one's own well-understood security interest.

Four factors contribute to this result in the nuclear security sector. The first one is the inclusive, even representative composition of initiative membership. Invitations to participate are broadly spread, bringing together developing and poorer industrialized countries with NWS and richer, further developed countries as donors. The lack of coercive measures levels power differences, thereby eliminating a key concern under justice perspectives and, in particular, neutralizes the devastating consequences of frustrated recognition. The focus on capacity building accepts the justice principle of need, one of the key justice demands of developing countries. By design or by default, the successful nuclear security initiatives can be read like model justice-based strategic institutions, and the amount of consent they command and the reasonable success they show may be the result of this feature.[59]

CONCLUSIONS

As the ancient philosophers knew, and as great thinkers have re-emphasized throughout the history of political thought, politics is heavily interwoven with human thinking and feeling about justice. This is not to say that politics are all about doing justice and erecting a just society. This would be nice, but this proposition fails already on the impossibility of arriving at a universal understanding of what justice means in principle and even more so in specific constellations.

Much of the old insights have been lost through the dogmas of our time, be they Marxist or neoliberal. Economic man and the selfish gene have largely dominated the debate and focused attention on preferences and interests rather than on justice concerns. This imbalance in the anthropological foundation of contemporary academic thinking on politics has done a lot of damage but apparently could be coming to an end (though not in politics and the media). Today, we can state with some certainty that in the evolution of the human species, the genetic disposition to care for justice and the cultural practice of developing ideas of justice, around which at times institutions were built, became part of the human condition. On this basis, we can safely assume that justice concerns, unfortunately for better *and* for worse, play an important role in politics and must be part of any analysis of conflict and its management between human collectives.

As in any policy field, we harbor this expectation in nuclear politics as well. It might seem like a hard case given the hard-core security aspects that characterize this field. In reality, it might be an easy case for research due to the inherent inequality in the global nuclear order and the legal/normative regime of nuclear nonproliferation that is its indispensable part.[60] The detailed analysis of the nonproliferation regime presented in this chapter reveals a cobweb of interconnected justice conflicts that pits groups of states against one another, prevents the regime from achieving optimal efficiency, and keeps states from pursuing nonproliferation (and, much less so and only occasionally, nuclear security) as a matter of rationally calculated national interests. The reason is the trick that justice plays with us. Once something has been flagged as a justice claim, an entitlement belonging to us, then pork barreling, compromising, engaging in specific or diffuse reciprocity, and other instruments from the rationalist negotiation toolbox become so much harder because emotions are involved. (By the way, the said toolbox may already be more justice infected than we tend to believe, but this is another matter.)

This analysis of the NPT and selected nuclear security initiatives confirms the expectation that justice conflicts make things more complicated and prevent actors at times from jointly and effectively pursuing objectives they say they share. On the other hand, barriers are neither absolute nor insuperable. The analysis of norm development in the NPT and of cooperative practices in nuclear security shows that cleavages can be overcome and prevented once justice problems are aptly and prudently addressed. This insight might contain an important lesson across many policy fields: justice might be called, rightly, a mixed blessing—but fortunately, it is not necessarily a Pandora's box.

NOTES

This work has been supported by Charles University Research Centre program UNCE/HUM/028 (Peace Research Center Prague, Faculty of Social Sciences).

1. Ernst Fehr and Klaus M. Schmidt, "A Theory of Fairness, Competition, and Cooperation," *Quarterly Journal of Economics* 114, no. 3 (August 1999): 817–68.

2. Paul W. Glimcher, Collin Camerer, Ernst Fehr, and Russell Alan Poldrack, eds., *Neuroeconomics: Decision Making and the Brain*, vol. 1 (London: Academic Press, 2009).

3. Alan G. Sanfey, James K. Rilling, Jessica A. Aronson, Leigh E. Nystrom, and Jonathan D. Cohen, "The Neural Basis of Economic Decision-Making in the Ultimatum Game," *Science* 300, no. 5626 (June 13, 2003): 1755–58.

4. Bryan Skyrms, *Evolution of the Social Contract*, 2nd ed. (Cambridge: Cambridge University Press, 2014).

5. On the concept of economic man, see John Kells Ingram, *A History of Political Economy*, (1888; repr., New York: Augustus M. Kelley, 1967). On the idea of the selfish gene, see Richard Dawkins, *The Selfish Gene* (Oxford: Oxford University Press, 1976).

6. On the work of evolutionary biologists, see Mark Bekoff and Jessica Pierce, *Wild Justice: The Moral Life of Animals* (Chicago: University of Chicago Press, 2009). On primate researchers, see Frans de Waal, *The Age of Empathy: Nature's Lessons for a Kinder Society* (New York: Harmony Books, 2009); Shinya Yamamoto and Tayaka Akimoto, "Empathy and Fairness: Psychological Mechanisms for Eliciting and Maintaining Prosociality and Cooperation in Primates," *Social Justice Research* 25, no. 2 (2012): 233–55. On anthropologists, see Christopher Boehm, *Hierarchy in the Forest: The Evolution of Egalitarian Behavior* (Cambridge, Mass.: Harvard University Press, 2001). On fairness rules, see S. F. Brosnan and Frans de Waal, "Fairness in Animals: Where to from Here," *Social Justice Research* 25, no. 3 (2012): 336–51.

7. Tania Singer, "The Neuronal Basis of Empathy and Fairness," *Novartis Foundation Symposium* 278 (2007): 20–30.

8. Stefan Liebig and Holger Lengfeld, eds., *Interdisziplinäre Soziale Gerechtigkeitsforschung: Zur Verknüpfung Empirischer und Normativer Perspektiven* (Frankfurt am Main: Campus Verlag, 2002).

9. Michael Tomasello, *Why We Cooperate* (Cambridge: Massachusetts Institute of Technology Press, 2009).

10. Nancy Fraser, *Scales of Justice: Reimagining Political Space in a Globalizing World* (Cambridge, UK: Polity Press, 2008).

11. Harald Müller and Carmen Wunderlich, eds., *Norm Dynamics in Multilateral Arms Control: Interests, Conflicts, and Justice* (Athens: University of Georgia Press, 2013); Harald Müller, Carmen Wunderlich, Marco Fey, Klaus-Peter Ricke, and Annette Schaper, "Nonproliferation 'Clubs' vs. the NPT," Swedish Radiation Safety Authority, Stockholm, February 14, 2014, http://www.stralsakerhetsmyndigheten.se/Global/Publikationer/Rapport/Icke%20spridning/2014/SSM-Rapport-2014-04.pdf; Marco Fey, Aviv Melamud, and Harald Müller, "The Role of Justice in Compliance Behavior: Germany's Early Membership in the Nuclear Nonproliferation Regime," *International Negotiations* 19, no. 3 (2014): 459–86.

12. Melvin J. Lerner, "The Justice Motive: Some Hypotheses as to Its Origins and Forms," *Journal of Personality* 45, no. 1 (1977): 1–52.

13. I. William Zartman, "Conflict and Order: Justice in Negotiation," *International Political Science Review* 18, no. 2 (April 1997): 121–38.

14. Harald Müller, "Justice and Peace: Good Things Do Not Always Go Together," in *Justice and Peace: Interdisciplinary Perspectives on a Contested Relationship*, ed. Gunther Hellmann (Frankfurt: Campus Verlag, 2013), 43–68.

15. Boehm, *Hierarchy in the Forest*.

16. Daniel Druckman, "Situations," in *Conflict: From Analysis to Intervention*, 2nd ed., ed. Sandra Cheldelin, Daniel Druckman, and Larissa Fast (New York: Continuum, 2008), 120–46.

17. Emma Hutchison and Roland Bleiker, "Theorizing Emotions in World Politics," in "Emotions in World Politics," ed. Bleiker and Hutchison, special issue of *International Theory* 6, no. 3 (2014): 491–514.

18. David Welch, *Justice and the Genesis of War* (Cambridge: Cambridge University Press, 1993).

19. David A. Welch, "The Justice Motive in International Relations: Past, Present, and Future," *International Negotiation* 19, no. 3 (2014): 410–25.

20. Zartman, "Conflict and Order."

21. Cecilia Albin and Daniel Druckman, "Distributive Justice and the Durability of Peace Agreements," *Review of International Studies* 37, no. 3 (2010): 1137–68.

22. Richard Ned Lebow, *Why Nations Fight* (Cambridge: Cambridge University Press, 2010); Richard Ned Lebow, *A Cultural Theory of International Relations* (Cambridge: Cambridge University Press, 2008).

23. Cecilia Albin, *Justice and Fairness in International Negotiation* (Cambridge: Cambridge University Press, 2001).

24. Harald Müller, "Between Power and Justice: Current Problems and Perspectives of the NPT Regime," *Strategic Analysis* 34, no. 2 (2010): 189–201.

25. Nina Tannenwald, "Justice and Fairness in the Nuclear Nonproliferation Regime," *Ethics and International Affairs* 27, no. 3 (2013): 299–317.

26. Biological, chemical, and nuclear weapons are usually called weapons of mass destruction. At the core of the respective international regimes are the Biological Weapons Convention, the Chemical Weapons Convention, and the NPT. Una Becker-Jakob, Harald Müller, and Tabea Seidler-Diekmann, "Regime Conflicts and Norm Dynamics: Nuclear, Biological and Chemical Weapons," in Müller and Wunderlich, *Norm Dynamics in Multilateral Arms Control*, 51–81.

27. Fey, Melamud, and Müller, "Role of Justice."

28. Jeffrey W. Knopf, "Nuclear Disarmament and Nonproliferation: Are They Linked?" *International Security* 37, no. 3 (2012/13): 92–132.

29. Mohamed I. Shaker, *The Nuclear Nonproliferation Treaty: Origin and Implementation, 1959–1979* (London: Oceana, 1980).

30. Jeffrey W. Knopf, ed., *Security Assurances and Nuclear Nonproliferation* (Stanford, Calif.: Stanford University Press, 2012).

31. William C. Potter and Gaukhar Mukhatzhanova, *Nuclear Politics and the Non-Aligned Movement* (London: IISS, 2012).

32. William C. Potter, "Disarmament Diplomacy and the Nuclear Ban Treaty," *Survival* 59, no. 4 (2017): 75–108.

33. Alexander Kmentt, "The Development of the International Initiative on the Humanitarian Impact of Nuclear Weapons and Its Effect on the Nuclear Weapons Debate," *International Review of the Red Cross* 97 (2015): 681–709, https://www.icrc.org/en/international-review/article/development-international-initiative-humanitarian-impact-nuclear.

34. Gunter Hildenbrand, "A German Reaction to U.S. Nonproliferation Policy," *International Security* 3, no. 2 (1978): 51–56.

35. Fey, Melamud, and Müller, "Role of Justice."

36. The NSG is a group of nuclear exporting states that coordinate export control policies in order to avoid undesirable transfers caused by a "race to the bottom" concerning export standards. The original guidelines (1977) covered special nuclear material and equipment only and permitted transfers to states with unverified (unsafeguarded) nuclear activities. The 1992 reform extended export controls to dual-use items and established "comprehensive safeguards" as a condition of supply: transfers were only legitimate to recipients where all nuclear material was under IAEA verification. The Additional Protocol complemented the original Verification System of the NPT after the revelations on Iraq's nuclear weapons program in

the aftermath of the Gulf War of 1991. It established broader reporting duties for the NNWS, more access of the IAEA to information beyond that provided by the inspected states, and more intrusive inspection rights. Altogether, these measures created for the first time a serious capability to uncover clandestine, nonreported nuclear activities by a "cheater".

37. A fifth country, South Sudan, is also a nonparty to the NPT. This is because South Sudan only recently became independent and has been in considerable internal turmoil since achieving statehood, rendering it incapable of completing the process to accede to the NPT. It is not considered at risk to acquire nuclear weapons.

38. Nabil Fahmi, "An Assessment of International Nuclear Nonproliferation Efforts after 60 Years," *Nonproliferation Review* 13, no. 1 (2006): 81–87.

39. The separation of plutonium through the reprocessing of spent fuel and the enrichment of uranium are called *sensitive technologies* because they can be utilized to produce weapons-useable fissile material.

40. P. R. Chari, "Introduction: The Indo-US Nuclear Deal," in *Indo-US Nuclear Deal: Seeking Synergy in Bilateralism*, ed. Chari (New Delhi: Routledge, 2009), 1–17.

41. Marc Hibbs, "The Future of the Nuclear Suppliers Group" (Washington, D.C.: Carnegie Endowment for International Peace, 2011).

42. Ian Anthony, Christer Ahlström, and Vitaly Fedchenko, "Reforming Nuclear Export Controls: The Future of the Nuclear Suppliers Group" (Stockholm: SIPRI, 2007).

43. Harald Müller, "A Nuclear Nonproliferation Test: Obama's Nuclear Policy and the 2010 NPT Review Conference," *Nonproliferation Review* 18, no. 1 (2011): 219–36.

44. Potter and Mukhatzhanova, *Nuclear Politics*.

45. On the following, see Harald Müller, "The NPT Review Conferences," in *The Nuclear Nonproliferation Regime at a Crossroads*, ed. Emily B. Landau and Azriel Bermant (Tel Aviv: Institute for National Security Studies, Memorandum No. 137, 2014), 17–26.

46. Theodore Hirsch, "The IAEA Additional Protocol: What It Is and Why It Matters," *Nonproliferation Review* 11, no. 3 (2004): 140–66.

47. Review Conference of the Parties to the Treaty on the Non-Proliferation of Nuclear Weapons, May 2015, 6, http://www.un.org/en/ga/search/view_doc.asp?symbol=NPT/CONF.2015/SR.4.

48. UNSC Res. 1540 was adopted in response to the 9/11 terrorist attacks in order to prevent terrorist groups from obtaining WMD and the technology, equipment, and materials to make them. The necessary majority of UNSC members chose to use this "shortcut" of adopting a legally binding UNSC Resolution rather than going through the cumbersome negotiation process for establishing a universal treaty to create universally binding rules for this objective. This bypassing of the more inclusive General Assembly met with criticism from many nonmembers of the UNSC.

49. Yuri Yudin, "Multilateralization of the Nuclear Fuel Cycle: A Long Road Ahead," Geneva, UN Institute for Disarmament Research, 2011, 35–37, 39–44, http://www.unidir.org/files/publications/pdfs/multilateralization-of-the-nuclear-fuel-cycle-a-long-road-ahead-378.pdf.

50. International Atomic Energy Agency, "Multilateral Approaches to the Nuclear Fuel Cycle: Expert Group Report Submitted to the Director General of the International Atomic Energy Agency," Vienna: International Atomic Energy Agency, 2005, https://www.iaea.org/publications/documents/infcircs/multilateral-approaches-nuclear-fuel-cycle-expert-group-report-submitted-director-general-international-atomic-energy-agency.

51. Pavel Podvig, "Global Nuclear Security: Building Greater Accountability and Cooperation," Geneva, UN Institute for Disarmament Research, 2011, http://www.unidir.org/files

/publications/pdfs/global-nuclear-security-building-greater-accountability-and-cooperation-383.pdf.

52. In 2010, the Obama administration introduced the Nuclear Security Summits in order to improve the security and safety of nuclear material and facilities. They brought together by invitation heads of states and governments of countries having or intensely planning for using civilian nuclear power. The aim was to obtain commitments at the highest level of state and government for plans of action and specific measures. Iran was not invited.

53. Müller, "Nuclear Nonproliferation Test."

54. Müller et al., "Nonproliferation 'Clubs' vs. the NPT."

55. Our findings are very similar to those of Wyn Bowen, Matthew Cottey, and Christopher Hobbs, "Multilateral Cooperation and the Prevention of Nuclear Terrorism: Pragmatism over Idealism," *International Affairs* 88, no. 2 (2012): 349–68.

56. On the impact of emotions on the course of negotiations, see Mara Olekalns and Daniel Druckman, "With Feeling: How Emotions Shape Negotiation," *Negotiation Journal* 30, no. 4 (2014): 455–78.

57. Fey, Melamud, and Müller, "Role of Justice."

58. Becker-Jakob, Müller, and Seidler-Diekmann, "Regime Conflicts and Norm Dynamics," 55–57.

59. Müller et al., "Nonproliferation 'Clubs' vs. the NPT," 82–94.

60. William Walker, *Weapons of Mass Destruction and International Order* (Oxford: Oxford University Press, 2004); William Walker, *A Perpetual Menace: Nuclear Weapons and International Order* (London: Routledge, 2012).

CHAPTER SEVEN

Constructing U.S. Ballistic Missile Defense

An Information Processing Account of Technology Innovation

ZACHARY ZWALD

Can the U.S. build a ballistic missile defense (BMD) system that enhances its national security? Ever since President Reagan's announcement of the Strategic Defense Initiative (SDI) on March 23, 1983, the policymaking and scholarly communities have passionately debated this question. Yet, despite the thought given to whether or not the United States should pursue and deploy various BMD technologies, the process by which actors assess information to arrive at a judgment on a candidate BMD technology has never been systematically examined. Scholars and practitioners alike typically focus on evaluating the military utility of a particular BMD technology and give only passing attention to the underlying capability. Typically, both advocates and critics of U.S. BMD treat a technology's capability as an objective fact, ignoring that the process by which anyone arrives at those "facts" is itself inherently subjective. In this chapter, I argue that scientific experts, military contractors, and government officials all rely on beliefs about the military utility of pursuing and possessing BMD as heuristics in order to assess the risk conveyed in technical data. Thus, judgments on a technology's capability are necessarily statements where social and objective facts are inextricably intertwined.

Today, significant doubts about both the capability and utility of U.S. BMD remain and, yet, official U.S. policy increasingly relies on BMD as a means to respond to nuclear proliferation and bolster the credibility of deterrence vis-à-vis rogue states.[1] It logically follows that policymakers' judgments on what U.S. BMD technology can do, physically and strategically, could now influence decisions about U.S. alliances, various treaty negotiations, and conventional force structuring and deployments throughout the world. Notwithstanding the significance of such judgments, however, we still have a limited understanding of how one determines the capability and utility of U.S. BMD technology.

Moreover, none of the potentially relevant existing academic literatures rigorously examines how one arrives at a judgment regarding military technology innovation writ large, let alone on U.S. BMD. The military innovation literature focuses on the effectiveness of organizations in harnessing technological developments as, or after, they occur.[2] Scholarship on the determinants of arms races usually examines the organizational dynamics that determine a state's arming decisions and, thus, marginalizes individual-level judgment and decision making.[3] International relations research that considers behavioral approaches to decision making tends to examine how members of the policymaking community reduce uncertainty about threat but has thus far taken as given the capability of military technology.[4] In light of these gaps in our understanding, therefore, in this chapter I aim to develop a conceptual framework for how key actors process information to arrive at a judgment on a candidate BMD technology. The information processing approach proposed in this chapter draws on insights from the fields of behavioral economics, science and technology studies (STS), and philosophy of science.

The remainder of this chapter proceeds in three parts. First, I present two alternative conceptual frameworks for how key actors arrive at judgments on BMD technology. Existing scholarship consistently implies or asserts a positivist "science versus politics" conventional wisdom in which one either arrives at an accurate judgment via the information-driven thinking of science, or one levies an inaccurate judgment based on the interest-driven thinking of politics. In contrast, I advance a scientific pragmatist framework in which BMD supporters and opponents, irrespective of expertise and material interests, arrive at a judgment on BMD technology by interpreting information in the context of their beliefs about the likely nuclear use scenario in which U.S. BMD would be employed. That is to say, supporters and opponents both tend to select and interpret available information about what a candidate BMD technology can and should do in a narrow manner that is consistent with their relative emphasis on one of two images of how a nuclear war would most likely begin. BMD supporters focus on mitigating calculated risk (from the rational and deliberate actions of an adversary that sees a gap in the U.S. deterrent posture and calculates it can gain an advantage from a nuclear strike), while BMD opponents give more weight to autonomous risk (arising from inadvertent and accidental actions that lead to nuclear use in conditions where neither side actually wanted the situation to escalate in this way).

Second, I provide an initial empirical evaluation of these frameworks by illustrating three trends exhibited in the historical record on U.S. BMD policy. These trends challenge the validity of the conventional wisdom's assumption that having material interests at stake is inversely correlated with the accuracy of technology assessments. This section shows that (1) the effect of BMD on an actor's material interests was often unclear; (2) information available to make a judgment of a technology's capability and utility was often incomplete and ambiguous; and (3) policymakers tend to narrowly interpret available information in a manner consistent with the logic of their stated national security beliefs.

Lastly, I conclude by briefly summarizing my findings, discussing the epistemological challenges to examining judgment and decision making on technology innovation, and by considering the implications of my analysis for how the policymaking community can increase the accuracy of those judgments that inform BMD development and procurement policy decisions. More specifically, I explain how material interests can both incentivize and disincentivize accurate technological judgments as well as why existing strategies to minimize the distorting influence of such interests are often counterproductive. The conclusion argues that encouraging a more robust political dialogue across policymakers, stakeholders, experts, and the public would be more conducive to reaching accurate judgments about BMD.

U.S. BMD TECHNOLOGY INNOVATION: AN INFORMATION-PROCESSING FRAMEWORK

Existing analysis of information processing dynamics on U.S. BMD does not comport with scholars' own intuitions on the matter. Many scholars note the pervasive uncertainty on both the capability and utility of BMD as well as the seemingly religious or ideological nature of policymakers' views; and, yet, their subsequent analysis typically implies that policymakers arrive at technological judgments via rational risk assessment. In light of this discrepancy, after first demonstrating the conventional approach, I will advance an alternative information-processing framework, rooted in pragmatic constructivism, that better captures long and widely held intuitions about how one's beliefs affect judgments under conditions of structural uncertainty.

The Conventional Wisdom

Scholars consistently advance the positivist perspective that the U.S. BMD technology innovation process is dictated by the push and pull of science versus politics, where science and politics are discrete spheres of activity. The underlying framework results from the scientific positivism that underpins realist international relations theory. As Bijker, Bal, and Hendriks summarize, in this "standard view of science" scholars proceed as though "scientific knowledge is true knowledge. True knowledge consists of facts. Facts are neutral, objective, and clearly distinguishable from values, and are discovered in empirical research"; then, once the scientific facts have been established, "politics is subsequently responsible for making choices on the basis of those facts."[5] With respect to existing analysis of

U.S. BMD, then, the dominant perspective is that BMD opponents—typically esteemed scientists without material interests at stake—engage in the information-driven thinking of science to arrive at critical judgments that accurately assess the data at hand, while BMD supporters—typically hawkish politicians, military bureaucrats, and government contractors with something to gain—engage in the interest-driven thinking of politics to levy positive judgments that distort that data.[6] Some scholars dissent from this dominant perspective and argue either in favor of the BMD supporter position or that both supporters' and opponents' judgments tend to distort available data. These analyses, too, put forward the science versus politics conventional wisdom that there is an inverse relationship between accuracy and material interests.[7]

This conventional wisdom on U.S. BMD is logically predicated on a unique conceptualization of information and information processing. First, with respect to information, scholars tend to treat the body of data on a technology's capability as distinct from the body of intelligence about the threat environment, and scholars describe both bodies of information as separate from how individuals assess a technology's capability and military utility.[8] James Lindsay and Michael O'Hanlon, for instance, assert that during the Sentinel, Safeguard, and SDI programs, respectively, the technological and strategic "obstacles" were separate from one another.[9] Numerous scholars argue that the technological "difficulties" of SDI were wholly separate from the strategic implications for U.S.-Soviet relations.[10] Likewise, Bradley Graham, Ernest Yanarella, and Stephen Cimbala each begin from the premise that whether or not the U.S. can "hit a bullet with a bullet" is separate from how BMD affects U.S. national security in the post–Cold War threat environment.[11]

On the one hand, information regarding the capability of U.S. BMD technology—both the required parameters and the course of development—is conceptualized as being in the realm of facts from fields in science and engineering. The dominant view is that the required capability of a candidate technology is a function of the offensive countermeasures (aka penetration aides or "penaids," for short) that *can* and *will* be integrated into an intercontinental ballistic missile (ICBM) that any adversary launches at the United States.[12] Within the existing scholarship, conventional wisdom on countermeasures has often been that "the problem isn't technology, it's physics.... No amount of development of the defense sensors or their associated analysis programs will allow discrimination of the warhead from a decoy."[13] During the Cold War, Charles Glaser concluded that the technology considered as part of SDI would be undone by countermeasures employed by the Soviet Union.[14] Following the 9/11 attacks, Glaser and Steven Fetter argued that even "reactive emerging missile states" such as North Korea, Iran, Iraq, and Libya could and would develop countermeasures capable of thwarting U.S. BMD.[15] In a similar vein, foundational to Columba Peoples's critique of U.S. BMD is the claim that "ICBMs, the proposed targets of the current BMD system, travel at a speed of 7 km per second and are *routinely* designed to deploy a range of countermeasures capable of overcoming defenses."[16]

When it turns from an adversary's countermeasures to the likely course of U.S. technological development, existing scholarship assumes that data on a candidate BMD technology conveys a discrete range of relative probabilities for the potential rate of progress between its current and future capability. Scholars typically imply that existing data on the *current* capability of a candidate technology, as well as the meaning and significance of that data for the probability of a given *future* capability, objectively describe the physical reality of what can be done. Uncertainty in that data, thus, is taken to refer only to the distance between what is known about the *physical properties* of that technology and what there is yet to know about those physical properties, which is due to limits and/or errors in testing, measurement, and data collection as well as the level of existing knowledge about associated building materials and engineering methods. A few scholars, such as Charles Zraket, are attentive to this uncertainty and note that determining the meaning of data is usually difficult "because of the early state of research [on potential missile defense technologies] and resulting uncertainties about their future performance."[17] More often, however, scholars marginalize such uncertainty and simply assert that "the poor test and evaluation record of missile defense to date ensures that doubts persist over the ability of proposed technologies."[18] It is routinely argued, for example, that the existing data, based on a limited number of tests conducted under artificial conditions, clearly indicate a likely lack of future success for BMD technology.[19]

On the other hand, scholars evaluate information on the military utility of BMD technology as though it follows from the necessary conditions for credible nuclear deterrence. More specifically, a technology's utility is said to be a function of how the pursuit and/or possession of such a system affects those conditions. The dominant perspective in international relations scholarship on BMD stipulates the necessary conditions for credible nuclear deterrence advanced in the nuclear revolution hypothesis. For instance, Robert Jervis's critique of what he called the "pre-nuclear thinking" underlying the Reagan administration's SDI is based on the premise that prudent nuclear strategy "must start with the realization that each side's civilization can be protected only by the other's cooperation. In such a world, the well-established idea that gaining a military advantage is necessary or sufficient for gaining security does not apply."[20] According to the nuclear revolution, a single set of conditions for credible nuclear deterrence logically follows from the capacity of a nuclear weapon to cause an unprecedented level of destruction and the mutual vulnerability between nuclear-armed states with the requisite delivery systems. That is to say, nuclear weapon states' national security necessarily requires a credible nuclear deterrent based solely on a retaliatory capability that provides an assured second strike. States that possess such a capability have a robust deterrent because no other nuclear-armed state has a rational incentive to launch a nuclear first strike. It follows that all such states are unavoidably in a condition of equilibrium with one another known as mutually assured destruction (MAD).

Frances Fitzgerald, for example, demonstrates this logic when she cites as a universal fact the conclusion reached by Herbert York and Jerome Wiesner in a 1962 article in *Scientific American*: the primary result of the U.S. pursuit of BMD will be to compel the Soviets to build up their offensive weapons.[21] Writing during the Cold War, Glaser argued that "less-than-near-perfect defense" would harm U.S. security by ending "serious arms control efforts" with the Soviet Union and intensifying the arms race between the two states.[22] More recently, Glaser and Fetter have asserted that deploying a limited missile defense system to address the emerging missile threat from rogue states would threaten Russian and Chinese retaliation capabilities and thus increase the likelihood of conflict via increased interstate tensions.[23] Similarly, Mitchell critiques the U.S. BMD program on the grounds that it "dismisses [the] cold war logic that led to massive buildups in offensive weapons."[24]

In sum, the first aspect of the conventional approach is a tendency to treat information about technology and military utility as separate issues. Second, the information-processing construct advanced in existing U.S. BMD scholarship follows from the rational choice model of human behavior. Scholars provide very little detail, if any, on the mechanisms that allow one to arrive at a technological judgment. Yet, they consistently imply that one engages in instrumental rationality in order to assign an expected utility value to each candidate BMD technology. One either engages in information-driven thinking and accurately depicts the structural conditions just described, or one engages in interest-driven thinking and distorts those conditions in a manner that furthers one's bureaucratic/electoral/financial ends. For instance, Gerald Steinberg describes how judgments by BMD opponents, such as Richard Garwin and Hans Bethe, "generally began with the technical conclusion" that an effective defense "was not feasible," while BMD supporters "began their arguments with statements concerning moral, political, or ideological statements in order to justify the need for the radical change embodied in SDI."[25]

BMD supporters' judgments are said to be motivated by a combination of the bureaucratic interests held by officials from the Defense Department and national laboratories, electoral interests held by Republican politicians and members of right-wing think tanks, and the economic interests of government contractors. They then supposedly pursue these material interests by instrumentally employing, in tandem, the narratives of "American exceptionalism" and "technological optimism" to exaggerate the significance of data for a candidate technology's rate of progress.²⁶

With respect to SDI, for example, scholars argue that positive technological judgments resulted from the combination of Dr. Edward Teller's pursuit of increased funding for Lawrence Livermore National Laboratory (LLNL), President Reagan's attempt to increase his standing with U.S. voters, and defense contractors' profit motive.²⁷ In the decade leading up to Reagan's announcement of SDI, scholars argue, these supporters' interest-driven thinking led them to instrumentally employ the above narratives in order to "render missile defense a realistic, desirable and necessary option for the USA."²⁸ Likewise, regarding George W. Bush administration officials, Peoples argues that despite the fact that U.S. BMD lacks technological promise and strategic value in the twenty-first century, the program persists because it "favors sectional political and industrial interests in the short-term and helps to sustain America's immense defense infrastructure in the post Cold War era."²⁹ Scholars then argue that the instrumental pursuit of those interests explains the pattern of overselling data exhibited in BMD supporters' judgments on the Patriot ground-based interceptor, which was used in the 1991 Persian Gulf war to try to stop Iraqi Scud attacks, as well as the current sea-based interceptors deployed on Aegis destroyers.³⁰

Ultimately, scholars substantiate their position that BMD supporters' judgments result from interest-driven distortions of fact by comparing them to those made by BMD opponents. Jervis makes his case against missile defense by referencing how the "overwhelming majority of scientific experts both in and out of government hold that the prospects for a successful ABM [anti-ballistic missile] system are extremely low."³¹ Reiss attempts to prove his contention that the "politics of influence" drove supporters' judgments of SDI technology by referencing the "ninety-eight percent of the U.S. Academy of Scientists" who expressed "disbelief in Reagan's vision."³² Peoples makes the argument that "missile defense advocacy" is based on distorting data about the actual capability of candidate technology by juxtaposing BMD supporters to the "American scientific community." In particular, Peoples references "scientific luminaries such as Richard Garwin (Nobel Prize–winning physicist) and Theodore Postol (Professor of Science and Technology at MIT)," who "remain highly skeptical" of BMD due to "strong arguments . . . that the physical limitations of such a project cannot be overcome."³³

There are, however, significant weaknesses in the conceptual framework undergirding existing U.S. BMD scholarship that undermine its conclusions about the relationship between material interests and judgment accuracy. Intuitively, it is clear that uncertainty about the required parameters of a candidate technology—and, the extent to which existing data suggests progress toward those parameters—is, to some degree, a function of irreducible uncertainty about the national security requirements for any weapon technology. Moreover, most everyone would also agree that uncertainty on these matters tends to be pervasive throughout the innovation process. Yet, for decades, scholars have advanced an information construct that inadequately conceptualizes the origin and character of uncertainty regarding a candidate technology's capability and military utility and an information-processing construct that marginalizes, if not ignores, how policymakers reduce uncertainty about a candidate technology from a condition of ambiguity to one of risk in order to arrive at a judgment.

The Pragmatist Approach

This chapter proposes an alternative information-processing model of military technology innovation, one that proceeds from a scientific pragmatist approach. In brief, this perspective conceives of science, politics, and psychology as overlapping spheres of activity. The challenge to arriving at accurate judgments is not minimizing the role of interest-driven thinking, as the positivist-based conventional wisdom advances. Rather, the actual challenge is to harness one's material interests to incentivize self-critical thinking. I term this "good politics," which is necessary in order to minimize "bad science," in which subjective interpretations of data are treated as strictly conveying material reality. Scientific pragmatism's evolutionary epistemology and consensus theory of knowledge allow for an analytic framework that synthesizes research in STS and behavioral approaches to decision making, two fields that typically do not speak to one another.[34]

First, contrary to the notion that information on the capability and military utility of a candidate technology are distinct structural conditions, this pragmatist model draws on STS scholarship to conceptualize information on a spectrum of sociotechnical complexity. At one end of the spectrum is the condition of low sociotechnical complexity, where uncertainty about a candidate technology may still be present, but there is enough information available so that the capability and utility of a candidate technology come close to resembling distinct structural conditions, and thus, members of the policymaking community can potentially determine the expected value of candidate technologies in a rational manner. However, most cases of military technology innovation more closely resemble the other end of the spectrum. Under high sociotechnical complexity, there is not only irreducible uncertainty on the scientific data but there is no consensus on national security requirements, and thus, judgments and decisions vary according to "differences in convictions, opinions on what is worthy of protection . . . and ideas on the future."[35]

To be clear, under high sociotechnical complexity, the capability of a candidate technology is rooted in "brute facts," that is, dynamics and materials with "intrinsic material capacities" independent of one's beliefs about them.[36]

Moreover, these brute facts have constraining and enabling effects on what can be built as well as what should be done to enhance national security.[37] Under these conditions, however, brute facts "do not directly serve as guides to action."[38] Rather, the relevant data are "hybrid facts," which is to say that the brute facts conveyed in data derive their meaning and significance for the capability of candidate technology from the context of "social facts" regarding the national security requirements to be fulfilled by that technology.[39] Social facts refer to ideas or beliefs that are shared among members of a community, and by virtue of being so accepted help construct the social reality for individuals within that community.

Specifically, the meaning of information regarding the capability and military utility of BMD technology follows from social facts about the likely nature of nuclear conflict and, thus, the necessary conditions for credible nuclear deterrence that one holds to be true. Contrary to the nuclear revolution hypothesis, which is a foundational assumption of the conventional wisdom in U.S. BMD scholarship, my pragmatist account proceeds from the premise that both terms (i.e., the nature of nuclear conflict and the requirements for credible deterrence) are irreducibly uncertain matters. The possible scenarios that could lead to a nuclear conflict in which U.S. BMD might be employed (i.e., the factors that lead to nuclear use and dictate the course of an exchange once it begins) vary wildly and unpredictably. Not only will the actions of each state in a nuclear conflict undoubtedly result from a unique combination of calculated and autonomous risk factors but each state's actions will also be contingent on the strategic interaction between states leading up to and during a nuclear conflict.

Given these uncertainties, I suggest that policymakers who evaluate U.S. BMD technology may consider available information in the context of two different belief sets. On the one hand, decision makers may operate from what I term the fear, misperception, and accident (FMA) belief set, which assumes that nuclear conflict is most likely to be initiated and escalate due to autonomous risk factors; that is to say, nuclear use would be an unintended consequence of FMA. In the context of autonomous risk-based scenarios, one finds it prudent to focus on minimizing the tension and anxiety that could give rise to inadvertent nuclear conflict. Thus, any incremental progress on BMD technology, along with the offense-defense arms race it may incite, are seen to only diminish U.S. national security by undermining the effectiveness of nuclear deterrence. On the other hand, decision makers may subscribe to what I term the rational deliberate action (RDA) belief set, which envisions nuclear war as likely to take the form of a calculated risk, in which an adversary state starts a contained tit-for-tat exchange dictated by a rational calculation that deliberate use of nuclear weapons would be advantageous.[40] In the context of calculated risk-based scenarios, even minimal progress on defensive technology and the prospect of an offense-defense arms race are viewed as developments that may complicate an adversary's attack calculus, which consequently increases U.S. national security by enhancing the credibility of deterrence.

Second, the pragmatist model conceptualizes information processing by synthesizing STS and behavioral decision-making research that shows how one arrives at a technological judgment under structural uncertainty. STS scholarship demonstrates that since "situations of high sociotechnical complexity" lack "an adequate empirical or theoretical basis for assigning probabilities to outcomes, ... conventional risk assessment is too narrow in scope ... [and] judgments about the right balance to strike in decision-making are laden with subjective assumptions and values."[41] Under such conditions, behavioral research on decision making shows how cognitive and affective dynamics lead one, regardless of expertise level or material interests, to exhibit a host of unmotivated and motivated biases.[42]

Daniel Kahneman and others have shown how one's limited cognitive capacity and subsequent need to conserve information processing energy usually result in intuitive "system 1" thinking (i.e., one usually employs belief sets as heuristics to quickly select and make sense of information). This typically prevents one from engaging in the deliberative "system 2" thinking, in which one conducts a thorough information search and updates one's established beliefs accordingly.[43] Jack Levy explains that "one key proposition arising from motivated reasoning is 'wishful thinking.' Whereas rational models of decision-making assume that the probability and utility of an outcome are analytically distinct, in wishful thinking probabilities are influenced by values: desirable outcomes are seen as more likely to occur while undesirable outcomes are seen as less likely."[44] Furthermore, Philip Tetlock shows how experts are at least as likely as laypersons to engage in motivated reasoning. In particular, his research demonstrates how motivated reasoning reflects people's general "aversion to probabilistic strategies that accept the inevitability of error."[45] The more confident experts are in their original judgment of a future event, he shows, the more threatened they are when faced with disconfirming evidence and, thus, the more motivated they are to employ belief system defenses.[46]

The information-processing challenge at hand, then, is that evaluating BMD technology requires one to simultaneously entertain the wide range of possible nuclear conflict scenarios (and concomitant conditions for credible deterrence), while also winnowing the potentials to the manageable size necessary for one to arrive at a finite technological judgment. Optimally, one initially conducts a comprehensive information search of available intelligence, arrives at a set of potential conflict scenarios comprised of both calculated and autonomous risk factors, and then adjusts one's operational conflict scenario set as new information comes to light. However, since this condition of structural uncertainty "is particularly uncomfortable psychologically," it is more typical for "leaders, just like experts," to fall short of processing information in the context of a range of potential scenarios, and instead, they "are likely to seek certainty, the false certainty, of order and control."[47] The interaction of cognitive, affective, and materialist factors and, as a consequence, numerous biases in information processing usually leads supporters and opponents to narrowly evaluate information on the capability and utility of BMD technology in the context of only either the RDA or FMA belief set, respectively. Specifically, RDA thinkers will have a bias toward favorable interpretations of ambiguous data on BMD technologies, while FMA thinkers will display the opposite bias.

U.S. BMD TECHNOLOGY INNOVATION: AN INITIAL EMPIRICAL EVALUATION

This section considers the relative plausibility of the conventional wisdom versus the pragmatist analytic framework for how key actors arrive at a judgment on U.S. BMD technology. Although it is not possible to measure exactly what someone knew or what someone was thinking as they arrived at a technological judgment, we can gain insight on the degree to which variation in the accuracy of judgments is better correlated with whether one has material interests at stake versus one's stated beliefs about the nature of the nuclear conflict in which a BMD system would be employed. Below, I illustrate three trends that, when considered in concert with one another, present a pattern that challenges the validity of the interest-accuracy correlation: (1) although supporters' judgments do tend to be consistent with their interests, the effect of supporting BMD on one's interests is often indeterminate at the time that a technological judgment is made, (2) the complexity of information about a technology's capability and utility means that judgments necessarily reflect a significant degree of subjective interpretation, and (3) supporters with interests and opponents without them both tend to narrowly interpret data and ignore that which defies their expectations in a manner consistent with their stated beliefs about nuclear conflict and credible deterrence.

Trend 1: U.S. BMD Typically Has an Indeterminate Effect on One's Material Interests

Consistent with the conventional wisdom's expectation of a negative correlation between accuracy and interests, those who perceive that it is in their material interests to support the pursuit of BMD do tend to interpret information about candidate technology in a manner that may stand to further those interests.

Some evidence also suggests that, at least on a few occasions, those with material interests levied positive judgments that contradicted brute facts. For instance, Columba Peoples discusses how a near miss during the June 10, 1984, Homing Overlay Experiment was reported as a direct hit.[48] Similarly, Graham shows how, in interpretations of the October 1999 flight test of the hit-to-kill interceptor, supporters seem to have instrumentally oversold the significance of test data by minimizing the role of a bright decoy in allowing the interceptor to see and hit the incoming warhead.[49] The tendency of supporters to exaggerate data matches the general trend described by scholars.

However, the contention that BMD supporters' technological judgments result from interest-driven thinking is undermined by the often indeterminate nature of the material interest structure. At any point in time, there are often multiple candidate technologies that could potentially enhance one's material interests; it is not always clear how a particular technology, if it comes to fruition, will affect those interests.[50] Also, fixed notions about how a candidate technology will affect one's material interests, when they do exist, are largely a function of the currently dominant beliefs about national security requirements and whether the candidate technology stands to address or contradict those requirements. Moreover, while the existing U.S. BMD scholarship often points to "obviously" wasteful spending as demonstrating the effect of material interests, persistent uncertainty about the capability and military utility of a candidate BMD technology means there is also often uncertainty about the amount of resources necessary to attain the required capability. Consequently, there is often no clear-cut evidence available to policymakers about when an investment crosses the line from not enough to too much. Therefore, policymakers' perceptions of their material interests and how best to pursue them are typically a function to some degree of cognitive and affective processes.

The existing literature on U.S. BMD actually demonstrates that the effect of BMD on one's material interests has often been indeterminate. For example, Fitzgerald shows that in the years leading up to President Reagan's announcement of SDI it was unclear how the pursuit of missile defense would affect his political interests and that it was only after that announcement that BMD eventually became a political winner.[51] Lindsay shows that congressional voting behavior on SDI procurement demonstrates that members' interest in securing government defense contracts for constituents was a less significant causal variable than a representative's beliefs about the use of military force.[52] Handberg shows that even when the pursuit of BMD technology may be economically beneficial to military contractors, they could just as easily support other far less controversial weapon technologies that are thus more likely to receive requested funding.[53] Moreover, Steinberg, Denoon, and Handberg each provide reasons for why, contrary to the expectation of a military interest in BMD, some DoD officials' bureaucratic interests led them to oppose the pursuit of BMD.[54] Ultimately, then, while none of this disproves that BMD supporters usually have material interests at stake, it does show that, contrary to conventional wisdom, contextual beliefs necessarily shaped supporters' perceptions of how BMD will affect those interests.

*Trend 2: Information about BMD Reflects
High Sociotechnical Complexity*

The content and the meaning of data on the capability of BMD technology are partly a function of information and beliefs about the military utility of a BMD system. More specifically, across the range of those technologies considered, information about both the required capability and likely rate of progress of candidate BMD technology is logically contingent on the beliefs one employs to seek out and interpret information.

For instance, the required parameters for any BMD technology are contingent on how one interprets incomplete intelligence to define three terms: the necessary interception percentage, the number of incoming missiles, and the quality of those missiles. The interception percentage that a BMD system has to achieve to be considered "effective" is a function of how one defines credible deterrence. Thus, since credible deterrence is a subjective term, any definition of BMD "effectiveness" is also subjective. The predicted number of missiles an adversary would launch in an attack—whether they will launch their entire arsenal in the opening moments of a nuclear war or just a few weapons with others held in reserve—is contingent on the beliefs one relies on to interpret incomplete information about adversaries' intentions and the likely nature of nuclear conflict. Likewise, the expected quality of an incoming ICBM (i.e., the probability that a U.S. BMD system will face offensive countermeasures as well as the significance of that probability for determining the required capability) is contingent on the beliefs one uses to interpret persistently incomplete intelligence regarding potential adversaries' capability and intent.

To demonstrate this point, consider the required capability of the hit-to-kill interceptor. This technology, which has been the centerpiece of U.S. BMD from the 1990s to the present, is contingent on the ability of so-called rogue states to develop countermeasures to evade midcourse interception. On this front, relevant information can be gleaned from the difficulties encountered by China, the UK, and the U.S. China, by many accounts, took almost a decade longer than expected to master MIRV (multiple independently targetable re-entry vehicle) technology, which illustrates the challenge of designing a decoy warhead that can properly separate from the host vehicle in outer space (rather than in the controlled environment of the laboratory).[55] James Lindsay and Michael O'Hanlon demonstrate that Britain "had considerable difficulty in developing ballistic missile countermeasures with its so-called Chevaline system."[56] Moreover, even the United States, with its unparalleled expertise in ICBM technology, has been unable to integrate simple decoys that consistently work as intended. Take, for example, the July 2000 BMD integrated flight test when a Mylar balloon that was to act as a decoy warhead failed to inflate properly. While none of this information demonstrates that offensive countermeasures cannot or will not be built, it does convey the irreducible uncertainty policymakers must make sense of in order to define the required capability of candidate BMD technology.

Similarly, the likely rate of progress is contingent on the subjective definition of "required capability" that one relies on to answer as yet "undecidable questions" about what can currently be built and what will be able to be built in the future.[57] That is to say, one's beliefs about a technology's required capability shape the content of data that is sought out and produced with respect to the current capability of any candidate technology as well as the meaning that it holds (with respect to progress or failure).[58]

The novelty of BMD technology has often led to challenges in designing instruments to collect data, followed in turn by difficulties in interpreting the meaning of that data once collected—all of which culminated in pervasive uncertainty about the likely rate of progress. Consistent with Thomas Kuhn's work on the scientific paradigm, then, beliefs regarding the military utility of a U.S. BMD system allow one to determine what information needs to be known (and, thus, what information is and is not sought) as well as shape the acceptable means to acquire data. It is the belief in the stabilizing effect of the Anti-Ballistic Missile (ABM) Treaty, for instance, that led scientists such as Sidney Drell and Richard Garwin to advocate avoiding tests of candidate BMD technology that would have violated the treaty.[59]

Through 2002, when the United States withdrew from the ABM Treaty, U.S. treaty compliance not only effectively limited the data that could be gathered—particularly on hit-to-kill technology and operationally deployed sensor technology—but also shaped the content of the data that was collected by imposing restrictions on the type of technology that the United States could pursue and prohibiting tests of any BMD technology against an actual ICBM "under realistic operation conditions." Treaty compliance thus magnified the already considerable uncertainty on the meaning and significance of existing data for any technology's likely rate of progress. Not only did artificial testing conditions limit the acquisition of data on the current capability of a candidate technology but the stylized tests also meant that one could never determine whether the capabilities indicated in the acquired data accurately depicted how the technology would perform under realistic operating conditions, for better or worse.

Trend 3: BMD Opponents and Supporters Each Tend to Narrowly Interpret Data

Irrespective of material interests, policymakers tend to narrowly interpret the range of probabilities conveyed by the data at hand in a manner consistent with their beliefs about credible nuclear deterrence. As noted above, available information on offensive countermeasures, potential adversaries' future capabilities and intentions, and the likely course of a technology's development is often ambiguous. Under these circumstances of structural uncertainty, neither BMD opponents nor supporters tend to integrate into their thinking potentially viable interpretations of that information that defy what their beliefs lead them to expect. Over time, opponents usually express the FMA belief set, emphasize the significance of potential countermeasures, and minimize the significance of data suggesting the potential for BMD breakthroughs. In contrast, supporters tend to articulate the RDA belief set, marginalize the significance of such countermeasures, and emphasize data suggesting breakthroughs.

BMD opponents' FMA-based thinking. From the Cold War to the present, BMD opponents' oft-stated requirement that a BMD system be "near perfect" to be effective is predicated on their stated belief that nuclear use will occur via autonomous risk factors: "The real risk of nuclear war does not lie in a cold-blooded decision to initiate one. . . . The more plausible situation would be a mounting crisis, in which both sides would wrestle with the fear that the opponent might strike first on rational or irrational calculation of advantage. And in the face of the apparent inevitability of nuclear war, a preemptive strike could appear better than awaiting the adversary's initial blow."[60] Likewise, BMD opponents such as Sidney Drell, McGeorge Bundy, Wolfgang Panofsky, and David Holloway advocated ABM Treaty compliance because it "removed from the calculation of both sides any fear of an early or destabilizing [BMD] deployment."[61] Since the end of the Cold War, opponents have tended to evaluate candidate technology in the context of inadvertent nuclear use resulting from the increased tensions of a multistate offense-defense arms race. For instance, a 2001 report opposed the George W. Bush administration's pursuit of a BMD system because such efforts were thought to increase the fears and anxieties of Russia and China, which would then spark an arms race and increase the potential for an accidental or inadvertent nuclear launch.[62] Similarly, a 2011 Federation of American Scientists report averred that fear of the military advantage conferred on the United States from a limited BMD system would compel Russia, China, and North Korea to modernize and increase the size of their nuclear arsenals, would force Iran to restart its nuclear weapon and ICBM programs, and, as a by-product of increased militarization in China, would lead to reciprocal actions in

India (and then in Pakistan)—all of which, ultimately, will increase the probability of nuclear conflict via autonomous risk.[63]

Opponents then determine the meaning of uncertainty in available data on U.S. BMD technology in the context of the 100 percent interception rate that would be necessary to mitigate the autonomous risk of nuclear use more effectively than maintaining a nuclear deterrent via assured destruction.[64] For example, Ashton Carter prefaces the technological analysis in his 1984 Office of Technology Assessment (OTA) report with the concern that the rise in autonomous risk of nuclear use from violating the ABM Treaty "would have to be weighed against the purely military and strategic benefit (if there were, in fact, any net long-term benefit) of a U.S. BMD deployment."[65] The influential Union of Concerned Scientists (UCS) report, *The Fallacy of Star Wars*, builds from the FMA-based concern that "SDI would make war more likely and cause an escalation in the nuclear arms race."[66] Likewise, the 2001 report by the Federation of American Scientists (FAS), UCS, and Natural Resources Defense Council, *Toward True Security: A U.S. Nuclear Posture for the Next Decade*, as well as the 2011 FAS report by Postol and Butt, *Upsetting the Reset: The Technical Basis of Russian Concern over NATO Missile Defense*, both proceed from the FMA belief set.

In defining the required capability for a candidate BMD technology, opponents subsequently marginalize, if not outright reject, the notion that there is any uncertainty regarding whether or not adversaries can and will build offensive countermeasures. Despite the numerous uncertainties regarding Soviet capability and intent, Carter's OTA report assumes it can and will take any measures necessary to "prevent itself from being effectively disarmed by a U.S. Defense."[67] A seminal UCS report ignored the known uncertainty about offensive countermeasures and stated they were "off-the-shelf weapons and techniques that exist today."[68] In another example, David Holloway discounted skepticism about the Soviet ability to develop fast-burn boosters and heat resistant shielding that could protect Soviet missiles against direct energy weapons and concluded that a more optimistic alternative estimate was "more realistic."[69]

Similar to how BMD critics expressed optimistic assessments of the Soviet ability to develop countermeasures, from the 1990s to the present, opponents' definition of the required capability for hit-to-kill BMD technology has tended to marginalize uncertainty about so-called rogue states' ability to develop offensive countermeasures in the same fashion. Influential critical judgments, by renowned experts such as Garwin and Postol, on the capability of hit-to-kill technology against such states are predicated on the definitive judgment that decoy balloons, or even enclosing a warhead in a Mylar balloon, are "all too simple" offensive countermeasures that any state can and will develop.[70] Such thinking engages neither the inconsistent reliability of Mylar balloon decoys in U.S. BMD field tests nor the widely held position that for countermeasures to function as expected (and not adversely affect the trajectory of the nuclear warhead) they must be repeatedly flight tested.

Regarding interpretation of available data on a BMD technology's likely rate of progress, scholars exhibit three patterns of biased thinking consistent with the logic of the FMA belief set. First, they tend to minimize incremental advancements on candidate technology (e.g., the confirmation of physical principles and foundational processes) by either comparing that data to the stringent required parameters to be achieved at the end of the research and development process or by emphasizing that the data do not provide insight on performance under "realistic operating conditions." In the report *BMD Technologies and Concepts in the 1980s*, Bethe, Boutwell, and Garwin conclude that "while many of the technological and systems problems associated with new BMD concepts are far from being solved[,] a large number of different types of countermeasures are available now."[71]

Second, opponents tend to amplify the significance of test failures by defining "failure" irrespective of the test's stated goal, by ignoring the cause for failure, and/or considering failure in isolation from other technologies that may be part of the BMD system under operational conditions. Third, opponents tend to interpret limits indicated in current data as substantiating the low probability of attaining the required capability in the future. In evaluating the effectiveness of U.S. BMD technology against a potential missile threat many years in the future (from North Korea or Iran), experts such as Postol, Butt, and Lewis stipulate that these adversaries will, if they so desire, eventually build, test, and miniaturize a nuclear warhead, develop ICBM technology, and integrate countermeasures; however, at the same time, their analyses project that current limitations of the hit-to-kill BMD technology demonstrated under scripted tests mean that they "will never be able to reliably function in real combat conditions."[72]

BMD supporters' RDA-based thinking. Supporters also evaluate candidate BMD technology in a manner that is logically consistent with their RDA belief set. Prior to President Reagan's announcement of SDI, the *U.S. Defense Guidance Plan, FY 1984–1988* asserted the need for the United States to be able to "prevail in a protracted nuclear war." This objective proceeded from an assumption of a tit-for-tat dynamic of conflict dictated by calculated risk, meaning deterrence depended on being able to convince the Soviet Union that the United States could defeat it at any level of nuclear escalation. During this period, Secretary of Defense Casper Weinberger consistently argued that a limited BMD system "would enhance deterrence by complicating the USSR's ability to gain a decisive advantage by initiating conflict."[73] Fred Hoffman, lead author of a report that provided the Reagan administration's authoritative account of how to proceed on BMD also exhibited RDA-based thinking in his testimony before the Senate Armed Services Committee on March 1, 1985.[74] Hoffman stated that the most likely nuclear conflict scenario was one in which the Soviet Union launched a limited strike in order to quickly terminate a conventional conflict with the United States. He went on to testify that "we need to evaluate SDI within a framework such as the preceding rather than that of MAD."[75]

Since the end of the Cold War, supporters usually assume an RDA-based scenario where a nuclear-armed rogue state utilizes its ballistic missile capability to overcome its conventional disadvantage vis-à-vis the United States, either through coercion or by launching a strike on forward-deployed U.S. troops in order to terminate a conventional conflict it is losing.[76] Throughout the 1990s, Keith Payne, who would go on to serve as deputy assistant secretary of defense for Forces Policy and, as such, the lead author of the 2002 U.S. *Nuclear Posture Review* (NPR), consistently examined a prospective U.S. BMD system in the context of a specific RDA-based scenario: one in which a limited BMD system is employed by the United States to deter or, perhaps, intercept "a challenger's [missile] strike while U.S. and allied forces are conducting successful military operations on the challenger's home soil."[77] The 2002 U.S. *NPR* thus articulated the rationale for seeking to attain a limited BMD system, as part of the so-called New Triad, as being to deter rogue states from attack by complicating their cost-benefit calculation (i.e., by the mitigation of calculated risk).

In the context of the RDA belief set, it makes sense to set only a minimal requirement for candidate BMD technology. The U.S. pursuit of BMD technology—and adversaries' pursuit of offensive countermeasures—is thought to occur as part of an ongoing process of each side mitigating calculated risk via the competition for relative military advantage: at minimum, committing resources to BMD demonstrates the will to maintain military strength, and if the United States has any degree of success, then adversaries may be dissuaded from the further pursuit of offensive and/or defensive technologies.[78] Furthermore, possessing a minimally effective BMD system signals to adversaries that they can no longer guarantee a given missile will strike its intended target.

During the Cold War, BMD supporters tended to focus on information suggesting that the Soviet Union would not be able to develop countermeasures to BMD for ten to fifteen years or more, at which point the United States might be able to find a solution to them.[79] Since the Cold War, supporters have usually acknowledged the challenge that even simple countermeasures pose to hit-to-kill BMD technology. Rather than an insurmountable obstacle, however, Stephen Hadley and others in the Bush administration argued that "many of these challenges already have solutions, or solutions can be found for them." Ultimately, they concluded that "the United States will never find them if it does not 'get in the business' of defending itself against ballistic missile attack."[80]

Supporters, consequently, exhibit three types of biases in their interpretation of available data about the likely rate of progress for BMD technology, all of which are consistent with the logic of their statements regarding the RDA belief set. First, they tend to amplify progress indicated in data by defining it as confirmation of previously theorized science/engineering processes, relative to other candidate BMD technology, or as the absence of disconfirming evidence. In Dr. Teller's December 1983 letter to presidential science advisor George Keyworth, for instance, his optimism regarding the X-ray laser was based on results showing that the "three parameters measured in the test were in 'quantitative agreement' with predictions, showing that scientists understood the physical principles underlying the laser's action"—a statement that a 1988 Government Accountability Office report found to be factually correct.[81]

Second, although supporters tend to acknowledge setbacks and test failures, the significance of those failures is marginalized. Specifically, supporters emphasize that failure is part of the learning process, that there is an expectation of failure at the early stages of complex technological feats, and/or that the cause of failure is tangential to the stated goals for the test.[82] The third bias exhibited by supporters is persistent agnosticism about the meaning and significance of existing data. They tend to express the sentiment that "it is generally not the position of science that a priori something won't work and shouldn't be pursued." They then compare BMD to other complex technological feats that succeeded, and during the period when the ABM Treaty was in force would emphasize the benefit of expanding tests beyond the ABM Treaty's limits to see what insights could be gained.[83]

CONCLUSIONS AND IMPLICATIONS

This chapter suggests that explaining how one arrives at a judgment on candidate BMD technology requires a more nuanced understanding of the dynamics between science, psychology, and politics. Scholars and practitioners both must recognize that the brute facts produced via science typically are based on probabilistic data that do not directly indicate how the state should proceed on a given technology. Therefore, it is necessary to understand how social facts—in this case, an actor's established beliefs regarding credible nuclear deterrence—necessarily shape technological judgments. Although such beliefs can serve as ideology that leads to rigid thinking and inaccurate judgments, those very same beliefs also serve as heuristics—or rules of thumb—that provide the necessary context for key actors to make sense of probabilistic technological data. Moreover, as they make sense of information regarding candidate BMD technology, material interests can either harm the accuracy of their judgments, by incentivizing individuals to skew information, or improve accuracy by providing an incentive to moderate the harmful effects of belief perseverance.

In short, rather than just minimizing the effect of politics on science, my analysis suggests that the actual challenge to arriving at accurate judgments on BMD technology is to incentivize self-critical thinking, which is what I've termed good politics, in order to minimize bad science, which is when subjective interpretations of data are treated as conveying fact. On the one hand, my analysis of BMD supporters demonstrates how interests, beliefs, and the agnosticism of good science can all act in concert to justify the continued pursuit of candidate military technology. It must be recognized that under these circumstances there are little to no objective criteria on which to invalidate the pro position and, thus, it is more difficult to identify and root out bad politics than previously thought. On the other hand, my analysis also demonstrates how patterns of thinking exhibited by both the pro and con positions on candidate technology can lead to bad science. BMD supporters' tendency to focus on mitigating only the calculated risk of nuclear use does not provide falsification criteria as they evaluate technology (i.e., according to their starting assumptions, there is never a point at which optimism about future technological developments is not warranted). Just as problematic, BMD opponents' tendency to focus on mitigating only the autonomous risk of nuclear use leads them to interpret technological data in a fashion that does not provide the necessary opportunity to learn from errors and mistakes.

It follows that the pursuit of depoliticization often hinders improving judgment accuracy by exacerbating the "dialogue of the deaf" on candidate military technology. My analysis of U.S. BMD demonstrates that even when strategies aimed at minimizing bad politics are fully implemented, uncertainty often remains: There are still multiple potentially valid trajectories that a candidate technology may follow in the future, intelligence regarding the capability and intent of adversaries remains indeterminate, and there is little consensus on the national security requirements for that technology. Under these circumstances, overconfident policymakers—expert and layperson—often use the pursuit of minimizing the role of politics in science as a political cudgel to enhance the validity of their own definitive, but inherently subjective, interpretations. In other words, the notion that the BMD technology innovation process can be objective allows one group to advance their technological judgments as "right," without contextual qualification, and then point to the other groups' judgments with which they disagree as conveying a politicized interpretation of the brute facts that is "wrong." Ultimately, this leads to further entrenchment between those with different beliefs regarding credible nuclear deterrence, which then hinders improving the accuracy of judgments on the capability and utility of BMD technology.[84]

The ensuing dialogue of the deaf results in a number of policy dynamics that have previously been attributed to politics. Since every new piece of test data tends to fan the flames—with proponents trumpeting how this demonstrates the technology's promise and opponents pouncing on every shortcoming and/or failure as proving the technology cannot be built—resources are often committed to conducting "safe" tests that yield little new data, rather than conducting riskier tests that will yield insights whether or not that test succeeds. Similarly, the dialogue of the deaf over procurement decisions results in wasted resources via stalemates, half-hearted research programs, and pendular swings in priorities over time.

Ultimately, then, my analysis suggests that arriving at accurate judgments on BMD technology requires that the technology innovation process be governed by new norms of professional behavior regarding the treatment of technological data and the role of scientific expertise. Specifically, the norm that prizes the pursuit of fact-based data in the innovation process must be replaced with a norm acknowledging the ubiquity of hybrid facts. This involves recognizing the limits of available information about the capability of BMD technology, admitting the role of national security beliefs in interpreting the meaning and significance of available technological information, and stipulating that the legitimacy of technological judgments rests on the internal consistency of social facts (as well as broader truth tests regarding the brute facts at hand).

Furthermore, the norm that holds expert-driven decision making as the goal must be replaced with a norm seeking horizontal dialogue across experts, government officials, industry stakeholders, and the public.[85] Popularizing this norm will require government officials, media, and the public to recognize that the fact some people have expertise on the physical capacities of candidate technology does not necessarily mean these individuals also have proportional expertise on matters of military strategy. In sum, to the extent that these changes in the norms of professional behavior occur, the ensuing dialogue between policymakers speaking from divergent national security beliefs stands a chance of yielding increasingly accurate points of consensus on the capability and strategic utility of BMD technology.[86]

NOTES

1. George W. Bush, "National Policy on Ballistic Missile Defense Fact Sheet," *American Presidency Project*, May 20, 2003, http://www.presidency.ucsb.edu/ws/?pid=80354; Kier Lieber and Daryl Press, "The Rise of U.S. Nuclear Primacy," *Foreign Affairs* 85, no. 2 (2006): 42–54; White House, "Ballistic Missile Fact Sheet," *New York Times*, September 17, 2009, http://www.nytimes.com/2009/09/17/us/politics/17shield.text.html; U.S. Department of Defense, "2010 Ballistic Missile Defense Review," February 1, 2010, https://www.defense.gov/News/Special-Reports/BMDR/; Barack Obama, "2013 State of the Union Address," U.S. Capitol,

Washington D.C., February 12, 2013, https://www.theatlantic.com/politics/archive/2013/02/full-text-president-obama-2013-state-of-the-union-address/318416/.

2. Emily O. Goldman and Leslie C. Eliason, eds., *The Diffusion of Military Technology and Ideas* (Stanford, Calif.: Stanford University Press, 2003); Risa A. Brooks and Elizabeth A. Stanley, eds., *Creating Military Power* (Stanford, Calif.: Stanford University Press, 2007); Michael C. Horowitz, *The Diffusion of Military Power* (Princeton, N.J.: Princeton University Press, 2010); Dima Adamsky, *The Culture of Military Innovation* (Stanford, Calif.: Stanford University Press, 2010).

3. On arms races, see Harvey Brooks, "The Military Innovation System and the Qualitative Arms Race," *Daedalus* 104, no. 3 (1975): 75–97; Ted Greenwood, *Making the MIRV: A Study of Defense Decision Making* (Cambridge, Mass.: Harvard University Press, 1975); Mary Kaldor, *The Baroque Arsenal* (New York: Hill and Wang, 1981); Matthew Evangelista, *Innovation and the Arms Race* (Ithaca, N.Y.: Cornell University Press, 1988); Charles L. Glaser, "The Causes and Consequences of Arms Races," *Annual Review of Political Science* 3 (2000): 251–76; Charles L. Glaser, "When Are Arms Races Dangerous? Rational versus Suboptimal Arming," *International Security* 28, no. 4 (2004): 44–84. Key examples of historical case studies include Michael H. Armacost, *The Politics of Weapons Innovation: The Thor-Jupiter Controversy* (New York: Columbia University Press, 1969); Harvey M. Sapolsky, *The Polaris System Development: Bureaucratic and Programmatic Success in Government* (Cambridge, Mass.: Harvard University Press, 1972); Edmund Beard, *Developing the ICBM: A Study in Bureaucratic Politics* (New York: Columbia University Press, 1976); Richard K. Betts, *Cruise Missiles: Strategy, Technology and Politics* (Washington, D.C.: Brookings Institution Press, 1981); Stephen Rosen, *Winning the Next War: Innovation and the Modern Military* (Ithaca, N.Y.: Cornell University Press, 1991); Michael E. Brown, *Flying Blind* (Ithaca, N.Y.: Cornell University Press, 1992). For seminal examples of case studies from a science and technology studies (STS) perspective, see Donald Mackenzie, *Inventing Accuracy* (Cambridge: Massachusetts Institute of Technology Press, 1990); Graham Spinardi, *From Polaris to Trident* (Cambridge: Cambridge University Press, 1994).

4. See, for example, Robert Jervis, *Perception and Misperception in International Politics* (Princeton, N.J.: Princeton University Press, 1976); and Janice G. Stein, "Rational Deterrence against 'Irrational' Adversaries?" in *Complex Deterrence*, ed. T. V. Paul, Patrick Morgan, and James Wirtz (Chicago: University of Chicago Press, 2009), 58–82.

5. Wiebe E. Bijker, Roland Bal, and Ruud Hendriks, *Paradox of Scientific Authority* (Princeton, N.J.: Princeton University Press, 2009), 24–26. This is also consistent with the "linear model of science" in Roger A. Pielke, *The Honest Broker* (Cambridge: Cambridge University Press, 2007), 12–13.

6. Robert Jervis, *The Illogic of American Nuclear Strategy* (Ithaca, N.Y.: Cornell University Press, 1984); Charles S. Glaser, "Why Even Good Defenses May Be Bad," *International Security* 9, no. 2 (1984): 92–123; Charles S. Glaser, "Do We Want the Missile Defenses We Can Build?" *International Security* 10, no. 1 (1985): 25–57; Barry O'Neill, "A Measure for Crisis Instability with an Application to Space-Based Antimissile Systems," *Journal of Conflict Resolution* 31, no. 4 (1987): 631–72; Alan Saperstein and Gottfried Mayer-Kress, "A Nonlinear Dynamic Model of the Impact of SDI on the Arms Race," *Journal of Conflict Resolution* 32, no. 4 (1988): 636–70; Edward Reiss, *The Strategic Defense Initiative* (Cambridge: Cambridge University Press, 1992); Francis FitzGerald, *Way out There in the Blue* (New York: Simon and Schuster, 2000); Charles S. Glaser and Steven Fetter, "National Missile Defense and the Future of U.S. Nuclear Weapons Policy," *International Security* 26, no. 1 (2001): 40–92; Craig Eisendrath, Melvin A. Goodman, and Gerald E. Marsh, *The Phantom*

Defense: America's Pursuit of the Star Wars Illusion (Westport, Conn.: Praeger, 2001); James H. Lebovic, "The Law of Small Numbers: Deterrence and National Missile Defense," *Journal of Conflict Resolution* 46, no. 4 (2002): 455–83; Roger Handberg, *Ballistic Missile Defense and the Future of American Security* (Westport, Conn.: Praeger, 2002); Ernest J. Yanarella, *The Missile Defense Controversy* (Lexington: University Press of Kentucky, 2002); Columba Peoples, *Justifying Ballistic Missile Defense: Technology, Security and Culture* (Cambridge: Cambridge University Press, 2010).

7. Some argue that an effective BMD system can be built and that the possession of such a system is necessary to enhance U.S. national security—for examples, see Colin S. Gray, "Moscow Is Cheating," *Foreign Policy* 56, no. 3 (1984): 141–52; J. C. Toomay, "The Case for Ballistic Missile Defense," *Daedalus* 114, no. 3 (1985): 219–37; Keith B. Payne, *Missile Defense in the 21st Century* (Boulder, Colo.: Westview Press, 1991); S. L. Quakenbush, "National Missile Defense and Deterrence," *Political Research Quarterly* 59, no. 4 (2006): 533–41; Stephan J. Cimbala, *Shield of Dreams* (Annapolis, Md.: Naval Institute Press, 2008). Other scholars argue that the U.S. BMD debate results from politically motivated distortions of fact by both supporters and opponents and then they prescribe depoliticization as a means to accurately assess what can and should be done—for examples, see James M. Lindsay and Michael E. O'Hanlon, *Defending America* (Washington, D.C.: Brookings Institution Press, 2001); James J. Wirtz and Jeffrey A. Larsen, *Rocket's Red Glare* (Boulder, Colo.: Westview Press, 2001); Bradley Graham, *Hit to Kill* (New York: Public Affairs, 2001).

8. Each of the following describe the challenge of reducing uncertainty about a candidate technology as a dual process: Armacost, *Politics of Weapons Innovation*, 266; Betts, *Cruise Missiles*, 550; Evangelista, *Innovation and the Arms Race*, 64–68; Rosen, *Winning the Next War*, 44–45, 226; Brown, *Flying Blind*, x, 14, 313.

9. Lindsay and O'Hanlon, *Defending America*, 4. The Sentinel antiballistic missile (ABM) program was announced by the Johnson administration in 1967; in 1969, the Nixon administration modified the program under the new name Safeguard. The ABM effort was then sharply limited by the 1972 ABM Treaty.

10. David B. Denoon, *Ballistic Missile Defense in the Post–Cold War Era* (Boulder, Colo.: Westview Press, 1995); Reiss, *Strategic Defense Initiative*, 56; Fitzgerald, *Way out There*, 19.

11. Graham, *Hit to Kill*, xxviii; Yanarella, *Missile Defense Controversy*, 195; Cimbala, *Shield of Dreams*, 14.

12. Generally, these are the offensive countermeasures at issue: to evade boost-phase interception, an adversary may be able to increase the speed of its ICBM booster, which would diminish its window of vulnerability to interception, and apply heat-resistant shielding to the booster shell, which would diminish its vulnerability to directed-energy BMD technology; to evade midcourse interception, an adversary may be able to employ numerous methods to prevent BMD sensor technology from locating incoming warheads (e.g., releasing decoys and/or chaff and/or masking the heat signature of the warhead via multiple means); and, to evade terminal phase interception, an adversary may be able to make adjustments so that a warhead does not follow its expected ballistic trajectory as it approaches its target.

13. Eisendrath, Goodman, and Marsh, *Phantom Defense*, 87.

14. Glaser, "Do We Want Missile Defenses," 53.

15. Glaser and Fetter, "National Missile Defense."

16. Peoples, *Justifying Ballistic Missile Defense*, 2. Emphasis added.

17. Charles A. Zraket, "Uncertainties in Building a Strategic Defense," *Science* 235, no. 4796 (1987): 1600–1606.

18. Peoples, *Justifying Ballistic Missile Defense*, 2.

19. Eisendrath, Goodman, and Marsh, *Phantom Defense*, 91, 92, 94, 99.

20. Jervis, *Illogic of American Nuclear Strategy*, 29.

21. FitzGerald, *Way out There*, 19.

22. Glaser, "Why Even Good Defenses May Be Bad," 123; Glaser, "Do We Want Missile Defenses," 53.

23. Glaser and Fetter, "National Missile Defense."

24. G. R. Mitchell, *Strategic Deception: Rhetoric, Science, and Politics in Missile Defense Advocacy* (East Lansing: Michigan State University Press, 2000), 283.

25. Gerald M. Steinberg, "Preaching to the Converted: The Role of Scientists in the SDI Debate," in *Lost in Space: The Domestic Politics of the Strategic Defense Initiative*, ed. Steinberg (Lexington, Mass.: Lexington Books, 1988), 99–100.

26. According to American exceptionalism, the United States holds a special moral distinction among nations and thus has a moral responsibility to pursue military capabilities necessary to be able to act unilaterally to maintain international stability. According to technological optimism, problems of national and international security can be solved via technological means and any candidate technology can be attained if enough political will and resources are devoted to its pursuit. See, for example Eisendrath, Goodman, and Marsh, *Phantom Defense*, xviii, 44; Yanarella, *Missile Defense Controversy*, 11, 194–95, 200; Handberg, *Ballistic Missile Defense*, 14, 18, 22, 23; Peoples, *Justifying Ballistic Missile Defense*, 4, 5, 66, 68.

27. Mitchell, *Strategic Deception*, 48, 52, 57; Reiss, *Strategic Defense Initiative*, 60–83.

28. Peoples, *Justifying Ballistic Missile Defense*, 94–98.

29. Ibid., 5.

30. Eisendrath, Goodman, and Marsh, *Phantom Defense*, 92.

31. Jervis, *Illogic of American Nuclear Strategy*, 55.

32. Reiss, *Strategic Defense Initiative*, 2.

33. Peoples, *Justifying Ballistic Missile Defense*, 198–99, 260.

34. This model is consistent with pragmatic constructivism. See the following: Emanuel Adler, "Seizing the Middle Ground: Constructivism in World Politics," *European Journal of International Relations* 3, no. 3 (1997): 319–63; Jorg Friedrichs and Friedich Kratochwil, "On Acting and Knowing: How Pragmatism Can Advance International Relations Research and Methodology," *International Organization* 63, no. 4 (2009): 701–31; Peter M. Haas and Ernst B. Haas, "Pragmatic Constructivism and the Study of International Institutions," in *Pragmatism in International Relations*, ed. Harry Bauer and Elisabetta Brighi (New York: Routledge, 2009), 103–23.

35. See Bijker, Bal, and Hendriks, *Paradox of Scientific Authority*, 159–62, and Pielke, *Honest Broker*, 24–29. On irreducible uncertainty, see Kenneth R. Hammond, *Human Judgment and Social Policy* (Oxford: Oxford University Press, 1996), 11, 13.

36. See John Searle, *The Construction of Social Reality* (New York: Free Press, 1995), 22–29, on the distinction between "brute" and "institutional" facts; also, see Alexander Wendt, *Social Theory of International Politics* (Cambridge: Cambridge University Press, 1999), 110–11, on "rump materialism."

37. According to literature on the offense-defense balance, for example, the material capacity of military technology can affect the probability of state's victory on the battlefield and, thus, its incentive to attack.

38. Haas and Haas, "Pragmatic Constructivism," 113; Thomas J. Pinch and Weibe E. Bijker, "The Social Construction of Facts and Artefacts; or, How the Sociology of Science and the Sociology of Technology Might Benefit Each Other," *Social Studies of Science* 14, no. 3 (1984):

349–441; Donald Mackenzie, *Inventing Accuracy* (Cambridge: Massachusetts Institute of Technology Press, 1990), 375.

39. Haas and Haas, "Pragmatic Constructivism," 114; Sheila Jasanoff, *The Fifth Branch* (Cambridge, Mass.: Harvard University Press, 1990).

40. The RDA-FMA distinction roughly corresponds to the framework advanced in David Goldfischer, *The Best Defense* (Ithaca, N.Y.: Cornell University Press, 1993), wherein he proposes that Jervis's deterrence versus spiral perspectives correspond to the pro and con positions on U.S. BMD, respectively. Also, the FMA-based thinking of BMD opponents is consistent with the arms control epistemic community as described in Emanuel Adler, "The Emergence of Cooperation: National Epistemic Communities and the International Evolution of the Idea of Nuclear Arms Control," *International Organization* 46, no. 1 (Winter 1992): 101–45, and the argument in Keir A. Lieber, *War and the Engineers* (Ithaca, N.Y.: Cornell University Press, 2005), 144–47, that BMD opponents "would not expect nuclear war to be long and indecisive, as with other defensive shifts in the balance, but they would expect it to bring so much destruction so rapidly that no state would ever initiate it in the first place."

41. Bijker, Bal, and Hendriks, *Paradox of Scientific Authority*, 24, 27, 157; Jasanoff, *Fifth Branch*, 7–8, 17, 232.

42. See Stein, "Rational Deterrence," on how "new research suggests that emotion precedes choice, emotions trigger choices, and emotion follows in the wake of choice to shape what people learn from their choices" (68).

43. The classic work on unmotivated biases is Daniel Kahneman, Paul D. Slovic, and Amos Tversky, *Judgment under Uncertainty: Heuristics and Biases* (New York: Cambridge University Press, 1982).

44. Jack S. Levy, "Political Psychology and Foreign Policy," in *Political Psychology*, ed. David Sears, Leonie Huddy, and Robert Jervis (New York: Oxford University Press, 2003), 268.

45. Philip E. Tetlock, *Expert Political Judgment* (Princeton, N.J.: Princeton University Press, 2005), 40, 137.

46. This is consistent with the point made by Friedrichs Kratochwil that, "trusting 'paradigms' might hinder rather than help with diagnosing the problem." Kratochwil, "Ten Points to Ponder about Pragmatism," in Bauer and Brighi, *Pragmatism in International Relations*, 13.

47. Stein, "Rational Deterrence," 66.

48. Peoples, *Justifying Ballistic Missile Defense*, 148–49.

49. Graham, *Hit to Kill*, 189–91.

50. Armacost, *Politics of Weapons Innovation*, 6, observes that it is "difficult to foresee the strategic implications of novel weapons and their impact upon established divisions of labor among the [armed] services."

51. As she notes, "Reagan and his supporters' much publicized efforts succeeded in making BMD deployment a partisan political effort. Indeed, they stitched it onto the ideological fabric of the Republican Party." Fitzgerald, *Way out There*, 20–21.

52. James M. Lindsay, "Testing the Parochial Hypothesis: Congress and the Strategic Defense Initiative," *Journal of Politics* 53, no. 3 (August 1991): 860–76.

53. Handberg, *Ballistic Missile Defense*, 28.

54. Steinberg, *Lost in Space*, 2; Denoon, *Ballistic Missile Defense*, 19; Handberg, *Ballistic Missile Defense*, 25, 28–29.

55. Lindsay and O'Hanlon, *Defending America*, 48, 94.

56. Ibid., 94.

57. Friedrichs and Kratochwil, "On Acting and Knowing," 704–5.

58. See Bijker, Bal, and Hendriks, *Paradox of Scientific Authority*, 28, 31–32, on the "backstage practice of scientific work."

59. *New York Times*, May 12, 1985.

60. Sidney D. Drell, Philip J. Farley, and David Holloway, *The Reagan Strategic Defense Initiative: A Technical, Political, and Arms Control Assessment* (Cambridge: Ballinger Publishing, 1985), 68.

61. McGeorge Bundy, George Kennan, Robert McNamara, and Gerard Smith, "The President's Choice: Star Wars or Arms Control," *Foreign Affairs* 60, no. 4 (1984/85): 273–74; Wolfgang Panofsky, "The Mutual-Hostage Relationship between America and Russia," *Foreign Affairs* 52, no. 1 (1973): 109–18; Wolfgang Panofsky and Sidney Drell, "The Case against Strategic Defense: Technical and Strategic Realities," *Issues in Science and Technology* (1984): 62–63.

62. Federation of American Scientists (FAS), National Resources Defense Council, and Union of Concerned Scientists (UCS), *Toward True Security: A U.S. Nuclear Posture for the Next Decade* (Cambridge, Mass.: UCS, June 2001), 26. Also see Richard A. Garwin, "A Defense That Will Not Defend," in *Contemporary Nuclear Debates*, ed. Alexander T. J. Lennon (Cambridge: Massachusetts Institute of Technology Press, 2002), 43.

63. Yousaf Butt and Theodore Postol, "Upsetting the Reset: The Technical Basis of Russian Concern over NATO Missile Defense," FAS Special Report No. 1, 2011, 11, 17, 30, 32; see also Yousaf Butt, "The Delusion of Missile Defense," *New York Times*, September 20, 2011.

64. Panofsky, "Mutual-Hostage Relationship," 112; Wolfgang Panofsky, "The Remaining Unique Role of Nuclear Weapons in post–Cold War Deterrence," in *Post–Cold War Conflict Deterrence* (Washington, D.C.: National Academy Press, 1997), 109; McGeorge Bundy, William J. Crowe, and Sidney D. Drell, *Reducing Nuclear Danger* (New York: Council on Foreign Relations Press, 1993), 93.

65. Ashton Carter, *Directed Energy Missile Defense in Space—A Background Paper* (Washington, D.C.: U.S. Congress, Office of Technology Assessment, OTA-BP-ISC-26, April 1984), 70, 77 (this background paper was written by Ashton Carter under a contract from OTA). In a study of the OTA, Bruce Bimber observed: "It is not the case that experts at OTA had no values, no opinions, no position on policies. What is interesting is that agency chose not to reveal those positions in its work. It is also not the case that OTA employed a special 'science' of policy analysis that somehow separated values from facts. OTA's formula was responsiveness to its institutional environment, not unique analytic methods or the employment of somehow apolitical experts." *The Politics of Expertise in Congress: The Rise and Fall of the Office of Technology Assessment* (Albany: State University of New York Press, 1996), 97

66. UCS, *The Fallacy of Star Wars* (New York: Vintage Books/Random House, 1984), 45.

67. Carter, *Directed Energy Missile Defense*, 77.

68. UCS, *Fallacy of Star Wars*, 5, 6, 40–43.

69. David Holloway, "The Strategic Defense Initiative and the Soviet Union," *Daedalus* 114, no. 3 (1985): 269.

70. See the following: Richard A. Garwin, "Theater Missile Defense, National ABM Systems, and the Future of Deterrence," in *Post–Cold War Conflict Deterrence* (Washington, D.C.: National Academy Press, 1997), 82, 184–85, 191, 196, 199; Garwin, "Defense That Will Not Defend," 31, 43; Garwin, "Holes in the Missile Shield," *Scientific American* 291, no. 5 (November 2004): 70–79.

71. Hans A. Bethe, Jeffrey Boutwell, and Richard A. Garwin, "BMD Technologies and Concepts in the 1980s," *Daedalus* 114, no. 2 (1985): 65.

72. Butt and Postol, "Upsetting the Reset," 7; FAS, Q&A Session on Recent Developments in U.S. and NATO Missile Defense with Dr. Yousaf Butt and Dr. George Lewis, March 20, 2013, https://fas.org/blogs/security/2013/03/qa-session-on-recent-developments-in-us-and-nato-missile-defense-with-dr-yousaf-butt-and-dr-george-lewis/.

73. This RDA-based conflict scenario was articulated in the *U.S. Defense Guidance Plan, Fiscal Years 1984–1988*, as cited in the *New York Times*, May 12, 1982, 12.

74. Fred S. Hoffman, study director, *Ballistic Missile Defenses and U.S. National Security: Summary Report*, prepared for the *Future Security Strategy Study* (Washington, D.C., October 1983.

75. Fred S. Hoffman, "The SDI in U.S. Nuclear Strategy: Senate Testimony," *International Security* 10, no 1 (Summer 1985): 13–24.

76. See Payne, *Missile Defense*, and Keith B. Payne, *Deterrence in the Second Nuclear Age* (Lexington: University of Kentucky Press, 1996) for an articulation of the post–Cold War scenario. For the post-9/11 scenario, see the following: White House, "National Security Strategy of the United States," September 2002, 15, http://nssarchive.us/national-security-strategy-2002/; Douglas J. Feith, "Statement of the Honorable Douglas J. Feith, Undersecretary of Defense for Policy to the Senate Armed Services Hearing on the Nuclear Posture Review," U.S. Capitol, Washington D.C., February 14, 2002, *https://fas.org/wp-content/uploads/media/State-of-the-Honorable-Douglas-J-Feith.pdf*; Stephen J. Hadley, "A Call to Deploy," in Lennon, *Contemporary Nuclear Debates*.

77. Payne, *Deterrence*, 31–32. Also, see Payne, study director, *Rationale and Requirements for U.S. Nuclear Forces and Arms Control*, (Fairfax, Va.: National Institute for Public Policy, January 2001)—Payne was primary author, and many of the key notions advanced in the 2002 NPR first appeared in this report.

78. Gerald Yonas, "The Strategic Defense Initiative," *Daedalus* 114, no. 2 (1985): 74; Casper Weinberger, "U.S. Defense Strategy," *Foreign Affairs* 64, no. 4 (1986): 691; Keith B. Payne and Colin S. Gray, "Nuclear Policy and the Defensive Transition," *Foreign Affairs* 62, no. 4 (1984): 839.

79. George Keyworth, "The Case for Strategic Defense: An Option for a World Disarmed," in *Issues in Science and Technology*, 1984, 42. Also, see William J. Broad, *Star Warriors* (New York: Simon and Schuster, 1986), 139, for an account of how Dr. Lowell Wood and his team of scientists at Livermore presented a similarly optimistic assessment of the U.S. ability to stay ahead of Soviet countermeasures.

80. Hadley, "Call to Deploy," 22.

81. U.S. General Accounting Office, *Strategic Defense Initiative Program: Accuracy of Statements Concerning DOE's X-Ray Laser Research Program*, June 1988, http://archive.gao.gov/d16t6/136334.pdf, 9–11.

82. According to Dr. James Fletcher, lead author of the 1984 Defense Technologies Study Team report on SDI, "the technological issues surrounding the development of effective defenses have many possible solutions and should not at this stage by the primary focus of the debate" ("The Technologies for Ballistic Missile Defense," *Issues in Science and Technology* 1, no. 1 (Fall 1984): 29. Similarly, President George W. Bush, in remarks at the National Defense University in May 2001, stated: "We recognize the technological difficulties we face and we look forward to the challenge." Quoted in Peoples, *Justifying Ballistic Missile Defense*, 182.

83. Peppi DeBiaso, interview with author, July 7, 2005. Also, see Keith B. Payne, "Action-Reaction Metaphysics and Negligence," *Washington Quarterly* 24, no. 4 (2001): 113.

84. See Jasanoff, *Fifth Branch*, 8, 231, on the inefficiencies that follow from attempting to artificially separate science from politics, and Pielke, *Honest Broker*, 6–10, on the role of scientists as "Stealth Issue Advocates" in generating political gridlock.

85. Jasanoff, *Fifth Branch*, 234. Also, this pragmatist notion of dialogue is consistent with Haas and Haas, "Pragmatic Constructivism," 111, as well as Levy, "Political Psychology and Foreign Policy," 265, on the role that "self-critical styles of thinking" can have in increasing the accuracy of one's beliefs.

86. Friedrichs and Kratochwil, "On Acting and Knowing," 709; Kratochwil, "Ten Points to Ponder," 13, 16, 24; Haas and Haas, "Pragmatic Constructivism," 104, 122; Bijker, Bal, and Hendriks, *Paradox of Scientific Authority*, 158.

CHAPTER EIGHT

Homo Atomicus, an Actor Worth Psychologizing?

The Problems of Applying Behavioral Economics to Nuclear Strategy

ANNE I. HARRINGTON AND JOHN DOWNER

The idea of the perfectly rational, utility-maximizing actor has done a lot of work for social scientists over the years. This is most visible in economics, where *homo economicus* has served as the hypothetical protagonist of innumerable models, theories, and formulae. Less visible but perhaps equally significant, however, has been the unnamed rational actor at the heart of modern nuclear strategy, invoked in the game-theoretic stratagems of Schelling and the many influential theorists and policymakers who followed in his wake.[1] Let us call this actor *homo atomicus*.

Homo atomicus enjoys considerable authority in the nuclear sphere, where rational actor models are still used to guide most strategy deliberations. This is perhaps surprising, however, since the authority of *homo economicus* has lately begun to wane[2]—in no small part due to the 2008 financial crisis, which dramatically undermined the rational actor models on which oversight of the global financial system had been premised.[3]

The 2008 crisis, along with other perceived failures of foresight and leadership, raised important questions about rational actor theories in economics and created space for a new model of economic man. Into it stepped the generation of behavioral economists such as Kahneman, Tversky, Thaler, Ariely, and Loewenstein. Drawing on a wide range of experiments in cognitive psychology, these thinkers exploded the notion of *homo economicus* as a perfectly rational actor by highlighting persistent irrationalities in common economic behaviors.

One reason this new approach found a home in mainstream economics was that, even while it critiqued the rational protagonist of common economic models, it simultaneously offered ways to rescue the models themselves. Its key contribution was not to show that humans were often irrational but to show that those irrationalities were shaped by consistent biases. This consistency allowed *homo economicus* to remain predictable even while he became irrational, which was crucial because it meant that economists could tailor their models to anticipate his irrationalities.[4] Behavioral economics did not kill the rational actor, in other words, it simply gave him quirks.

If the models of economists can be improved by finessing their protagonist, however, then why not those of nuclear strategists? *Homo economicus* closely resembles *homo atomicus*, after all, and nobody imagines that the irrationalities identified by cognitive psychologists apply exclusively to the economic sphere. It seems intuitive, at least, that the models of nuclear strategists might evince the same shortcomings as those of economists and, as such, that they might equally learn from cognitive psychology. Perhaps there is potential for a discipline of "behavioral deterrence," akin to behavioral economics.

This is the question that motivates this chapter. The goal is to evaluate the viability of cognitive and behavioral approaches to nuclear strategy.[5] Our conclusion strikes a skeptical note. Contra many of the contributions to this volume, we will argue that cognitive psychology is markedly less useful to nuclear strategists than it is to economists. We do not doubt that nuclear strategic thought might gain from looking beyond its (unquestionably problematic) commitment to rational actors and from incorporating psychological considerations more directly in its analyses. We believe, however, that there are a priori reasons to imagine that insights into human irrationality have less purchase in the context of nuclear strategy than in economics.

The argument, in essence, is that economists and nuclear strategists understand and justify their rational actor models in meaningfully different ways, with the effect that insights from cognitive psychology are more useful to one than the other. These differences in the ways that economists and strategists approach rational actors, and their significance, become visible if we unpack the specific meaning of *rational* and *actor* in each context. To this end, the crux of the chapter is divided into two parts.

In the first part, we look critically at the notion of rationality. The chapter begins by asking why it is, exactly, that economists and nuclear strategists felt comfortable assuming rational behavior for so long. It then looks at the specific circumstances under which it is logical for theorists to modify their rationality assumptions to accommodate cognitive biases. The conclusion of this part is that it is only logical to adjust for cognitive biases under specific circumstances because these circumstances pertain to many economics problems but very few (if any) nuclear strategic problems. The upshot being that cognitive psychology has significantly less to offer strategists than it does economists, even if there remains scope to imagine it playing a role.

The second part looks critically at the notion of actors. It examines who, or what, those actors represent in the relative contexts of economics and nuclear strategy. It then examines the applicability of cognitive psychology to these actors at different levels of analysis. Its conclusion, similar to that above, is that psychology has a more complicated relationship to the actors that populate nuclear strategic models than it does to the models invoked by many economists. By drawing on studies that have examined similar issues, however, it concludes by suggesting possible avenues for future research into cognitive psychology and nuclear strategy.

ON RATIONALITY

An Unlikely Premise

In many schools of economics and nuclear strategy, rationality has become such a foundational premise that theorists often forget that it requires justification at all. This can be surprising to outsiders because, on some level, it seems intuitively obvious that people routinely behave in ways that would challenge even the most expansive definition of rationality. "All men are, at times, influenced by inexplicable sentiments," as the American novelist Charles Brockden Brown once put it.[6] Public health experts, for instance, have long struggled with the realization that most smokers already understand that their expensive habit is killing them.

Yet neither economists nor strategists are as blind to human nature as their critics sometimes suggest. Both have logical justifications for assuming rational actors despite the undeniable capriciousness of actual people.[7] Their argument, in essence, is not that all people act rationally, or even "boundedly rationally," all the time, but that theoretical models are able to transcend the messiness of real behavior.[8] This argument tends to invoke at least one of four distinct justifications or mechanisms, each loosely corresponding to a specific construal of rationality and its purpose. For want of better labels we will call these: (1) Rationality as normative prescription, (2) Rationality as product of special circumstances, (3) Rationality as product of systemic selection, and (4) Rationality as emergent mean or mode. In what follows, we will discuss these justifications in turn. In each case, we will briefly outline the essential logic, its relationship to cognitive psychology, and its applicability to economic and strategic models.

Rationality as Normative Prescription

Some models invoke rational actors not to describe how actors *do* behave but to explain how they *should* behave. Construed in this way, rational behavior is aspirational, and rational actor models are justified because they allow theorists to identify optimal solutions for problems that can then guide decision making.[9] In economics, for example, the game-theoretic Nash Equilibrium has been used to design auctions.[10]

This rationale is important to nuclear strategic models, many of which justify their invocation of rational actors in these terms (i.e., as a tool for exploring and guiding optimal decision making). Scholars routinely argue that deterrence theory served a normative function, for example.[11] From the earliest days of the Cold War, writes Morgan, "we needed instruction on how to do our best, to be rational, to avoid disaster but not lose."[12]

Crucially, however, cognitive psychology has little to offer models premised on this justification and for a straightforward reason. Psychology can help researchers identify common biases, but in this context—where models are being used for guidance—the explicit purpose of formulating rational solutions is to *avoid* such biases.[13] Simply put, the fact that people tend to be poor at certain problems does not, in most instances, fundamentally change the optimal solution to those problems.

Rationality as Product of Special Circumstances

A second justification for assuming rational actors conceives of models as being "descriptive" rather than "normative" (as in the justification above). It argues that even though actors often act irrationally, they nevertheless act rationally in special circumstances, such as when (1) they are incentivized to act rationally, (2) the interpretation of what is rational is relatively clear and consistent to all, and (3) they are provided resources—stratagems, information, advice, and so on—that promote and facilitate rational decision making.[14] Where objectives are clear, stakes are high, and actors are uncommonly judicious (or judiciously advised), in other words, then many theorists would argue that rationality becomes a more viable premise than it would be otherwise.[15] In economics, for example, the objectives of many financial decisions are relatively tightly defined, and where large sums are at stake and professional businesspeople involved, it arguably makes sense for economic models to assume that certain key decisions will be made on predictably rational grounds.

As with the previous rationale, the invocation of "special circumstances" offers a plausible justification for modeling nuclear strategic interactions in rational terms. This is because such interactions almost exclusively occur in circumstances where well-resourced actors are incentivized to make carefully considered decisions.[16] In questions of deterrence, for example, the high stakes of nuclear conflict undoubtedly create an incentive for states to reflect carefully on their decision making, defer to experts, and to formulate (and then follow) "rational" prescriptions. As Waltz succinctly puts it, "nobody but an idiot can fail to comprehend [the] destructive force [of nuclear weapons]. How can leaders miscalculate?"[17]

As with the previous rationale, however, the insights of cognitive psychology have significant limitations in this context and for straightforward and intuitive reasons. Simply put, situations that incentivize deliberate reflection by well-resourced actors about problems with clear stakes are not conducive to unthinking cognitive errors. The most fateful nuclear strategic decisions have unambiguous and carefully explored consequences, in other words, and nobody makes them without due consideration.

Rationality as Product of Systemic Selection

A third justification for invoking rational actors in models of human behavior assumes the existence of a selective process that actively favors rational outcomes.[18] Such processes are usually assumed to take the form of an external sorting mechanism—an "invisible hand," such as the free market—that advantages rational behaviors.[19] In economics, for instance, we might reasonably imagine that small businesses disproportionately fail when they make irrational economic decisions, and disproportionately prosper when they make rational economic decisions. And in these (eminently plausible) circumstances, it is logical to assume that economically rational businesses become more prevalent over time—boosted by the market's internal selection processes.[20] (Or, framed slightly differently, it would be reasonable to assume most established businesses to be rational actors because if they were not rational then they would not be established businesses.)

While such assumptions are plausible in economic scenarios like that above, however, it is difficult to imagine that nuclear strategic models could realistically invoke the same justification. This is because the stakes of failure are too high. In the context of deterrence, for instance, the sorting mechanism would presumably be nuclear annihilation, which is far too blunt and final an instrument to be effective in fashioning rationality. Even if nuclear strategists could make a case for rationality on these grounds, however, the point would still be moot insofar as we are interested in the applicability of cognitive psychology. This is because cognitive psychology, again, has little application to models that assume rationality on this basis.

Cognitive psychology has no bearing on selection-based models of rational behavior because such models are operationally indifferent to the psychology of the actors involved. The truth of this becomes clear if we consider that such models do not even require that actors *have* a psychology.[21] Take, for example, evolutionary biology, which has had great success using game-theoretical (i.e., rational actor) models justified on these grounds. When biologists explain the behaviors of fish with reference to the (evolutionary) rationality of those behaviors, they are not saying that fish make consciously rational decisions.[22] They are asserting, rather, that certain instincts proved more rational when aggregated over time—in the sense that they conferred slight but meaningful advantages to reproductive success—and, as a consequence, were favored by natural selection.

Rationality as Emergent Mean or Mode

A final justification for invoking rational actors in theoretical models focuses on trends rather than individuals and assumes that actors behave rationally on average even if they can be capricious as individuals. This claim can more accurately be thought of as two distinct justifications with different mechanisms, which are grouped together here because they are functionally equivalent in their relationships to nuclear strategic models and cognitive psychology. These are (1) to suppose that individual behaviors cluster around a rational *mode* and (2) to suppose that individual behaviors converge on a rational *mean*.

To say that behaviors cluster around a rational mode is to assume that more people make the rational choice than any other. For example, consider a group of individuals who are shopping for a new car and are reduced to choosing between two options that are identical in all meaningful ways except their price. In these circumstances some individuals might choose the more expensive—economically irrational—option for personal and circumstantial reasons (perhaps it is being sold by a friend or relative). Yet, it is nevertheless reasonable for economists to expect the majority of shoppers to choose the cheaper—economically rational—option, which will therefore become the modal choice.

To say that behaviors converge on a rational mean is to assume that the irrational behaviors of individuals cancel each other out in the aggregate, making the decisions of the collective (expressed, for instance, in the price of a stock) more rational than those of the individuals of which it is composed. Economists routinely make this assumption. A consequential example would be Hayek's argument that free markets efficiently integrate individual behaviors in ways that reveal optimal (and thus rational) distributions and prices.[23]

It is primarily in this context—where models are basing a rational actor assumption on the justification that rationality lies in means and modes—that economists have found cognitive psychology to be valuable. As outlined at the beginning of this chapter, the core insight of behavioral economics is that biases often *do not* cancel each other out or cluster around a rational mode but can instead converge toward "predictably irrational" outcomes.[24] Identifying such irrationalities, along with their intensity and the circumstances in which they occur, has allowed economists to hone their models and interventions in many ways—informing the designs of everything from retirement schemes to gambling machines.[25]

Crucially, however, it is difficult to imagine that the models of nuclear strategists can be justified (and therefore modified) on these grounds. The key point here is that these justifications for assuming rationality only apply when theorists are interested in means and modes (in the form of trends, for example, or stock prices) and are relatively indifferent to isolated data points (such as individual choices or bids), which they assume to be messy and unpredictable. Yet individual incidents *matter* in nuclear strategic models, which cannot afford to treat them as inherently unpredictable. In this sphere, the fate of civilization can hinge on a single decision by a single actor: be it a parliament, a president, or even a midlevel functionary like Vasili Arkhipov or Stanislav Petrov.[26] And where an isolated data point could mean a war that rendered all models and stratagems moot forever, it seems illogical for theorists to dismiss specific interactions as "noise" and look past them to a "signal" in their aggregate.[27]

Rationality Revisited

This is all to say that cognitive psychology is only valuable to models that make specific assumptions about rationality, and that the models of nuclear strategists (unlike those of many economists) cannot afford to make these assumptions (see table 8.1). It follows from this that strategic models should have little use for cognitive psychology. Indeed, nuclear strategists might gain more from doubling down on their rationality assumptions than from questioning them.

Although we believe the essential logic of this argument to be sound, we freely concede that it deserves more nuance than can be afforded here. Let us therefore close this section with two caveats. The first is to note that some of the models deemed irrelevant to cognitive psychology above might at the margins find some value in explorations of human irrationality. Where models are intended to be normatively prescriptive, for example, there might be scope for cognitive psychology to highlight areas where people are most in need of guidance. The second is to note that even if strategic models are unlikely to benefit from insights into cognitive biases, strategic thinkers might still gain from looking to psychology more broadly. Prominent cold warriors have come to believe that rational actor models are poor tools for guiding nuclear strategy in a world of "rogue states" and terrorist organizations.[28] In such circumstances, it may be valuable to abandon game-theoretic models entirely and to look for strategic insights in aspects of psychology that economists have largely ignored.

Table 8.1
Justifications for Assuming Rationality and Their Implications for a Behavioral Approach to Nuclear Strategy

Justification for rational actors	Relevant to nuclear strategic models?	Amenable to behavioral adjustment?
Normative prescription	Yes	No
Special circumstances	Yes	No
Systematic selection	No	No
Emergent mean/mode	No	Yes

ON ACTORS

Methodological Individualism and the Problem of Aggregates

In the previous section, we examined the different justifications that rational choice theorists invoke for ascribing rationality to economic and strategic actors. In this section, we more directly examine the actors to which they ascribe that rationality.

In nuclear strategic discourse, theorists apply theories of rational choice to many different types of actors, about which they require little substantive knowledge.[29] As long as the actor can be treated as unitary, rationality is equally as applicable to organizations, such as nation-states and firms, as it is to individuals. Behavioral economics, by contrast, is rooted in experimental fields that exclusively take individual human cognition to be their object of inquiry.[30] As such, its findings are not only specific to the behavior of individual beings but often also linked to the underlying biology of the human brain. In *Thinking, Fast and Slow*, for instance, Kahneman argues that people often depend on simple heuristics because slower and more deliberate thought processes require physiological effort and resource expenditure.[31] (So it is, for example, that scientists have found that people are more likely to engage in rigorous analysis instead of making a snap judgment after rather than before lunch.) The fact that this approach is based on the study of individual human behavior, however, raises question about what applicability, if any, these findings have to the collective and aggregate actors often invoked by nuclear strategists.

That there is a problem with applying findings based in methodological individualism to collectives and aggregates is widely recognized.[32] In the conclusion to a recent special issue on "The Behavioral Revolution and International Relations," for instance, Janice Stein argues that psychological explanations of international behavior are undermined by processes of aggregation. She concludes that the methodological individualism of cognitive psychology creates an inference problem because "theoretical propositions drawn from individual-level analysis do not move easily to 'higher-level' units such as states."[33] In a similar vein, economists Bruno Frey and Jana Gallus have proposed that aggregation processes may produce different outcomes than those observed at the individual level and that the problem of understanding these differences is substantial enough to constitute a new field of research.[34]

Behavioral researchers have generated a number of specific insights that pertain to strategic planning and decision making but have struggled to integrate these insights into a single, comprehensive framework.[35] This could be, at least in part, due to the fact that theories of deterrence and nonproliferation typically take the state as the primary actor, and treating a state as if it behaves like an individual is to commit what is known as a category mistake.

A category mistake, in its most general sense, is when someone mistakenly ascribes qualities to an object or entity that it clearly does not possess. The mid-twentieth-century philosopher Gilbert Ryle introduced the term to describe the false equation of two entities that do not share the same ontological status, or the misattribution of characteristics to an entity that cannot, by definition, exhibit such characteristics. He offers several examples, such as the following, which revolves around the ontological status of the university: "A foreigner visiting Oxford or Cambridge for the first time is shown a number of colleges, libraries, playing fields, museums, scientific departments and administrative offices. He then asks 'But where is the University? I have seen where the members of the Colleges live, where the Registrar works, where the scientists experiment and the rest. But I have not yet seen the University in which reside and work the members of your University.'"[36] The category mistake here is to expect that the university will be a discrete building rather than a collective entity that is the association of these discrete parts. States are made up of individuals, but to treat them as if they possessed the characteristics of a human being is to make the same mistake as Ryle's tourist. The state does not exhibit the characteristics of a human body any more than the university exists as a single building.

Avoiding category mistakes is one of the challenges of applying the insights of behavioral economics to questions of nuclear deterrence and nonproliferation. Unlike the rational actor assumption, which, in some circumstances, is equally applicable to states, organizations, and individuals, the findings of behavioral economics are based on observations of human behavior and rooted in the physical processes of the brain. The experimental basis of those observations, meanwhile, grants them a different ontological status than that of an a priori assumption. But whereas an assumption is easily transported from one domain to another, the substantive findings of psychological and neurobiological experiments are not so readily transferred. Claiming that a state might be predictably irrational in the same way as a person is a significant and problematic leap. So it is that the problem of aggregate actors offers a second reason to doubt there is a straightforward application of findings from behavioral economics to the realm of nuclear strategy.

Toward a Reconciliation?

The complexities of collective behavior undoubtedly raise important questions for deterrence strategists looking to invoke behavioral insights. As with the discussion of rationality above, however, and probably to a greater degree, it is possible to envisage ways that nuclear strategists might grapple productively with the problems of applying cognitive psychology to collective actors. To this end, it is worth looking to other research programs that have faced the challenges of reconciling methodological individualism with aggregate subjects. There are at least two such examples: (1) the study of affect in international relations and (2) the study of decision making in bureaucratic organizations. We will briefly examine each in turn.

Affect and the State

Scholars interested in the role of emotions in international relations contend with a problem similar to the one identified above.[37] Like cognitive biases, emotions are individual-level phenomena that are understood in relation to their biological basis and that have a complex relationship to institutional actors. Although emotions such as anger, sympathy, and guilt are easily observable in the rhetoric of international interactions, the focus on state-level behavior in dominant theories of international relations excludes such emotions from consideration. While it is easy to observe emotion at the individual level in the behavior of leaders and members of the public, it is difficult to theorize it as a driver of state behavior.

Political scientists Todd Hall and Andrew Ross have tackled the problem of linking microlevel emotions to macrolevel behaviors. They theorize three pathways for collective affective experience: bottom-up through shared concerns and dispositions, horizontally across individuals through contagion, and top-down as a result of social harmonizing processes.[38] In exploring these pathways they describe "affective waves," which occur in response to an event that elicits strong emotions across individuals. The shared experience of the emotions further intensifies the response and becomes capable of overriding preexisting goals and concerns.[39] They also speak of "emergent collective solidarities," wherein the political identities of groups are shaped through shared emotional responses.[40] (For an illustration of these collective dynamics, we might look to the Arab Spring, where a shared response to Mohamed Bouazizi's self-immolation in Tunisia inspired a series of protests across the Middle East, resulting in major social uprisings.)

By providing a connection between the individual experience of emotion and the collective phenomena of "affective waves" and "emergent collective solidarities," Hall and Ross show how theorists might grapple with the relationship between individual-level phenomena and state-level behavior. It is not implausible, moreover, that the pathways they outline might offer a tool for ascribing biases to collective actors. While some of the biases and heuristics identified by behavioral economists are cognitively driven rather than rooted in affective experience, others have a clear emotional basis.[41] Take, for example, loss aversion (a stronger desire to avoid losses over realizing equivalent gains) and the endowment effect (a tendency to overvalue goods we already own), both of which are readily identifiable as being linked to feelings of attachment.[42]

One could easily imagine pathways and collective-level phenomena through which loss aversion and the endowment effect make it easier for a state to forego building nuclear weapons than for it to give them up after having crossed the nuclear threshold.[43]

Bureaucracies

An alternative approach that scholars have taken to the problem of extrapolating from individual to collective actors is to take an explicitly organizational approach and ask how institutional structures interact with individual-level decision-making biases and heuristics. This approach recognizes that key individuals (with all their biases) can have real agency even within large organizations and seeks to explore how and where that agency is exercised.

The organizations that are most pertinent from the perspective of nuclear strategy are the state bureaucracies that frame and process key decisions (about whether or not to send information about a possible attack up the chain of command, for example).[44] The question of how institutional incentives interact with biases and heuristics to shape decisions in bureaucratic contexts could potentially constitute an important avenue of behavioral research.[45]

CONCLUSION

Sigmund Freud is often said to have deemed the Irish to be entirely immune to psychology. It is unlikely that the same could be said of *homo atomicus*. Yet, the insights of psychologists undoubtedly have a complicated relationship to nuclear strategy. In this chapter, we presented two critiques of the "behavioral revolution" as it applies to nuclear strategic thought.

In the first part, we evaluated applying the findings of cognitive psychology in light of justifications that theorists invoke for assuming rational actors. Cognitive psychologists have shown that people have biases, which, in the aggregate, lead to consistent and predictable outcomes. Economists—who often build models on the assumption that people behave rationally in the aggregate and isolated events can profitably be ignored—have found this insight to be useful. Nuclear strategists, by contrast, do not build models on assumptions about the aggregate behavior of groups and the insignificance of isolated cases. They build models that speak to isolated cases and do so on the belief that those models can inform and/or usefully explain the behavior of informed actors. As such, we argued, they are less likely to either want or need to correct for unconscious biases.

In the second part, we addressed the challenge of applying individual-level findings to state-level behaviors. Unlike the rational actor assumption, which moves relatively easily across different levels of analysis, we argued, simply transferring the results of cognitive psychological experiments to more complex social actors is not so straightforward. The substantive claims that cognitive psychologists make about heuristics and biases are rooted in the biological processes of the human brain. Organizations do not share this physiology, however, and we contended that to treat more complex social actors, such as states, as if they would display the same biases as an individual is to commit a category mistake.

Neither critique is definitive, as we explain, and it is possible to imagine research programs that attempt to navigate the limitations they describe. We do, however, believe that both are foundational and far reaching. There are compelling reasons to believe that the insights of behavioral psychology will not map easily or straightforwardly onto the problems of nuclear strategy; it is important that scholars remain alive to this.

NOTES

1. E.g., Thomas Schelling, *Arms and Influence* (New Haven, Conn.: Yale University Press, 1966).

2. *Homo economicus* was never entirely uncontroversial, however, and predictions of his demise have been around for decades. See Joseph Persky, "Retrospectives: The Ethology of Homo Economicus," *Journal of Economic Perspectives* 9, no. 2 (Spring 1995): 221–31.

3. Testifying before Congress, former U.S. Federal Reserve chairman Alan Greenspan admitted to making foundational mistakes about rational actors in the financial system. See Andrew Clark and Jill Treanor, "Greenspan—I Was Wrong about the Economy. Sort Of," *Guardian*, October 28, 2008, https://www.theguardian.com/business/2008/oct/24/economics-creditcrunch-federal-reserve-greenspan.

4. This is conveyed clearly in the title of Dan Ariely's book, *Predictably Irrational* (London: Harper Collins, 2008).

5. Our intention is to speak specifically to cognitive psychology's relationship to nuclear strategy, not to its relationship with international relations or political science more broadly. Many of our points will apply across these contexts, but the unique nature of nuclear weapons also creates specificities that will be significant to our argument.

6. Charles Brockden Brown, "Somnambulism, A Fragment," in *American Gothic: From Salem Witchcraft to H. P. Lovecraft*, ed. Charles L. Crow (Malden, Mass.: Wiley-Blackwell, 2013), 26.

7. There are complex debates around the question of whether nuclear strategic models *should* be premised on rationality (especially given that its strategies routinely call for displays of irrationality); see Patrick Morgan, *Deterrence Now* (Cambridge: Cambridge University Press, 2004), 42–79. Such questions are beyond the scope of this chapter, however, and in the following discussion we limit ourselves to the question of whether (and how) rational agent theories of deterrence (such as they are) stand to gain from the insights about psychology that feature in behavioral economics.

8. "Bounded rationality," a phrase coined by Herbert Simon, is the idea that individuals attempt to act rationally but are constrained by limited information, time, cognitive ability, etc. Herbert Simon, "A Behavioral Model of Rational Choice," in *Models of Man, Social and Rational: Mathematical Essays on Rational Human Behavior in a Social Setting* (New York:

Wiley, 1957); Herbert Simon, "Human Nature in Politics: The Dialogue of Psychology with Political Science," *American Political Science Review* 79, no. 2 (1985): 293–304.

9. In discussing the behavioral revolution and its applicability to international relations, for example, Hafner-Burton et al. make an explicit point of excluding "normative" (as opposed to "positive") theories of human behavior. Emilie M. Hafner-Burton, Stephan Haggard, David A. Lake, and David G. Victor, "The Behavioral Revolution and International Relations," *International Organization* 71, issue S1 (Supplement 2017): S1–31, 7.

10. For further examples of rationality being invoked in this fashion by economists, see, for instance, Leonard J. Savage, *The Foundations of Statistics*, 2nd ed. (1956; repr., New York: Dover Publications, 1972). This justification for rational actors is particularly prominent in fields like ethics and the philosophy of practical reason. See, for instance, R. L. Cunningham, "Ethics and Game Theory: The Prisoner's Dilemma," *Papers on Non-Market Decision Making* 2 (1967): 11–26.

11. Evidence for deterrence theory's normativity can be found in the fact that many of its core recommendations were highly counterintuitive, suggesting that they were only adopted because the theory itself was authoritative. See James DeNardo, *The Amateur Strategist: Intuitive Deterrence Theories and the Politics of the Nuclear Arms Race* (Cambridge: Cambridge University Press, 1995).

12. Morgan, *Deterrence Now*, 42.

13. Although, in principle, it might be useful to understand the common biases that lead people astray—to ascertain where explicit rules would be most useful, for instance.

14. It is worth noting here that this justification for assuming rational actors can easily be combined with the previous justification. This is simply to observe that in circumstances where the stakes of a decision are very high, it becomes more likely that actors will model optimal solutions and more likely that they will adhere to the prescriptions of those models.

15. Indeed, many institutions are actively designed to mitigate biases—for example by facilitating the expression of dissent. See Elizabeth Saunders, "No Substitute for Experience: Presidents, Advisers, and Information in Group Decision Making," *International Organization* 71, issue S1 (Supplement 2017): S219–47. See also Michael Taylor, "When Rationality Fails," in *The Rational Choice Controversy: Economic Models of Politics Reconsidered* ed. Jeffrey Friedman (New Haven, Conn.: Yale University Press, 1995), 223–34; John Ferejohn and Debra Satz, "Unification, Universalism, and Rational Choice Theory," in Friedman, *Rational Choice Controversy*, 71–84; Stanley Kelley Jr., "The Promises and Limitations of Rational Choice Theory," in Friedman, *Rational Choice Controversy*, 95–106.

16. Morgan, *Deterrence Now*, 42, 66; John Mueller, *Retreat from Doomsday: The Obsolescence of Major War* (New York: Basic Books, 1989).

17. In Scott Sagan and Kenneth Waltz, *The Spread of Nuclear Weapons: A Debate* (New York: W. W. Norton, 1995), 98.

18. See for instance Morgan, *Deterrence Now*, 70–72.

19. Such models invariably define rationality in relation to themselves, such that it makes sense to speak of a "market rationality," which might differ significantly from any intuitive sense of rationality.

20. E.g., Lawrence Blume and David Easley, "If You're So Smart, Why Aren't You Rich? Belief Selection in Complete and Incomplete Markets," *Econometrica* 74, no. 4 (2006): 929–66.

21. We might say that the agency in such models resides in the system rather than the actors themselves.

22. See for instance Peter Buston and A. Zink, "Reproductive Skew and the Evolution of Conflict Resolution: A Synthesis of Transactional and Tug-of-War Models," *Behavioral*

Ecology 20, no. 3 (2009): 672–84. Nor are they saying that every irrational fish fails to prosper, only a disproportionate number in the aggregate (on this, see our next point).

23. Friedrich Hayek, "The Use of Knowledge in Society," *American Economic Review* 35, no. 4 (1945): 519–30. This assumption also has some surprising applications beyond markets. Consider, for example, a group of individuals trying to guess the weight of an ox at a county fair. Some guess too high and others too low, but if every guess is added together and then divided by the number of guesses to obtain a mean, then that mean tends to be closer to the correct weight than any of the individual guesses (to the extent that we might want to call it the most rational guess). This counterintuitive phenomenon has been well documented in a range of contexts, having been first recognized by Francis Galton in 1909 (in the context of guessing the weight of an ox). James Surowiecki, *The Wisdom of Crowds* (New York: Random House, 2004).

24. Ariely, *Predictably Irrational*.

25. Richard Thaler and Cass Sunstein, *Nudge: Improving Decisions about Health, Wealth, and Happiness* (New Haven, Conn.: Yale University Press, 2008).

26. On Vasili Arkhipov, see for instance Noam Chomsky, *Hegemony or Survival: America's Quest for Global Dominance* (New York: Owl Books, 2004), 74. On Stanislav Petrov, see for instance Tony Long, "Sept. 26, 1983: The Man Who Saved the World by Doing . . . Nothing," *Wired*, September 26, 2007, https://www.wired.com/2007/09/dayintech-0926-2/.

27. It should be recognized that in some respects nuclear strategy is undoubtedly an iterated game with emergent norms. Nye, for example, argues that the U.S.-Soviet relationship became more stable over time as parties learned from each other. But such learning cannot be the fundamental justification for invoking rational actors, as rational theories of strategy assume actors "get it right" from the start and do not need to undergo a learning process. Joseph S. Nye Jr. "Nuclear Learning and US-Soviet Security Regimes," *International Organization* 41, no. 3 (1987): 371–402.

28. See Philip Taubman, *The Partnership: Five Cold Warriors and Their Quest to Ban the Bomb* (New York: Harper Perennial, 2013).

29. A notable exception is the literature on strategic culture. See for instance Jeffrey S. Lantis, "Strategic Culture and Tailored Deterrence: Bridging the Gap between Theory and Practice," *Contemporary Security Policy* 30, no. 3 (2009): 467–85.

30. Daniel Kahneman, *Thinking, Fast and Slow* (New York: Farrar, Strauss and Giroux, 2011), references both the cognitive psychology and cognitive neuroscience literature extensively.

31. The nervous system consumes more glucose than other systems in the body, and cognitive function is especially sensitive to its availability. See Matthew T. Gailliot et al., "Self-Control Relies on Glucose as a Limited Energy Source: Willpower Is More than a Metaphor," *Journal of Personality and Social Psychology* 92, no. 2 (2007): 325–36. See also Kahneman, *Thinking, Fast and Slow*, 43.

32. See for instance Robert Powell, "Research Bets and Behavioral IR," *International Organization* 71, issue S1 (Supplement 2017): S265–77; Bruno S. Frey and Jana Gallus, "Aggregate Effects of Behavioral Anomalies: A New Research Area," *Economics Discussion Papers*, no. 2013-51, Kiel Institute for the World Economy, 2013, http://www.economics-ejournal.org/economics/discussionpapers/2013-51. For a related discussion of a research program for the application of findings about emotions to aggregates, see Todd Hall and Andrew Ross, "Affective Politics after 9/11," *International Organization* 69, no. 4 (Fall 2015): 847–79; Todd Hall, *Emotional Diplomacy: Official Emotion on the International Stage* (Ithaca, N.Y.: Cornell University Press, 2015).

33. Janice Stein, "The Micro-Foundations of International Relations Theory: Psychology and Behavioral Economics," *International Organization* 71, issue S1 (Supplement 2017): S249-63, quote at S255.

34. Frey and Gallus, "Aggregate Effects."

35. This was also the finding of a recent special issue in *International Organization*. See Hafner-Burton et al., "Behavioral Revolution and International Relations," 1.

36. Gilbert Ryle, *The Concept of Mind*, 60th anniversary ed. (London: Routledge, 2009), 6.

37. On emotion and international relations, see Hall and Ross, "Affective Politics after 9/11"; Hall, *Emotional Diplomacy*; Jonathan Mercer, "Human Nature and the First Image: Emotion in International Politics," *Journal of International Relations and Development* 9, no. 3 (2006): 288-303; Jonathan Mercer, "Emotional Beliefs," *International Organization* 64, no. 1 (2010): 1-31; Jonathan Mercer, "Emotion and Strategy in the Korean War," *International Organization* 67, no. 2 (2013): 221-52.

38. Hall and Ross, "Affective Politics after 9/11," 848.

39. Ibid., 859.

40. Ibid.

41. As an example, anchoring effects (a tendency to over-rely on early information) are primarily cognitive in nature because the radical contingency of the anchor precludes their effects from being motivated by emotional experience.

42. A common example of a state-level endowment effect that likely operated through these emotive pathways is the Falklands War in which the UK fought a costly war to preserve possession of a resource-poor remote South Atlantic archipelago. By arousing nationalistic sentiments, Prime Minister Margaret Thatcher was able to generate the support for defending the islands against Argentinian attack, though making a similar case to occupy the islands were they not already under British administration would be hard to imagine. See Frey and Gallus, "Aggregate Effects," 3-4.

43. See also the chapter by Etel Solingen in this volume, which makes a similar argument for why sanctions and positive inducements are more likely to persuade a state to give up a nuclear weapons program the earlier the stage of the development program at which these tools are applied.

44. See for instance the chapter by Janice Gross Stein and Morielle I. Lotan in this volume.

45. By taking Kahneman's model of "two systems" within the brain, for example (i.e., a "fast" associative system of shortcuts, and a "slow," analytical system), we might imagine a form of analysis that maps these systems onto different bureaucratic structures. For instance, they might match up with different sections of the political and military bureaucracy that are responsible for rapid response and longer-term planning, respectively. (This approach is inspired by Slovoj Žižek's recovery of Lacanian psychoanalysis for the study of political phenomenon. See Žižek, *The Sublime Object of Ideology* [New York: Verso, 1989]). In this context, one could imagine that systematic biases (manifest at the collective rather than the individual level) might be more prevalent in structures that work with shorter timeframes.

CONTRIBUTORS

JEFFREY D. BEREJIKIAN is a Josiah Meigs Distinguished Teaching Professor at the University of Georgia and senior fellow at the university's Center for International Trade and Security (CITS). His scholarship on cognitive science and foreign policy has appeared in multiple journals, including the *American Political Science Review*, *Political Psychology*, and the *Journal of Conflict Resolution*. His research on prospect theory and deterrence is referenced in the U.S. *Deterrence Operations Joint Operating Concept* (2006) and has been translated into Korean. His book *International Relations under Risk* (State University of New York Press) outlines a theory of international relations grounded in cognitive principles. Dr. Berejikian was invited to consult on the role of cognitive science and deterrence policy for the Cross-Domain Deterrence Initiative (Assistant Secretary of Defense, Global and Strategic Affairs) and has been invited to speak on cognitive science and deterrence at the annual USSTRATCOM Deterrence Symposium. His current funded research includes an experimental study of human risk processing and cross-domain deterrence stability (a joint project with Zachary Zwald, another contributor to this volume).

JOHN DOWNER is on the faculty of the University of Bristol's School of Sociology, Politics and International Studies (SPAIS), where he occasionally gets roped into writing about nuclear weapons by his friends, but spends most of his time not finishing a book about managing complex, safety-critical technologies. Downer received his PhD in 2007 from Cornell University's Department of Science and Technology Studies. On graduating, he worked for three years as a researcher at the London School of Economics' ESRC Centre for Analysis of Risk and Regulation (CARR) and then at Stanford University, where he lectured for the Science, Technology and Society program and undertook research at the Center for International Security and Cooperation (CISAC).

JEAN-PIERRE DUPUY is professor emeritus of social and political philosophy, Ecole Polytechnique, Paris, and professor of political science, Stanford University. He is a member of the French Academy of Technology, a spinoff of the Academy of Sciences, and of the Conseil Général des Mines, the French High Magistracy that oversees and regulates industry, energy, and the environment. He chairs the Ethics Committee of the French High Authority on Nuclear Safety and Security. He is the director of the research program of Imitatio, a San Francisco foundation devoted to the dissemination and discussion of René Girard's mimetic theory. He is author of forty books, including, in English, *The Mechanization of the Mind* (Princeton University Press, 2000), *On the Origins of Cognitive Science* (Massachusetts Institute of Technology Press, 2009), *The Mark of the Sacred* (Stanford University Press, 2013), *Economy and the Future: A Crisis of Faith*

(Michigan State University Press, 2014), *A Short Treatise on the Metaphysics of Tsunamis* (Michigan State University Press, 2015), and *Enlightened Doomsaying* (Michigan State University Press, to be published in 2019).

ANNE I. HARRINGTON is a lecturer in the Department of Politics and International Relations at Cardiff University. Since earning her PhD from the University of Chicago in 2010, she has held academic fellowships at the Center for International Security and Arms Control at Stanford University, the James Martin Center for Nonproliferation Studies at the Middlebury Institute of International Relations at Monterey, and the Center for Security Studies at ETH Zürich. In 2013–14, she worked for the U.S. Congress as an American Political Science Association Congressional Fellow, first in the office of Sen. Kirsten Gillibrand and then at the Congressional Research Service, where she coauthored a report on "DOD Cyber Operations." Her publications have appeared in a variety of academic journals, including the *Nonproliferation Review*, *Millennium*, and *Critical Studies on Security*. Her research interests are located at the nexus of international relations and science and technology studies. They include nuclear deterrence, disarmament and nonproliferation, cybersecurity, and women in combat.

FLORIAN JUSTWAN is an assistant professor of political science at the University of Idaho. Justwan earned his PhD from the University of Georgia. His research interests are in the fields of international conflict, conflict management, and political psychology. In particular, he focuses on the roles of heuristics and cognitive biases in the formulation of foreign policy and the formation of public opinion. Dr. Justwan's work has been published in a variety of academic journals, including *Journal of Conflict Resolution*, *International Interactions*, and *Journal of Elections, Public Opinion & Parties*.

JEFFREY W. KNOPF is a professor at the Middlebury Institute of International Studies at Monterey (MIIS), where he serves as chair of the MA program in nonproliferation and terrorism studies. He is also a senior research associate with the institute's James Martin Center for Nonproliferation Studies (CNS). Dr. Knopf is the author of *Domestic Society and International Cooperation: The Impact of Protest on U.S. Nuclear Arms Control Policy* (Cambridge University Press, 1998) and the editor of *Security Assurances and Nuclear Nonproliferation* (Stanford University Press, 2012) and *International Cooperation on WMD Nonproliferation* (University of Georgia Press, 2016).

MORIELLE I. LOTAN is an American-Israeli academic and entrepreneur. She received a master's degree from the Interdisciplinary Center (IDC) in Israel. Her research on the dilemmas of nuclear operators, titled "Strategic Dilemmas of WMD Operators," was published in *Comparative Strategy* in 2016. She is currently the director of innovation for US Grid Company, a New York–based utility company working on carbon reduction and the optimization of energy sources.

HARALD MÜLLER served as executive director of the Peace Research Institute–Frankfurt (PRIF) for twenty years and professor of international relations at Goethe University, Frankfurt. Dr. Müller also taught as a guest professor at the Johns Hopkins Center for International Studies (Bologna, Italy); University of Potsdam, Germany; Sciences

Politiques, Paris; and Hebrew University of Jerusalem. He served on the German delegations to the NPT Review Conferences from 1995 to 2015. From 1999 to 2005, he was member of the UN Secretary General's Advisory Board for Disarmament Matters, which he chaired in 2004. In 2004–2005 he worked in the IAEA Expert Group on Multilateral Nuclear Arrangements. From 2011 to 2016, he was vice-president of the European Union Consortium for Non-proliferation and Disarmament. He cochaired the working group on peace and conflict research at the German Foreign Office's Planning Staff, 1999–2016. Currently, he is senior associate fellow at PRIF and external supervisor at the Peace Research Center Prague of Charles University. His latest books are *Norm Dynamics in Multilateral Arms Control: Interests, Conflicts, and Justice* (University of Georgia Press, 2014, coedited with Carmen Wunderlich), *WMD Arms Control in the Middle East: Prospects, Obstacles and Options* (Ashgate, 2015, coedited with Daniel Müller), and *Great Power Multilateralism and the Prevention of War: Debating a 21st Century Concert of Powers* (Routledge, 2017, coedited with Carsten Rauch).

ETEL SOLINGEN is the Thomas and Elizabeth Tierney Chair in Peace Studies at the University of California–Irvine (UCI) and a Distinguished Professor at UCI. She was also president of the International Studies Association (ISA) and the recipient of the 2018 William and Katherine Estes Award from the National Academy of Sciences, recognizing basic research on issues relating to the risk of nuclear war. Her book *Nuclear Logics: Contrasting Paths in East Asia and the Middle East* won the American Political Science Association's Woodrow Wilson Award and the Robert Jervis and Paul Schroeder Award. Her other books include *Regional Orders at Century's Dawn*; *Comparative Regionalism*; and *Industrial Policy, Technology, and International Bargaining*. She also edited *Sanctions, Statecraft, and Nuclear Proliferation* and *Scientists and the State*.

JANICE GROSS STEIN is the Belzberg Professor of Conflict Management in the Department of Political Science and the founding director of the Munk School of Global Affairs at the University of Toronto. She is a fellow of the Royal Society of Canada and an honorary foreign member of the American Academy of Arts and Sciences. She was the Massey Lecturer in 2001 and a Trudeau Fellow. She was awarded the Molson Prize by the Canada Council for an outstanding contribution by a social scientist to public debate. She has received an honorary doctorate of laws from four universities and is a member of the Order of Canada and the Order of Ontario.

NICHOLAS WRIGHT is an affiliated scholar at Georgetown University, honorary research associate at University College London (UCL), fellow at New America, and consultant at Intelligent Biology. His work combines neuroscientific, behavioral, and technological insights to understand decision making in politics and international confrontations in ways practically applicable to policy. He has conducted work for the UK government and the U.S. military's Joint Staff. He was previously an associate in the Nuclear Policy Program, Carnegie Endowment for International Peace, Washington, D.C. Before this, he examined decision making using functional brain imaging at UCL and in the Department of Government at the London School of Economics. He worked clinically as a neurologist in Oxford and at the National Hospital for Neurology in London. He has published academically (e.g., in *Proceedings of the Royal Society*), in general publications such as the *Atlantic* and *Foreign Affairs*, and with the Pentagon Joint Staff (see www.nicholasdwright.com/publications) and has appeared on the BBC and CNN. Wright received a medical degree from UCL, a BSc in health policy from Imperial College London, has membership of the Royal College of Physicians (UK), and has an MSc in neuroscience and a PhD in neuroscience, both from UCL.

ZACHARY ZWALD is an assistant professor in the Political Science Department at the University of Houston. His research examines judgment and decision making on issues where matters of national security and technology overlap. Dr. Zwald is associate director of the UH Center for International and Comparative Studies and director of the university's degree minor in national security studies. Previously, Dr. Zwald was an assistant professor jointly appointed in the U.S. Air War College and the USAF Counterproliferation Center. Dr. Zwald's current research empirically examines how level of military experience, threat clarity, and conflict domain affect the relationship between risk disposition and deterrence signaling preferences. He is also completing a book manuscript on military technology innovation, which provides the first systematic examination of how policymakers arrive at judgments and decisions on the probable capability and utility of candidate technology. Zwald received his PhD in political science from UC Berkeley and has held posts as a postdoctoral fellow at the Mershon Center at the Ohio State University and as a junior faculty fellow at Massachusetts Institute of Technology's Security Studies Program.

INDEX

ABM Treaty. *See* Anti-Ballistic Missile (ABM) Treaty
acceptance, risk, 9, 25, 28, 29–31, 32, 68, 70
active defense, 86–88
actors: aggregate, 194–97; unitary, 59
Additional Protocol (AP), 143, 147, 151
affective waves, 196
aggregate actors, 194–96
Ahmadinejad, Mahmoud, 120, 123–24
Albin, Cecilia, 139–40, 149
alliances: ban treaty, 142; BMD technologies, 159; defensive, 27, 37; framing/frames, 38–40; offensive, 37, 39–41, 44, 48–50; patterns, 33–36
anchoring heuristic, 67
Andropov, Yuri, 61–62
anger, 11, 136
anomalies, 120–21
Anti-Ballistic Missile (ABM) Treaty, 172–74, 177
AP (Additional Protocol), 143, 147, 151
Arkhipov, Vasili, 60
Article IV, NPT, 144, 148
Article VI, NPT, 12, 141, 150–51
Article X, NPT, 146
assurance game, 105–6, 110
audience costs, 27, 37, 40, 119–20
autonomous risk-based scenarios, 160, 167–68, 173–74, 178
availability heuristic, 67
aversion, risk, 9, 25, 29, 32, 68, 69–70. *See also* loss aversion

backward induction paradox (BIP), 105–7, 110
Bal, Roland, 161
ballistic missile defense (BMD): capability of, 159–60; conventional approach, 161–66; debates about, 5, 159–79; empirical evaluation, 169–77; FMA-based thinking, 173–75; material interests, 169–71; narrow interpretation of, 173; pragmatist approach, 166–69; RDA-based thinking, 175–77; sociotechnical complexity, 171–72
ban treaty negotiations, 119, 142–43
bargaining, 115–16
behavioral economics: decision making, 115, 135–36; deterrence, 6–7, 19; emotions, 10–11; framing/frames, 30; justice, 135–36; nuclear strategies, 187–97; predictions of, 19–20; rational choice theory (RCT), 82–83; review of, 5–12, 18–21. *See also* prospect theory
Berejikian, Jeffrey, 10, 30
Bethe, Hans, 173
biases: behavioral economics, 19–20; bounded rationality, 8–9; bureaucracies, 197; cognitive, 4, 7, 115, 124, 126, 128, 168; cognitive psychology, 67, 190, 197–98; collective actors, 196; decision making, 7, 168; deterrence, 4, 7–9; excessive coherence, 121–26, 131; fairness, 12; fear, misperception, and accident (FMA), 175; framing/frames, 30, 34; irrationalities, 187, 192; motivated, 4, 7, 168; rational deliberate action (RDA), 169, 177; systematic, 115, 121–25, 130
Bijker, Wiebe, 161
BIP (backward induction paradox), 105–7, 110
Blasko, Dennis, 79
BMD. *See* ballistic missile defense
bounded rationality, 8–9
Boutwell, Jeffrey, 175
Brazil, 147
Brodie, Bernard, 3, 104, 111
Brzezinski, Zbigniew, 58
Budapest Agreements, 120
Bueno de Mesquita, Bruce, 33
bureaucracies, 197
Bush administration, 145, 148, 165, 173
Butt, Yousaf, 174

calculated risk-based scenarios, 160, 167–68, 175–76, 178
campaign deterrence practices, 86–87
candidate missile defense technologies, 159–60, 162–67, 169–79
capabilities: BMD technologies, 159–67, 169–76, 178–79; British maritime, 35; cognitive theory of deterrence, 38–40, 42, 44–45, 48–50; disarmament, 140–41; endowment effects, 119; existential deterrence, 104; justice claims, 138; justice conflicts, 140; misperception, 42; operational, 86; second-strike, 58–59, 72–73; Soviet, 61; structural deterrence, 27, 36–37; weapons, nuclear, 120
Carter, Ashton, 174
category mistakes, 18, 194–95, 198
causal base rate, 128
causal mechanisms, 115–16, 125–27, 130, 139
Center for Defense Information, 58–59
Chile, 34
China, 118–19, 124, 129–30. *See also* doctrine, U.S. and Chinese
Cimbala, Stephen, 162
Clare, Joe, 33, 36, 40, 42
cognitive biases, 4, 7, 115, 124, 126, 128, 168
cognitive psychology, 66–67, 70, 111–13, 187–97
cognitive theory of deterrence: American approach, 38; argument testing, 33–37; evaluative framing, 31; findings, 38–42; international relations, 46–47; misperception, 42–45; nuclear vs. non-nuclear deterrence, 45; prospect theory, 28–31; status quo assessments, 28–31, 45–46; traditional scholarship, 26–28
coherence bias, 121–26, 131
Cold War, 61, 65, 72, 164
collective actors, 192, 194–96
compatibilism, 101–2
complexity, 126–27, 166
conflict initiation, 40–45
consilience, 93
conventional campaigns, 86–87
conventions, social, 70–71
coordination by means of the future, 109
counterfactual power over the past, 102, 108–10, 112–13, 126

counterforce strategy, 61
countermeasures, 162–63
countervalue strategy, 61
credibility of deterrence: audience costs, 27; backward induction paradox (BIP), 106–7; BMD technologies, 159, 163, 167–76; capabilities, 36; doctrine, 80; existential deterrence, 104; heuristics, 67, 177; judgments, 177–78; mutual assured destruction (MAD), 103, 163–64; nuclear operators, 57–59, 72; projected time, 110; risk dispositions, 25; status quo assessments, 45–46
crisis management, 90–91
Cuban missile crisis, 60

Danilovic, Vesna, 33, 36, 40, 42
decision making: of adversary, 92; behavioral economics, 5–7, 135–36; bureaucracies, 197; conventions, social, 71; deterrence, 25–28, 78, 92; emotions, 20; further research, directions for, 94; nuclear operators, 71; perceptions, 42; pragmatism, 166–69; procedural justice, 145–46; prospect theory, 28–31; psychological components, 82–83; science and technology studies, 168; time horizons, 20–21; uncertainty, 64–68, 71, 115; unfairness, 88–89
DEFCON (defense-condition), 60
defensive alliances, 27, 37
Denoon, David, 170–71
denuclearization, 118–20
determinism and free will, 101–2
deterrence: backward induction paradox (BIP), 107; behavioral economics, 6–7, 19; biases, 4, 7–9; category mistakes, 194–95; cognitive psychology, 190–91; conventional campaigns, 86–87; decision making, 78, 92–94; defined, 80; disarmament, 140–43; doctrine, U.S. and Chinese, 80–82, 86–87, 89–94; emotions, 69; existential, 103–5; fear, 11; framing/frames, 46–47; indeterminacy, 111; mutual assured destruction (MAD), 72, 103; non-nuclear, 45; nuclear operators, 56–64; nuclear security, 148; prevention of nuclear war, 71–73; projected time, 110; prospect theory, 68; psychological component, 80–82, 91–94;

rationality, 3–5, 18–19, 100, 104, 190–91; Russian concepts of, 94; stability, 25–28, 32, 33, 35–37, 40–46, 72–73; structural theories of, 26–27; surprise, 85–86; tailored, 3, 19, 25–26, 46; unfairness, 88–91. *See also* cognitive theory of deterrence; credibility of deterrence
disarmament, 12, 140–43, 147, 149, 150–53
distributive justice, 136–37, 141
doctrine, U.S. and Chinese, 78, 79, 80–82, 84–88, 89–91, 91–94
DO-JOC. *See* U.S. *Deterrence Operations Joint Operating Concept*
domestic politics, 5, 37–41, 44, 48–50
Druckman, Dan, 139, 149

Early, Bryan, 30
economic nationalism, 117
economic sanctions. *See* sanctions
ED (existential deterrence), 103–5
Egypt, 152
emergent collective solidarities, 196
emotions: anger, 11, 136; behavioral economics, 10–11; decision making, 20; deterrence, 69; fear, 19, 69–70, 71; framing/frames, 30; international relations, 196–97; justice, 138–39, 142, 150, 154; nuclear operators, 68–70
endogenous fixed point, 109, 111
endowment effects, 119–21, 196–97
enrichment, uranium, 120–21, 147
equal security, 140
EU/P5+1 (UN Security Council plus Germany), 122–24, 126, 128–29
evaluative framing, 31–32
evolutionary biology, 136
evolutionary game theory, 135
excessive coherence bias, 122, 125–26, 131
excessive discounting, 8
existential deterrence (ED), 103–5

fairness, 11–12, 20, 88–91, 92–93, 135–36
The Fallacy of Star Wars (report), 174
false alarms, 58–60, 62
false certainty, 56, 66
FAS (Federation of American Scientists), 174
fate, 105
fear, 11, 69–70, 71

fear, misperception, and accident (FMA) belief set, 167–69, 173–75
Fearon, James, 28
Federation of American Scientists (FAS), 174
Fehr, Ernst, 135–36
Fetter, Steven, 162–64
Fey, Marco, 140
Fitzgerald, Frances, 164, 170
FMA (fear, misperception, and accident) belief set, 167–69, 173–75
foreign policy, 29–31
framing/frames: behavioral economics, 30; decision, 20, 29–32, 34, 41–42; defining, 31–32; deterrence, 32, 46–47; evaluative, 31–32; overview, 20; prospect theory, 28–31, 68; security, 26, 30–36, 42–47; strategic, 34–35, 43–46. *See also* gains frames; loss frames
Fraser, Nancy, 136, 139
Frey, Bruno, 194
fuel cycle technology, 143, 147–48
Fuhrmann, Matthew, 27, 30
full spectrum dominance, 140
future capabilities, BMD technologies, 163, 175
future catastrophe, 110–11
future contingents, 108–9
future in projected time, 107–8, 110

gains frames, 20, 28–30, 32, 33–35, 35–46, 68
Gallus, Jana, 194
game theory, 82–83, 105–6, 135
Garrison, Jean A., 30
Garwin, Richard, 175
geopolitical interests, 35–36
Germany, 34–35, 140
Glaser, Charles, 162–64
Graham, Bradley, 162, 170
Great Britain, 35

Hadley, Stephen, 176
Hafner-Burton, Emilie, 10
Haggard, Stephan, 125
Hall, Todd, 196
Handberg, Roger, 170–71
Hayek, Friedrich, 192
Hendriks, Ruud, 161
Henley, Lonnie, 88

heuristics: anchoring, 67; availability, 67; behavioral economics, 8–9; BMD technologies, 159; bureaucracies, 197–98; cognitive psychology, 56, 67; credibility of deterrence, 67, 177; emotions, 70, 196; information processing framework, 7, 168; nuclear taboo, 65; rational actor models, 19; representativeness, 67; simple, 194; unitary actor assumptions, 116
HI (Humanitarian Initiative), 142–43
hit-to-kill technology, 170–75
Hobbes, Thomas, 105
Hoffman, Fred, 175–76
Holloway, David, 174
Hughes, D. Alex, 10
Humanitarian Initiative (HI), 142–43
Hume, David, 105
Huth, Paul, 37
hybrid facts, 167
Hymans, Jacques E., 10

IAEA (International Atomic Energy Agency), 129–30, 145–46
ICBMs (intercontinental ballistic missiles), 58, 162–63, 171–72
indeterminacy, 110–11
India, 144–45
individualism, 194–96
inducements: causal mechanisms, 125–27; demand side, 116–18; systematic biases, 121–25; uncertainty, 115; unitary actor assumptions, 116–17
information processing framework, 162–64, 168–69
intercontinental ballistic missiles (ICBMs), 58, 162–63, 171–72
interest-accuracy correlation, 169
International Atomic Energy Agency (IAEA), 129–30, 145–46
internationalization, 117–20, 122
International Organization (journal), 6
international relations, 5–6, 92–94, 139–40, 160, 196
intra-northern conflict, 151–52
inward-looking models, 117, 119–20, 122–24, 129
Iran, 120, 122–30, 173
Iraq, 143
IRGC (Islamic Revolutionary Guard Corps), 117

irrationalities, 6–7, 57, 105, 112, 187–88, 190–93, 195
Islamic Revolutionary Guard Corps (IRGC), 117
Israel, 144

JCPOA (Joint Comprehensive Plan of Action), 120
Jervis, Robert, 7, 115, 163, 165
JOAC (Joint Operational Access Concept), 79, 89–90
Johnson, Jesse C., 37, 40
Joint Comprehensive Plan of Action (JCPOA), 120
Joint Operational Access Concept (JOAC), 79, 89–90
Jonas, Hans, 108
judgments, 162, 164–66, 168, 169, 177–78
justice: behavioral economics, 135–36; claims, 137–39, 140, 145, 147, 150, 154; distributive, 136–37, 141; emotions, 138–39, 142, 150, 154; formula, 139; international relations, 139–40; linkage, 146–50; motive, 137–38, 139; and politics, 137–39; procedural, 137, 145–46; recognition, 137, 139, 145
justice conflicts: disarmament, 140–43; nonproliferation, 143–44; nuclear security, 148–49; peaceful uses of nuclear energy, 143–44; procedural justice, 145–46; universalism, 144–45

Kahneman, Daniel, 6–8, 9, 29–30, 69, 128, 168, 194
Kant, Immanuel, 105
Katzenstein, Peter, 71
Kerr, Walter, 35
Khamenei, Ayatollah, 124, 126–27
Khatami, Mohammad, 122–23, 129
Kim Jong Un, 121, 124
Knopf, Jeffrey W., 11–12
Kuhn, Thomas, 172

launch on attack (LOA), 58
launch on warning (LOW), 58–59
learning and unlearning, 127–29
Lebow, Richard Ned, 7, 126, 139
Leeds, Brett A., 37, 40
Lerner, Melvin, 137–38, 139
Levy, Jack, 30, 168

Lewis, David K., 101–2, 104
Lindsay, James, 162, 170–72
LOA (launch on attack), 58
loss aversion, 9, 28, 70, 119, 196–97
loss frames, 20, 28–30, 32, 33–35, 38–45, 45–46, 68
LOW (launch on warning), 58–59

MAD (mutual assured destruction), 57–60, 72, 100, 103, 106–7, 164
Mao Zedong, 91, 129
material interests, 11–12, 160–62, 164–66, 169–71, 177–78
McNamara, Robert, 100, 111
Mearsheimer, John, 27
Melamud, Aviv, 140
MFG (multilateral nuclear fuel guarantees), 147
militarized interstate dispute (MID), 33
military technology innovations, 160–61, 166, 178–79
military utility, 159, 162–67
Mintz, Alex, 31
MIRV (multiple independently targetable re-entry vehicle), 171
misperception, 4, 7, 9, 79, 92, 167
missile defenses. *See* ballistic missile defense
Mitchell, G. R., 164
MNA (multilateral nuclear fuel cycle arrangements), 147–48
Morgan, Forrest, 88
Morgan, Patrick M., 80, 190
Mossadegh, Mohammad, 128
motivated biases, 4, 7, 168
Müller, Harald, 140
multilateral nuclear fuel cycle arrangements (MNA), 147–48
multilateral nuclear fuel guarantees (MFG), 147
multiple independently targetable re-entry vehicles (MIRV), 171
mutual assured destruction (MAD), 57–60, 72, 100, 103, 106–7, 164

NAM (nonaligned movement), 140, 142, 143–45, 147–49
national security, 159, 161, 162–64, 166–68, 170, 178–79
Natural Resources Defense Council, 174

negative inducements, 115–16, 121–26
Nelson, Stephen C., 71
neuroscience, 30, 70, 82–88, 92–93. *See also* behavioral economics; cognitive psychology
New Agenda Coalition, 151
Newcomb, William, 111–13
Nincic, Miroslav, 127
NNWS. *See* non-nuclear weapon states
Noland, Marcus, 125
nonaligned movement (NAM), 140, 142, 143–45, 147–49
noncompliance, 128, 145–46
non-nuclear deterrence, 45
non-nuclear weapon states (NNWS), 12, 141–45, 149, 150–51, 152
nonproliferation: behavioral economics, 6–7, 10; category mistakes, 194–95; China's position on, 129; excessive coherence bias, 125; material interests, 11–12; nuclear strategies, 3; positive inducements, 121; psychological component, 5; rational actor models, 18; regime, 136–54
Non Proliferation Treaty (NPT): Article IV, 144, 148; Article VI, 12, 141, 150–51; Article X, 146; and denuclearization, 119–20; and disarmament, 141–42, 150–52; and Germany, 140; NAM countries, 147–48; nonproliferation, 143–44; and norm development, 152, 154; and North Korea, 130; and nuclear aspirants, 118; and nuclear security, 149, 152–53; overview of, 12; and peaceful uses of nuclear energy, 143–44; and procedural justice, 145–46; and RevCons, 12, 145–47, 149, 150; and universalism, 144–45
NORAD (North American Aerospace Defense Command), 58, 60
North Korea, 119–22, 124–25, 129–30, 144
Norway, 64
NPR (*Nuclear Posture Review*), 176
NPT. *See* Non-Proliferation Treaty
NSG (Nuclear Suppliers Group), 143, 145–46, 147
nuclear ban treaty. *See* ban treaty negotiations
nuclear disarmament, 140–43
nuclear energy, 48, 130, 143–44, 148, 149, 152–53
nuclear inequality, 144

nuclear operators: conventions, social, 70–71; deterrence, 56–64; emotions, 68–70; overview, 56; prevention of nuclear war, 72–73; prospect theory, 68; uncertainty, 64–68
Nuclear Posture Review (NPR), 176
nuclear security, 3, 148–50, 152–54
nuclear strategies: behavioral economics, 19–21; bureaucracies, 197; collective and aggregate actors, 194–95; models of, 187–89; rationality, 3–5, 189–93. *See also* deterrence
Nuclear Suppliers Group (NSG), 143, 145–46, 147
nuclear taboo, 65, 71, 72–73
nuclear war: autonomous risk-based scenarios, 173; BMD technologies, 160, 171; calculated risk-based scenarios, 175; and fear, 70; humanitarian consequences of, 142; nuclear operators, 59–61; prevention of, 71–73; rational actor models, 3; rational deliberate action (RDA), 167; and uncertainty, 56, 64–67. *See also* deterrence
nuclear weapons. *See* weapons, nuclear
nuclear weapon states (NWS), 12, 119, 140–43, 145, 146, 150–53

Obama administration, 123, 129, 148
occurring time, 102, 107–9
offensive alliances, 37, 39–41, 44, 48–50
Office of Technology Assessment (OTA), 174
O'Hanlon, Michael, 162, 171–72
opportunity cost, 93
OTA (Office of Technology Assessment), 174
overconfidence, 56, 66, 128

P5+1. *See* UN Security Council plus Germany
PALs (permissive action links), 59–60
Payne, Keith, 176
peace agreements, 139
peaceful uses of nuclear energy, 143–44, 148
Peace Research Institute Frankfurt, 149
peace years, 37–38
Peoples, Columba, 163, 165, 170
People's Liberation Army (PLA), 79–80
People's Liberation Army Rocket Force (PLARF), 80
perceptions, 34, 42–45, 69
permissive action links (PALs), 59–60
personnel reliability programs (PRPs), 59–60
Petrov, Stanislav, 61–66, 70
PLA (People's Liberation Army), 79–80

Plantinga, Alvin, 102, 112–13
PLARF (People's Liberation Army Rocket Force), 80
policy tools, 3–5
politics, 37, 40–41, 137–39, 161–62
Posen, Barry, 79
positive inducements, 115, 121–25, 126–27, 130
Postol, Ted, 174
power transition theory, 31
pragmatist approach, 166–69
prediction errors, 83–88, 92–93
preference reversal, 9
prevention, 107–8
probability of conflict initiation, 40–41, 43, 45, 47
procedural justice, 137, 145–46
procedural rationality, 6–7
projected time, 107–8, 110
proliferation, nuclear: and behavioral economics, 115–16; and BMD technologies, 159; China's position on, 129; and emotions, 69; and internationalization, 118; noncompliance, 146; and prospect theory, 10; and rationality, 19; and statecraft, 131
prospect theory: and decision making, 28–31; and deterrence, 68; and deterrence outcomes, 26; and evaluative framing, 31–32; and international relations, 94; and nuclear operators, 68; and nuclear weapons, 118–21; overview of, 9–10
PRPs (personnel reliability programs), 59–60
Psychology and Deterrence (Jervis, Lebow, and Stein), 7

rational actor models, 3–4, 6–8, 11–12, 18–20, 187–93
rational choice theory (RCT), 82–83, 100, 106
rational deliberate action (RDA), 167–69, 173, 175–77
rationality: assumptions, 193; assurance game, 106; and behavioral economics, 6–9; and BMD technologies, 164; bounded, 8–9; debates about, 3–5; and deterrence, 3–5, 18–19, 100, 104, 190–91; and emotions, 10; and existential deterrence, 104–5; inducements, 115–16; means and modes, 192–93; and normative function, 189–90; as premise, 189; and special circumstances, 190–91; and systemic selection, 191
rationality of irrationality theory, 57, 105

RCT (rational choice theory), 82–83, 100, 106
RDA (rational deliberate action), 167–69, 173, 175–77
Reagan, Ronald, 61, 165, 170
recognition conflict, 142
recognition justice, 137, 139, 145
Redd, Steven B., 31
reference dependence, 28
reference points, 9, 28–31, 68
regime stability, 149–50
Reiss, Edward, 165
Renshon, Jonathan, 30
representativeness heuristic, 67
reputations, 27, 36, 40, 42
RevCons (NPT Review Conferences), 12, 145–47, 149, 150
risk-as-feeling argument, 70
risk dispositions: decision frames, 29–31; and emotions, 68–70; foreign policy, 30–31; overview, 25–26; and prospect theory, 9, 29–31; and risk acceptance, 9, 25, 28, 29–31, 32, 68, 70; and risk aversion, 9, 25, 29, 32, 68, 69–70; shifts in, 27–28, 30, 45–46; and uncertainty, 56–57, 64–68
rivalries. *See* strategic rivalries
Ross, Andrew, 196
Rouhani, Hassan, 122–24, 126, 129–30
Russett, Bruce, 37
Russia: and China, 89; and disarmament, 140–41; doctrine, 94; and endowment effects, 120; and FMA-based thinking, 173–74; and mutual assured destruction (MAD), 164; and nonproliferation, 143; nuclear operators, 57–64, 71–72; and rational actor models, 3–4; and rational deliberate action (RDA), 175–76
Ryle, Gilbert, 195

sacred values, 11
sanctions, 115, 120, 121–27, 129–30
Schell, Jonathan, 103
Schelling, Thomas, 27, 57, 105
Schmidt, Klaus M., 135–36
science and technology studies (STS), 160, 166–68
The Science of Military Strategy, 80, 81–82, 86, 90–92
The Science of Second Artillery Campaigns, 80, 81–82, 86–87, 90

Scientific American (magazine), 164
SDI (Strategic Defense Initiative), 162–65
Sechser, Todd, 27
Second Artillery. *See* People's Liberation Army Rocket Force
second-strike capabilities, 72–73, 164
security: and internationalization, 117–19; justice issues, 140–42; national, 159, 161, 162–64, 166–68, 170, 178–79; and noncompliance, 145–46; and North Korea, 121–22; nuclear, 3, 148–50, 152–54; and prediction errors, 85
security frames, 26, 30–36, 42–47
seizing initiative, 85–88
signaling, diplomatic and military, 83–88
Simon, Herbert A., 8
Skyrms, Brian, 135–36
social constructivism, 4
social conventions, 70–71
social facts, 167
social utility, 11
sociotechnical complexity, 166, 168, 171–72
soft determinism, 101
South Africa, 119–20
Spain, 33–34
Stalnaker, Robert, 101–2
statecraft, 116–17, 122, 124–25
Stein, Janice Gross, 7, 194
Steinberg, Gerald, 164, 170–71
strategic bombing, 84
strategic culture, 3–4, 19, 70–73
Strategic Defense Initiative (SDI), 162–65
strategic frames, 34–35, 43–46
strategic rivalries: capabilities, 37; conflict initiation, 41–42, 44, 47–50; deterrence, 27, 40, 42–43, 46; geopolitical interests, 35–36, 38–40; reputations, 36, 40, 42, 47–50; risk dispositions, 46; security position, 31–32
Strategy of Conflict (Schelling), 105
structural deterrence, 26–27
structural uncertainty, 161, 168–69, 173
STS (science and technology studies), 160, 166–68
supply side, 116–17
surprise, 84–88
systematic bias, 115, 121–25, 130

tailored deterrence, 3, 19, 25–26, 46
Tannenwald, Nina, 140
Teller, Edward, 165, 177

temporality, 101–2, 107–10
Tertrais, Bruno, 80
Tetlock, Philip, 66, 126, 168
"Theory of Fairness, Competition, and Cooperation" (Fehr and Schmidt), 135
Thinking, Fast and Slow (Kahneman), 6–7, 194
Thompson, William, 33
time horizons, 20–21
Tobey, William, 128
Toward True Security: A U.S. Nuclear Posture for the Next Decade, 174
Trump administration, 128–29
Tversky, Amos, 8, 9, 29–30

UCS (Union of Concerned Scientists), 174
ultimatum game, 11, 88–90, 135
uncertainty: BMD technologies, 161, 163, 165–70, 172–74; decision making, 71; inducements, 115; learning and unlearning, 127–29; probability estimates, 61, 63; and risk, 56–57, 64–68; structural, 161, 168–69, 173
unfairness, 88–91
Union of Concerned Scientists (UCS), 174
unitary actor assumption, 116–17
United Kingdom, 148–49
United Nations Security Council (UNSC), 129–30, 145–46
United States: deterrence approach, 3, 25–26; deterrence stability, 32; disarmament, 140–41; fuel cycle technology, 148; justice linkage, 152; nonproliferation, 143; nuclear operators, 57–63; nuclear security, 148–49; P5+1 process, 128–29; positive inducements, 121–23; as target of challenges, 46–47, 50. *See also* ballistic missile defense (BMD); doctrine, U.S. and Chinese
universalism, 144–45
unmotivated biases. *See* cognitive biases
UNSC (United Nations Security Council), 129–30, 145–46
UN Security Council plus Germany (the EU/P5+1), 122–24, 126, 128–29
Upsetting the Reset: The Technical Basis of Russian Concern over NATO Missile Defense (Postol and Butt), 174

U.S. *Deterrence Operations Joint Operating Concept* (DO-JOC), 25, 46, 79–81, 85, 89–90, 92

value(s): of actors, 3–4, 19; anchoring, 67; biases, 8–9; BMD technologies, 164–65; candidate technologies, 166; conflict initiation, 41–42; decision making, 82–83, 168; deterrence stability, 27; distributive justice, 137; emotions, 10; endowment effects, 119; facts, 161; fairness, 88–89; material interests, 11–12; reference points, 29–30; status quo, 32; weapons, nuclear, 57, 65, 118
Victor, David G., 10

Waltz, Kenneth, 190
Wang Jisi, 91
The War Trap (Bueno de Mesquita), 33
Washington Post, 63
weapons, nuclear: and decision making, 18; demand side, 116–18; disarmament, 141–42; and emotions, 10, 20; and endowment effects, 119–21, 196–97; and inducements, 115–16; and internationalization, 117–19; nuclear operators, 56–64; nuclear taboo, 71; nuclear vs. non-nuclear deterrence, 45; prospect theory, 68, 119; sanctions, 120, 122–23, 129–30; and second-strike capability, 72–73; time horizons, 21; and uncertainty, 65
weapons of mass destruction (WMD), 11–12, 140
Weeks, Jessica, 27
Weinberger, Casper, 175
Welch, David, 139
Wen Jiabao, 130
Whyte, Glen, 30
Wiesner, Jerome, 164
WMD (weapons of mass destruction), 11–12, 140

Yanarella, Ernest, 162
Yeltsin, Boris, 64
York, Herbert, 164

Zartman, Bill, 139, 149
Zraket, Charles, 163

www.ingramcontent.com/pod-product-compliance
Lightning Source LLC
Chambersburg PA
CBHW030649230426
43665CB00011B/1017